At Home on the Slopes of Mountains

At Home on the Slopes of Mountains

The Story of Peggy Pond Church

by Sharon Snyder

Los Alamos Historical Society Publications
Los Alamos, New Mexico
2011

Second Printing

Library of Congress Cataloging-in-Publication Data

Snyder, Sharon, 1946-
   At home on the slopes of mountains : the story of Peggy Pond Church / by Sharon Snyder. -- 1st ed.
      p. cm.
   Includes bibliographical references and index.
   ISBN 978-0-941232-39-5 (softcover : alk. paper)
   1. Church, Peggy Pond, 1903-1986. 2. Poets, American--20th century --Biography. 3. Women poets, American--Biography. 4. New Mexico --Biography. I. Title.
   PS3505.H946Z87 2011
   811'.52--dc23
   [B]
                        2011039635

Graphic Design by Shirley Veenis, Comuniqué
Cover photograph courtesy of Don Taylor's Photography, Los Alamos, NM

Los Alamos Historical Society Publications
P.O. Box 43
1050 Bathtub Row
Los Alamos, New Mexico 87544
www.losalamoshistory.org

Printed in Canada

To

Theodore Spencer Church
(1925–2011)

and

Karen Pond Krone
(1939–2011)

Contents

Acknowledgments

First of all, I have to thank my friend Phyllis Wallis at whose home I encountered *Foretaste*, the volume of poetry by Peggy Pond Church that inspired this project in 1996. If I hadn't been packing boxes of books for her move to Oppenheimer Place, this biography might never have come about.

Without the many contributions of Peggy's family, this book would have remained only a good idea. So, to Peggy's sons—Ted, Allen, and Hugh Church—and to Hugh's wife, Kathleen, a huge "Thank you!" You gave me such a gift in allowing me to write this biography, and you were there whenever I needed you every step of the way. To Peggy's nieces and nephew—Joan Pond, Karen Pond Krone, Gretchen Pond Lofgren, and Ashley D. Pond and his wife, Katherine—you have been exceptional. To Peggy's grandchildren—Robyn Church Hatton, Nancy Church Whetstone, Janet Church Harrison, Julia Church Hoffman, Eric Church, and Leigh Church—I appreciate your input and shared memories. And to those of you in the next generations, I say thank you as well. It is in part because of you that I wrote this book, so that you will know this remarkable woman who is your ancestor and appreciate your family's unique place in history.

For support, suggestions, shared memories of Peggy, and sometimes just for listening, I thank Linda Aldrich, Shelley Armitage, Ann Baumann, Nina Baym, Terry Brewer, Patrick Burns, Liz Cunningham, Nancy Hayes, Hedy Dunn, John and Toni Gibson, Dorothy Hoard, David Laird, Betty Lilienthal, Florence Lister, Judy Machen, Michael Mauldin, Frances McAllister, Heather McClenahan, Edwina McConnell, Philip Morrison, Ann O'Bryan and Rick Buettner, George and Nancy O'Bryan, Larry O'Bryan, Pam O'Bryan, Janie O'Rourke, Teresa and Walter Pickett, Lucille Pond, Corina Santistevan, Nancy Steeper, Georgia and Gerry Strickfaden, Theresa Strottman, Tom Trusky, Jean Wallis, Pam Wallis, Sarah Wider, Susan Wider, and Nancy and John Wirth.

I am grateful for the excellent assistance from the following institutions: Arizona Historical Society, Bentley Historical Library, Boise State University's Albertson Library, Detroit Public Library, City of Las Vegas Museum and Rough Rider Memorial Collection, Columbia University's Department of Music, Las Vegas Citizens Committee for Historic Preservation, Los Angeles Public Library, Marlborough School, Museum of Northwest Colorado, Palm Springs Public Library, Pasadena Public Library, Rancho Valmora, University of California at Los Angeles, University of California at Riverside, University of Iowa Libraries, Raton Museum, Smith College Library, University of New Mexico's Center for Southwest Research, and the Ransom Center at the University of Texas.

With graditude I acknowledge Terry Brewer and Brian and Karin Boyd for numerous visits to the site of the old brick house and Ashley Pond's first ranch school on the Black Willow Ranch in Shoemaker Canyon; Claudette and Chester Norman for visits to the old Clyde Ranch; Charlotte Whaley for hiking with me to Peggy's Holy Place; Bud Kelly and Jim Baker for tours of the former Pond homes on East Palace Avenue; Sal Hemmo of Charles Restaurant, Tucson, for his knowledge of Stone Ashley history, and his hostess, Julie Essroger, for her memories of Florence Pond; The Mountain Oyster Club, current owner of Stone Ashley, for subsequent visits; and Skip Dunn for recognizing a 1909 Hupmobile Runabout!

My special thanks to Dick Albright for the amazing research connections and your steadfast friendship and to Owl for putting up with my computer and research papers all over your dining room table!

To the Los Alamos Historical Society I am indebted for the years of support. I especially thank archivist Rebecca Collinsworth for gathering and scanning photographs and my editor, Jeannette Mortensen, for the hours of time she put into making this a better book. And last, but far from least, I wish to thank Bill Bradley for his generosity to our society through the years and in particular for his kindness in helping to make this book a reality.

Introduction

"This is a good place to grow up in."

Those words from the movie adaptation of Richard Bradford's *Red Sky at Morning* are the foundation of his classic, coming-of-age novel set in northern New Mexico. For those of us who had the good fortune to grow up here in real life, the words hold a special truth.

At the age of twelve, I moved to the Pajarito Plateau, an expanse of canyons and mesas on the eastern slopes of the Jemez Mountains northwest of Santa Fe. The year was 1959, and my father had been hired by the Los Alamos Scientific Laboratory. I remember the first time I looked westward from the Santa Fe highway to the Pajarito country. The mountains were an outline against the late afternoon sky, and all around me was a flood of light and color, an atmosphere so clear and bright that it hurt my eyes. My parents and I had traveled all day from the flat lands of northern Texas. Perhaps, in all fairness, they were rolling flat lands, but they had done nothing to prepare me for the landscape that lay before me.

We passed Camel Rock and turned west at the village of Pojoaque to climb gradually through an open terrain dotted with dark junipers. Clumps of grayish green sage and bright yellow chamisa added touches of color, though I didn't know the names of those plants at the time, and as we crossed the two-lane bridge over the Rio Grande, the billowing golden leaves of cottonwoods along the river created a dividing line between the valley we had passed through and the rising volcanic cliffs.

The road continued to climb until it had only a tenuous hold on the steep side of a deep canyon. We leveled out on the plateau at approximately 7,200 feet and for the first time saw the town of Los Alamos and its western horizon of forested mountains. For someone from the Texas plains who had never experienced anything higher than 1000 feet, it was an amazing sight. We had arrived at our new home, one that represented more than just a change of houses. It was a change of worlds.

Within days I had become a part of that new world, exploring canyons and following trails through ponderosa pines. In my youthful imagination, I was sure the trails had been made by Indians, but I learned later, with some disappointment, that they were paths used by boys who had attended a ranch school on the plateau in the years before World War II. With newfound friends, I went hiking, explored caves, restored an old sheepherder's hut, and encountered deer, skunks, and, on one almost-too-exciting afternoon, a bear! As a teenager I could imagine nothing more special than my world of trees and rocks and animals.

Then one day during my college years, while reading a book called *The House at Otowi Bridge*, I discovered a different Pajarito Plateau. I learned the story of someone else who had known the bond I felt with that place but who had a prior claim to what I had come to think of as *my* world. The book was a dual memoir of its author, Peggy Pond Church (1903–1986), and her friend Edith Warner (1892–1951), and it introduced others who had deeply loved the beauty and nature that surrounded me. The plateau as I knew it was the backdrop for a modern town and a scientific laboratory complex, even though I understood that Pueblo Indians and homesteaders had been there long before. The author of the book had come to the Pajarito Plateau as a young girl, just as I had, but more than fifty years earlier. For the young Peggy Pond, the plateau setting included the same forests and high mountain meadows that I knew, but they overlooked sparsely populated mesas and canyons. The area was reached by a precarious dirt road and occupied by only a few ranchers and seasonal farmers from the valley below. What had it been like to live on the plateau then, I wondered. There would come a time when I had to know the answer to that question—and many more.

I loved *The House at Otowi Bridge* and read it more than once, but I wasn't stirred to action until years later, in the spring of 1996, when I read a small volume of poems called *Foretaste*. Published in 1933, it was Peggy Pond Church's first book. The poems were about the land and the people of northern New Mexico, and they touched emotions deep within me. Suddenly, I experienced a need to learn more about the woman who wrote the poems and the memoir I'd read years before. Who was Peggy Pond Church? I soon discovered that satisfying my curiosity wouldn't be easy. Though she had eventually written eleven books and her name was known by almost everyone in Los Alamos and Santa Fe, not much had been written about her. I found a few short interviews in old newspapers and magazines and a brief introduction in her book *Wind's Trail: The Early Life of Mary Austin*. There was also a monograph published by Boise State University as part of their Western Writers Series, but even that didn't come close to answering all my questions. What I wanted was a biography, but that didn't exist. Then I understood. I was going to be the one to write it.

I had a unique advantage. A few years before, I had worked with Kathleen Church, Peggy's daughter-in-law. I phoned her to explain what I wanted to do.

She liked the idea but wanted to talk it over with her husband and his two brothers. With their approval two days later, a treasure trove of information opened to me. The family had most of Peggy's personal journals, files of her correspondence, newspaper clippings, address books, photograph albums—the kinds of resources I would need if I were to become truly knowledgeable about Peggy Pond Church. An extraordinary adventure was beginning.

To write biography is to take on the responsibility of revealing a life not one's own. It demands time and commitment that can't be fully understood by anyone who hasn't done it, but it reaps rewards far beyond anything imagined in the beginning. Soon I was co-existing with Peggy by reading her journals and experiencing the things she experienced. Through those journals I took morning walks with her, went on picnics, cooked dinner, argued, loved, heard the bird songs at sunrise, weeded the garden, struggled to find just the right phrase to end a poem. I learned Peggy's complexities. To understand her, I had to retrace some of my own steps and then take new ones. I hiked the Pajarito Plateau again, as I had when I was young, but I looked at every rock and tree and ruin anew. I read Colette, Pablo Neruda, and the fairy tales of Andrew Lang, authors who had been some of Peggy's favorites. I checked out books on Carl Jung and the I Ching. I had to know what it was like to live in the Santa Fe of the 1920s and to reflect on Mary Austin and Haniel Long and Alice Corbin Henderson. I traveled to Tucson, Flagstaff, Boise, San Francisco, Los Angeles, and as far away as England to learn from people who had known her. I visited the ranches of her ancestors and the isolated canyon where she was born. Peggy was taking me to places I never dreamed I would go, and some of them were inner places.

In reading Peggy's journals and letters, I sometimes felt as though I were trespassing or, at the very least, eavesdropping on a private conversation. At the same time, I knew it was those resources that would give me the best insight. Peggy understood such sanctioned intrusions, for she had done extensive biographical research on Mary Austin as well as delving into her own family history. Eventually, with enough investigation, all of the pieces come together, and a bond forms between biographer and subject. "This strange resurrection that we give to the dead," Peggy once described it, "pondering their lives at such a distance in time, yet able to communicate." After several years of research and "communicating," I felt I knew Peggy well enough to begin writing the book.

Peggy was born on a cold December night in 1903 in a remote ranch house in the Territory of New Mexico. She was premature, and her worried father wrapped her in cotton batting and placed her in a closet that he warmed with a small oil stove. The tiny infant survived and lived to be eighty-two years old, completing a journey of wondrous observation and discovery—the journey of a poet.

"As a girl, her eyes always had a direct, long-range expression," Mabel Dodge Luhan once said of the young Peggy Pond, "as in one who gazes from a mountain top across wide valleys to a far-away distance. And always she had time. Out in the world, one has everything else but hardly anyone has time! Time to experience the overlooked, the important natural things that escape us in our hurry."[1] Those elements of time and keen observation combined with a love of the southwestern landscape to create the sensitive writer and poet Peggy became.

The quest for discovery was not an easy one. Peggy struggled to cope with being "woman," to find an independence that was demanded by her being but not often allowed by society in her formative years. She married a young schoolmaster at the Los Alamos Ranch School and raised three sons, but she was continually torn between her family responsibilities and her desire to spend time writing. She needed to express the love she held inside and to be worthy of love in return, but she imagined herself falling short on both counts. There were endless questions longing for answers. She read and studied in order to learn from other writers and poets who came into her life, both on the printed page and as friends and acquaintances. Haniel Long was her mentor. She idolized Alice Corbin Henderson. Friendships with May Sarton, Lawrence Clark Powell, Witter Bynner, Edith Warner, Erna Fergusson, Corina Santistevan, and many others provided opportunities for sharing and experiencing life's lessons.

Despite her talent and the respect and admiration of her peers, Peggy had her quota of human frailties and problems. She fought low self-esteem and couldn't always control a bad temper. Her parents didn't understand her, and she thought her sister was prettier than she was. She suffered a nervous breakdown in her thirties and had an affair. In many ways Peggy was like thousands of other women, but there was also that part of her that saw things on another level and needed to share her insights in beautiful and sensitive poetry.

In the years following World War II, Peggy found herself at a crossroads in history, attempting to span the gap between the ancient pueblos she explored as a child and the nuclear laboratory that evolved from the Manhattan Project. "When I was a child I climbed here / at sunrise, barefooted among the grasses," she wrote in one of her most famous poems. "I searched for arrowheads among the ruins / and stood wondering on the rims of the broken kivas."[2] The setting of her childhood was a peaceful one, but within three decades World War II had ended with an atomic bomb built on the same spot where men had once fashioned those arrowheads. Searching for the answers to questions that sprang from that enormous discrepancy, she turned to her poetry, but rather than reflecting on mysteries of the past, her words related a deep concern for the future. "Love is no longer a theme for eloquence, or a way of life for a few to choose whose hearts can decide it. / It is the sternest necessity; the unequivocal ultimatum."[3] As the world had changed, so had Peggy's perceptions. Her verse matured and gained strength. In the words of author and poet Stanley Noyes, Peggy Pond Church was no longer merely an outstanding southwestern poet, "she was a significant American voice."[4] It is a voice that is still relevant.

Essentially, that was the woman I came to know, but as with any life, it takes the small, intimate details to complete the picture, to fill in the character, the personality, the memories, and the reasons. And only with all of that could I come close to answering my question. Who was Peggy Pond Church?

"Strange how the imagination strives to breathe life into these long-gone persons. What survives is never our earthly being but an essence that lives in memory."

— *Peggy Pond Church, 1976*

Preface

When I first considered how I would write this biography, I knew that to present the life of Peggy Pond Church without the experience of place would be to leave out the heart of her story. I wanted the reader to enter her world, to feel the heat of a canyon on a summer day, to hear the wind in the ponderosas of Pajarito Canyon, and to appreciate the solitude of a mountain trail. I needed to present the essence of the land, the culture, and the history of northern New Mexico as well as Peggy's sensitivity to it. Only then could the reader fully understand the beauty and the depth of Peggy's poetry and comprehend why so many people agree that *The House at Otowi Bridge* could have been written only by a poet. With those thoughts in mind, I wrote portions of this biography in a way that allows the reader to more fully experience Peggy's life and emotions. These passages are set apart in visual design and in writing style. While they may read like fiction, these vignettes are constructed with facts. The scenes they portray are accurate in historical details, quotes, and settings. They are taken from the recollections of family and friends and from journals and poems. Peggy's life was so connected to the beauty and the history of New Mexico, in particular with the Pajarito Plateau, that her biography must be, in some regard, a biography of the place as well. Of her poetry Peggy once remarked, "It is the land that wants to be said."[1] It is my hope that this biography will tell both their stories.

Sharon Snyder
Rio Rancho, New Mexico
2011

Chapter 1

A Sense of Place

"The land there has a soul, and my own soul is somehow mixed with it."

The New Mexico sky was a clear and brilliant blue. Beneath it, tan cliffs radiated heat as a young girl rode her horse through the freedom of a summer afternoon. Her chestnut mare stepped lightly through the canyon, avoiding rocks and clumps of grama grass and sage to plod almost silently through powdery soil. Only the tops of the nearby ponderosas caught enough breeze to sway slowly. She reined her horse to the north side of the canyon where there were cliff dwellings in the volcanic rock. Hollowed partly by erosion, the caves had been further shaped by the hands of Indians who lived in the canyon long before.

The girl dismounted, tied her horse to a juniper branch, and climbed cautiously among the broken rocks. Huge, jagged boulders of tuff, the hardened ash of prehistoric eruptions, sat embedded in the talus slope. They had separated from the canyon wall and crept downward through the centuries to stand as sentinels below the abandoned dwellings. Narrow spaces allowed passage between the rocks, but the surface of the tuff was raspy to the touch, even sharp in places. She made her way to the canyon wall and used toeholds to enter one of the caves. It was a familiar place. She came here often to write in her journal and sometimes add to a cache of potsherds and arrowheads hidden there. She sat for a while at the cave's entrance, absorbing the canyon's beauty and solitude. Shaded from the sun, the back of the cave was comfortable, but where she sat was too hot in the late afternoon, especially where her legs dangled over the edge and touched the rock. She left the cave to find a cooler place. She walked her horse farther up the canyon and found some shade for the little mare. From there, a path led to the rim of the mesa where a large petroglyph, a seven-foot-long plumed serpent, pointed to the ruins of an ancient pueblo above. The figure etched in the rock was the Awanyu, the deity of clouds and rain, of the flowing water that sustained life.

Atop the mesa, the breeze was stronger and brought relief from the late afternoon sun. As she sat down in the welcome shade of a piñon, the flight of a hawk caught her eye. With outstretched wings, it glided high above the remnants of rock walls still held together with crumbling adobe. Those walls were all that remained of the once thriving pueblo of Tshirege.[1] *The whispers of the wind and the scent of chamisa blended with the spirits of the mesa, and her imagination soared with the hawk. She became one with the rocks and trees, the ragged forms of the piñons, and the flower-shaped cones that held the seeds of a past season. Short pine needles littered the ground, mingling with broken bits of pottery and chips of obsidian. Far below, the Rio Grande flowed through time, and across its valley the Sangre de Cristo Mountains would soon take on the blood-red hue they turned each evening when the sun began to set behind the Jemez Mountains and the Pajarito Plateau. It was a magical realm, a place that filled her every sense of being and determined her destiny.*

The year was 1914, a time poised between the ancient world of the Pueblo Indians and a modern era in which the isolated plateau would lose its innocence, but on that afternoon, the canyon held only summer heat, blue sky, and peace. In years to come, far from New Mexico, a young woman would remember that time and the special view from the mesa that had been hers.

Sangre de Cristo

I did not even ask to understand;
That night the mesa was so still, so still,
Half lost in shadows. Mists crept up until
They breathed pale incense through the aisle of trees.
Even the wind was hushed; somehow it seemed
Like a great dim cathedral filled with prayer
And my soul kneeling for communion there.

Till breathlessly the mountains seemed to glow
Like a great grail, holy and wonderful,—
Up swept a tide of fire, nor did I know
How I could sense the beauty of the Lord!
Wine that was blessed, at twilight so out-poured!
Almost, I saw His face and felt His hand—
Nor did I even need to understand.[2]

     — Peggy Pond Church
      Written at age seventeen,
      Hillside School, Norwalk, Connecticut

Today, a road connects the town of Los Alamos with its suburb of White Rock as it passes through the canyon where the young girl rode that day. The intervening decades shaped the sensitive and observant child into the woman who would one day be called the "First Lady of New Mexico poetry."³ Those years hold the story of Peggy Pond Church, and the winds will gladly tell it to all who stand beneath a tall pine in Pajarito Canyon, touch its bark, breathe in its fragrance, and listen.

It is not uncommon for a writer to become inseparably linked with a place. Isak Dinesen will forever be a part of Africa, just as the poems of Robert Service will forever haunt the gold fields of the Yukon. For Peggy Pond Church the *place* was a high plateau of pine-covered mesas and deep canyons bordering the Jemez Mountains in northern New Mexico.

"I remember the very first sight of it," Peggy said longingly in 1982 as

Young Peggy Pond stands in the middle of the ruins of Tshirege Pueblo, a place she loved to explore. Even as a child, she felt a reverence there. Years later she would write "I had no words to say what it was that moved me / A wisdom of rocks and old trees, of buried rivers, / of the great arcs and tangents of sky and mountain / and always the grass that whispered upon the ruins" (from "Morning on Tshirege"). Courtesy Los Alamos Historical Museum Archives.

she presented a talk about her early days on the Pajarito Plateau. It was "a world in itself," she told her listeners, "elevated above the arid and steeply sloping Rio Grande Valley. We drove down the stony hills, across dry water courses, and came to the edge of a dark brown river, treeless and uncommunicative. On the other side of the river, the steep hills of gravel were capped by fortress-like walls of black basalt."[4]

When Peggy's father, Ashley Pond Jr., moved his family to Pajarito Canyon in 1914, the route they traveled was not the paved, four-lane highway it is today, heading north from Santa Fe and turning west at the village of Pojoaque. It was a rugged dirt road that took the traveler west through deep ruts and arroyos to cross a questionable bridge over the Rio Grande at a railway siding called Buckman.

"When we crossed the rickety, narrow wooden bridge and climbed up and up in the panting car," Peggy said, "I could look down, appalled at the tiny silver thread of the river engulfed by its steep canyon, a desert river bordered not by trees and green grass but by rolled gravels and tumbled black rocks."

She recalled the long, hot ascent of the plateau and the frequent stops to allow the engine to cool. They carried canvas bags of water that hung alongside the car so that the radiator could be refilled. Her father had brought his family to a land of broad canyons cutting through mesas that spread out toward the Rio Grande Valley like fingers from the 11,000-foot Jemez range. The canyons were steep-sided and sandy, with remnants of old stream beds visible but mostly dry. The mesas were covered with piñons, junipers, and ponderosa pines. "Not that I knew the names then of what I looked at," she added. "I only knew it was a world unlike any I had ever seen before."

"'This was the ranch,' my father said. The Ramon Vigil Ranch. There were 32,000 acres of land just like this piece of it. He liked to give everyone the impression that he and his family owned it," Peggy explained, "and I didn't find out until many decades later that he owned only a fifth part of it and that for him it was both the fulfillment of a dream and an eventual source of heartbreak."[5]

From the moment he saw it in 1913, Ashley Pond was in love with the Pajarito Plateau, but his attempt at ranching on the Ramon Vigil Land Grant failed after only two years. Unwilling to leave the secluded plateau, he found a way to continue living in the Pajarito country by starting a boys' ranch school on a nearby mesa, but within a year, World War I had drawn him from his commitment to the school to serve in France. Like her father, Peggy, too, had fallen in love with the plateau, and when Ashley Pond left the boys' school in 1918, it meant that her ties to the Pajarito country were severed as well, though she was not to be separated from it for long. Even without its founder, Los Alamos Ranch School succeeded, and within six years Peggy had made her way back by marrying one of the school's masters.[6] She had returned to the canyons and forests of her childhood, the place she loved above all others, but Fate can change even the most perfect of circumstances. Despite the isolation, the small mountain school was not, as Peggy put it years later, "beyond the reach of history."[7]

Dreams and heartbreak. In time, destiny attached those words to Peggy as well, for the land of the Pajarito spelled both joy and sadness for her as it had for her father. In the life of Peggy Pond Church, there were two defining moments—coming to live on the Pajarito Plateau and being forced to leave it.

The afternoon sun offered no warmth as Peggy stepped out the door of Spruce Cottage on a December day in 1942. It had been just more than a year since the bombing of Pearl Harbor, and she thought about the war and the troubled world that was about to encroach on the peaceful plateau that was her home. She walked through shadows cast by the pines, heading for Pueblo Canyon and the small cabin where she had found privacy to write her poetry. It was a walk she had taken many times, but this visit was different. It would be the last. Only days before, a letter from Washington had confirmed what she and others at Los Alamos Ranch School had suspected for weeks. The government was taking over the property—all land and all buildings. The staff and students must leave immediately. The seclusion that was perfect for her writing was also perfect for an isolated, top secret project. She opened the door of the tiny wooden hut and went inside, quickly closing the door against the cold. No need to light a fire in the small wood stove. She wouldn't be there long.

Almost nineteen years had passed since she came to live at the Ranch School as a young bride. Her father had established his boys' school on the plateau in 1917, when she was thirteen years old. How angry she had been at him for designing his school for boys only! Peggy spent months away from home each year attending boarding schools, and she passed the summers at Camp Aloha in Vermont or in Santa Fe, where her father had relocated the family. Then, in 1924, she found a way to return to the plateau. She came home that summer from her second year at Smith College and married Fermor Spencer Church, a young master at the Ranch School. Together, they had built a comfortable log home and raised three sons.

She looked out the window to the north. The shadows were lengthening across the canyon, but in the windowpane other images seemed to take shape. She saw a red rose climbing next to the front door of a log and stone house. Three little boys slept on a screened porch covered by honeysuckle vines, and the forest beyond her garden was bathed in moonlight. Delphiniums and marigolds surrounded an old sunken bathtub that held goldfish and lilies. She saw herself at the piano as young men practiced a Gilbert and Sullivan operetta. A family of skunks played once more beneath the crabapple tree in her backyard.

"And in the late afternoon / I go down to the edge of the canyon and watch the swallows," she whispered, reciting a phrase from one of her poems. Two volumes of poetry and a children's book had been created, at least in part, in the small room where she stood. "And I forget that I am mortal / and torn with mortal griefs."[8]

Good times mingled with sadness and struggle would be remembered from the years at the school. Peggy looked slowly around the room one more time before she turned and left the cabin, closing the door behind her. She looked westward to the familiar outline of the Jemez Mountains silhouetted against the sunset. Tomorrow she would leave and take the first uncertain steps in a new life.

Peggy was well acquainted with uncertain steps and new homes from her childhood years. By the time ten-year-old Peggy Pond moved to the Pajarito Plateau, she had lived in five different homes in New Mexico, Michigan, and California, and attended boarding schools in Detroit, Albuquerque, and Los Angeles. She would be sent to three more such schools before graduating and moving on to Smith College. And though the separation from her beloved plateau brought pain, she was used to that, too. As an adult, Peggy still felt the frustration that remained from a childhood with parents to whom she could not relate and from whom she felt little love. She recalled that her mother "endlessly criticized and disciplined and found fault" with her and her siblings. Her father thought she had an "irrational temperament" and berated her for "poetic absentmindedness." Though her parents undoubtedly loved her, they failed often to show it. They were wrapped up in their own frustrations with life.

Peggy was a sensitive child and was frequently misunderstood. As she grew older, her sensitivities created a feeling of isolation from the main stream, and because she hadn't learned love as a child, Peggy was uncomfortable showing it outwardly. It remained locked inside until it would emerge in the words of her poems. She felt tears she could not show, needs that were not met, and often experienced moments of frustration and fiery temper. In a letter to her friend May Sarton in 1951, Peggy observed, "It's a hard world for sensitive people to live in."[9]

Throughout her life, Peggy struggled with inner conflict. She continually searched for self, trying everything from Jungian analysis to in-depth study of other poets and authors. She read constantly, looking for answers in the poetry of William Blake and Pablo Neruda, in the writings of Doris Lessing and Colette, and in the wisdom of Thomas Merton, Meister Eckhart, and a host of other philosophers. She examined religions and sought solitude for reflection, but in the end, she realized that all of the places and events she had·experienced were simply steps in a journey. In her poem "East of the Sun and West of the Moon," she put her fate into words: "She must wander, questioning, through the wide world."[10]

Pajarito Canyon was a private playground for the Pond children when they lived at the Pajarito Club. This view of the lower canyon was taken ca, 1915. Courtesy Los Alamos Historical Museum Archives.

Chapter 2

Roots in New Mexico
"The story of this life is not this life only."

Life takes a person down many paths, and for Peggy some of the most important ones led to places of long ago and to ancestors who had been lured to the West. Establishing a connection with those ancestors not only helped with her self-understanding but inspired some of her finest poetry. "It is as though a released bird / remembered the use of wings. The sloping grasslands / waken ancient nomadic dreams."

She was inspired to write those words in 1983 as she looked across the prairie where her family had lived in northeastern New Mexico eighty years earlier. Strong emotions stirred within. "Visions of grazing herds begin to shimmer; / the horseman wakens."[1]

The poem "Return to a Landscape" resulted from a visit to her birthplace in Mora County, land to which she was drawn in later years by a need for continuity, not only within her own life but between generations.[2]

Peggy traced her family's ranching history on the western edge of the Great Plains by reading old newspapers, letters, and diaries and sometimes by listening to old-timers tell stories of the region. She was told that it took a whole day to travel the twenty miles from the ranch to nearby Las Vegas, New Mexico, in a wagon! And when her Uncle Homan went to town for a haircut, it was *news* in the *Las Vegas Optic*. Peggy had always known that her great-grandfather's ranch, the Clyde, was named for the Clydesdale horses he raised there, but what else could she learn? She returned to the ranch in 1976 to experience for herself the land and what remained of the buildings, though they no longer belonged to the family. She found that the hay smelled as sweet as her mother had always said and that her parents' house of handmade bricks still stood nearby in Shoemaker Canyon.[3] The pieces of an old puzzle began to fall into place. "The story of this life is not this life only," Peggy wrote in notes for her poem "Preface to an Autobiography." "The story of a tree is not the story of half a summer and the blossoming of one spring remembered. The story of this life, the story of any life, is a river flowing."[4]

The house on the Clyde Ranch was atypical of ranch houses in its day. It was built in 1864 of adobe brick and mortar, but accent materials such as lumber, windows, frames, paneling, and hardware were brought from Missouri over the Santa Fe Trail, which passed through the property right next to the house. Courtesy Peggy Pond Church estate.

Hazel Hallett was an active young girl when this photograph was taken on the Clyde, ca. 1898. Along with her brother, Homan, she visited during every summer vacation until she married Ashley Pond Jr. in 1903, at which time she moved to a ranch five miles to the east in Shoemaker Canyon. Courtesy Peggy Pond Church Estate.

Margaret Hallett Pond, to be known as Peggy, was born December 1, 1903, near the frontier town of Watrous, Territory of New Mexico, at a place known as Valmora. She was the first of her family to be born in New Mexico, but the love she was to feel for her native land was shared by ancestors on both sides, pioneers who made their way west in the late 1800s to buy ranches.

Ozro A. Hadley, a former governor of Arkansas, was the first of Peggy's ancestors to arrive. In 1878, Hadley cast his lot with an infamous United States senator named Stephen Dorsey and came to New Mexico looking for business opportunities.[5] Hadley was Peggy's great-grandfather, and despite many admirable accomplishments in his life, she was always skeptical about "his connection with that land-grabbing politico and rancher, Senator Dorsey."[6] Regardless of what Peggy suspected to be "financial shenanigans," ranches were bought and sold and stock companies were formed. The goings-on would have made a spirited plot for a dime western, but whether or not the land ventures and a dubious involvement with the Maxwell Land Grant were unscrupulous, Dorsey *was* responsible for bringing the Hadley relatives to the West.

Hadley was fifty-six years old when he arrived in New Mexico. He represented the seventh generation of Hadleys in America and was the first to move away from a family of staunch New Englanders who had lived in Massachusetts for more than two hundred years. The first Hadley landed in Boston as an indentured servant in 1628, and despite the one relative hanged as a witch in Salem in 1692, there were Massachusetts towns that bore the family name.[7] By the time he was seventeen, Ozro Hadley had assumed responsibility for his mother, a brother, and two sisters because of his father's poor health. He gave up his dream of studying law and settled instead for work in insurance and farming. In 1849, he married Mary Cordelia Kilbourn of New York, and five years later, freed by the death of his father, he moved his wife; their baby daughter, Addie; and his mother to a farm in Rochester, Minnesota. A second daughter, Altie, who would become Peggy's grandmother, was born there. The farming and some minor endeavors in county politics were successful for Hadley, but, by the end of the Civil War, opportunities in the commission business in Arkansas attracted him to Little Rock, where he became engaged in purchasing cotton. In addition to his business ventures, he again took an interest in politics and eventually became a state senator from Pulaski County. His work in the senate earned him enough respect that when Arkansas Gov. Powell Clayton was elected to the U.S. Senate in 1871, Hadley was unanimously chosen by his fellow state

Ashley Pond Jr. holds his baby daughter, Peggy, in 1904 at Valmora. Courtesy Los Alamos Historical Museum Archives.

Peggy poses with Princess, the Great Dane, in the brick house in Boone Valley, Shoemaker Canyon, summer of 1904. Courtesy Peggy Pond Church Estate.

senators to fill the vacated position. He served for the next two years as the governor of Arkansas. After that, it wasn't long before another adventure presented itself in the form of Sen. Stephen Dorsey's offer of a trip to the New Mexico Territory.[8]

Hadley liked what he saw in the way of business possibilities in the territory and teamed up with Dorsey in 1879 to purchase the Eagle Tail Ranch in Colfax County near Raton, where the two planned to run a small herd of Galloway and Aberdeen Angus cattle. By the time Hadley relocated his family to New Mexico, both of his daughters were married, Addie to Civil War general Keyes Danforth and younger daughter, Altie, to William Henry Hallett, a railroad clerk. The Danforths were living in Colorado Springs, and William and Altie were settled in Little Rock, where Altie had given birth to Hadley's first grandchild, William Hadley Hallett. Consequently it was Ozro Hadley, his wife Mary, and his seventy-seven-year-old mother who settled in at the Eagle Tail. Four years later, however, he was on the move again, this time to Chico Springs to manage another ranch for Stephen Dorsey. While still owning his share of the Eagle Tail and running the Chico Springs Ranch, Hadley continued to build his influence in the region. By 1888 he had bought yet another ranch, taking his son-in-law William Hallett as a partner. The *Las Vegas Optic* reported the substantial transaction on December 1, 1888: "Ex-governor O. A. Hadley has purchased the Tipton place of 15,000 acres, situated some 22 miles from Las Vegas and one and a half miles from Watrous, for a large consideration. He intends to beautify the place, put every convenience in the dwelling and buildings, and embark on the business of raising thoroughbred horses on a considerable scale, using for his purpose imported Norman-Percherons, Clydesdales, and other improved breeds." Hallett was an absentee owner, but Hadley resigned from Chico Springs and moved to his new ranch at Tiptonville, an upstart town south of Ft. Union. He saw the frontier army post as a market for the horses he intended to raise.

Mary Hadley and her mother-in-law presided over a splendid mansion "in the midst of a wide lawn, the grassy carpet stretching away for some distance and shaded by beautiful and noble trees, the whole having much the appearance of an old English manor."[9] However, the grandeur was somewhat of an illusion. Life on the Clyde was a lonely existence for the women of the "manor." Peggy would reflect years later, as she looked back on the life of her great-grandparents, that "it was not a life or a time in which women could be very happy. The men could ride the ranges and go out wheeling and dealing . . . while the women were shut up at home, tending their big houses, trying to keep some atmosphere of elegance, lonely and awed into terror by the solitude." That description may not have been true for all the women on the vast New Mexico ranches of the 1890s, but it was accurate for Mary Hadley. "She was a porcelain great-grandmother whom I never saw," Peggy wrote of the small, pure-complexioned, fastidious woman. "Did she finally die, I wonder, of homesickness too long endured? She hated the country. The horses frightened her. The meat brought in to be butchered sickened her. She was too delicate, too feminine for this wilderness. She busied herself all day long at tasks she hated, performing them each meticulously and beautifully, with great pride shirking nothing." She was determined to maintain a semblance of the elegance she had known in her home in New York State. When visiting cowboys came to the ranch, usually two or three at a time, they were put up in the bunkhouse and were welcome at Mary Hadley's table, but she "made them wear coats!"

Isolation was a fact of life for the women of the Clyde, and travel possibilities were limited. A visit to Las Vegas, the nearest town, usually took three days. They would drive down behind a team the first day, rest the horses, and drive back on the third day. However, a stay at the Plaza Hotel or the newer Hotel Casteñeda and perhaps the purchase of a hat or fabrics for sewing helped to counter the loneliness of life at the ranch. The needs of the women were in vast contrast to those of the men who settled northeastern New Mexico, those "aggressive masculine spirits," Peggy called them, "buying and selling land, dealing in cattle, dreaming of profit, of riches, as the Spanish conquistadors dreamed of gold, of power . . . ."[10] She felt a close bond to the frontier women in her family, their spirit and fortitude, the life they endured. In "Return to a Landscape" she wrote,

> I still wear my mother's silver thimble
> that was her grandmother's before;
> when I prick my finger
> the drop of blood is theirs.[11]

The routines of ranch life at the Clyde were periodically broken for the Hadleys by visits from their daughters. By the time William and Altie Hallett bought an interest in the Tiptonville ranch, they had added three more children to their family. A second boy, Homan, was born in Little Rock in 1881. Their only daughter, Hazel, Peggy's mother, was born in 1885 in St. Louis, and another son, Horace, followed in 1888. Addie Danforth moved to New Mexico after losing her husband to consumption, and she eventually married Louis C. Tetard of Las Vegas, co-owner of the town's cigar store and a dealer in real estate. The Hadleys must have felt a certain warmth and security as their extended family gathered at the Clyde, but that was to be an illusion, too.

After the death of Keyes Danforth, a string of losses plagued the family. In May of 1889, the oldest grandson, William Hadley Hallett, died of diphtheria at age nine. Six weeks later, the birth of a daughter, Mary, to Addie and Louis Tetard brought joy to counter the grieving, but the recovery was short lived. Only a few days after celebrating her daughter's first birthday in June of 1890, Addie died of heart failure. A period of mourning descended on the Clyde, but there was more to come. Another of the Hadley's grandsons, five-year-old Horace, contracted diphtheria and died in March of 1893, an event followed soon after by the death of Hadley's mother. Eunice Bates Hadley, age ninety, had lived with her son's family for thirty-six years.

Despite their fine home and the success of the ranch, Ozro and Mary Hadley were experiencing the harshness that accompanied life on the frontier in the late 1800s. Still, there were some lighter moments at the Clyde. The Hadleys were able to watch two grandchildren grow during frequent visits. Homan and Hazel Hallett came from Los Angeles, where their family had moved, to spend summer months at the ranch.

Peggy stood in a vast front yard overgrown with wild grasses and looked up at the fan-shaped window in the second story of an imposing house. A porch with tall pillars lined the front of the house, but its white trim was peeling badly. A breeze rustled through tall, aging trees. Did she really smell the scent of a barnyard, the scent of horses hot with sweat from their work in the fields? Did she hear the sound of heavy hooves stamping? She visualized the horses. Huge horses. How large must they have seemed to my mother when she played in this yard, Peggy wondered. She had returned to her roots, the ranch her mother had loved as a child.

As a six-year-old, Peggy's mother, Hazel, rode a pet burro when she stayed at the Clyde in the early 1890s. She remembered him fondly in stories she told her children. "My burro Lightfoot," she used to begin with a chuckle. "The men always groaned when told we were on the way out and it was time to bring in Lightfoot." It always took several days to round him up. "He'd climb up and down the side of a cliff, while the men on horseback had to go around. Nobody could get near him." One wrangler grumbled, "Don't tell me a little girl six years old is going to ride that burro!" But when Hazel went to the fence and called, he would come to her and put out his head to have his bridle put on. "He had a saddle and a harness," Hazel told Peggy, "and he pulled a little wagon with two seats, a model of a spring wagon."[12]

It had been almost thirty years since Peggy's first visit to the Clyde. The property had no longer belonged to the family even then, but the place was filled with feelings and emotions and memories that were hers. She thought of the words she wrote after that first visit. *"There is a house on the east slope of New Mexico mountains I never saw before I was grown. Yet I remember it more intimately, more eagerly than any house I have ever lived in. I had never been in this house before, but I remembered instantly the tall square walls and the spaced windows, the dark-grained wood paneling . . . the rooms opening from the dark halls . . . the wide beds angled against the walls, the smooth wall paper, the color and texture even of the paper. It was not I who ran in and out of this house, a child intoxicated with summer . . . It was my mother. Why then do I remember, as if she had never told me, the sun on the pastures, the fields with the ripe grain . . . the cool alfalfa, the willow trees . . . the dense grove of them where the ditch ran? Why should I remember that large man, that immense man, the man called 'Grandpaw' who laughed and was kindly but with whose laughter no liberties were ever taken? Afternoons, memory said, or my mother, he would take a small girl driving beside him, high on the seat of the buckboard, he filling the side of the seat and overflowing and weighing it down, she springing beside him down up, up down, small and insubstantial, as the horse trotted over the rutted road, over the road with the deep summer dust on it, past the willow grove and the river, two miles to town and back to bring the mail in. Grandpaw had been governor of a state once, but that was long past him. He was an old man sitting in the sun now, proud of his countless acres and his cattle, remembering his life. Remembering whatever trails had brought him westward out of New York and through Minnesota, down into Arkansas, and at last to this ranch on the slope of New Mexico mountains, on the Mora River . . ."*[13]

⟨⁓⟩

"Oh proud house!" Peggy called the Clyde when she wrote "Preface to an Autobiography" in 1933.

> Here my own heart returns to its beginnings,
> remembering these mountains, strangely remembering them,
> feeling at home here,
> feeling with my great-grandfather's heart at home
>   in these meadows,
> feeling with my great-grandmother's heart
>   the pang of homesickness
> when the sharp light mellows in the polished pewter,
> mellows in the clear surface of the stately table
> that reflected once the patriarchal beard of Grandpaw,
> and Grandmaw's fragile hands that poured the coffee,
> and the eager face of my mother browned in the summer sun.[14]

During one of her summer visits to the Clyde, the young Hazel Hallett met a handsome rancher. His name was Ashley Pond Jr.

Ashley was the only surviving son of an eminent Detroit attorney and had grown up in a well-to-do family, attending the best private schools and socializing with the children of the power figures in the emerging automobile industry. Despite the advantages, in the cold and humid northern climate, Ashley was plagued by repeated colds and bronchitis that too often kept him away from classes and hampered his education. Following such episodes, Ashley would spend days or weeks at his father's cabin at the Huron Mountain Club, a private hunting and fishing resort near Marquette, where he recuperated in the fresh air. To young Ashley, "recuperating" often meant spending time on the Pine River in his father's motor boat with his two boyhood friends, Roy Chapin and Henry Joy.[15] At age fifteen, Ashley was sent to the prestigious St. Paul's School in New Hampshire, but again his studies were interrupted by frequent illness. He returned home to Detroit several times for bed rest.[16]

Because of his educational setbacks, Ashley wasn't accepted to Yale University until 1891, when he was twenty years old. Throughout his life, Ashley showed pride in his association with Yale. He frequently mentioned his membership in the Class of 1896, leading people to believe he graduated with that class. In reality Ashley entered Yale's Sheffield College but never earned a degree. The greatest honor achieved in his time there came not from his studies but on the playing fields. He excelled in track events, particularly the 220-yard dash. In the summer after his freshman year, he traveled to London with the Yale team to compete in an international meet at Oxford. Though he failed to win in any of his events, the glamour and prestige of the competition remained with him for a lifetime. In 1895 Ashley left Yale. Seemingly at loose ends for the next three years, he fought the usual respiratory problems, briefly enrolled in medical school, and spent time traveling. Then, in 1898, the battleship *Maine* exploded in Havana Harbor, and the United States declared war on Spain. In a characteristic gesture of patriotism, Ashley joined Teddy Roosevelt's Rough Riders. It was a move that suited his longing for action and adventure, but before the unit could travel to Cuba, he fell victim to typhoid fever. Ashley remained in Tampa while his comrades charged to their glory up San Juan Hill. He once again returned to Detroit until his father could make arrangements to send him west to continue his recovery.

In 1899, Ashley found himself in the unlikely destination of Catskill, New Mexico. A small lumber boomtown that had existed for less than a decade, Catskill was the end of the line for the Union Pacific Railroad out of Trinidad, Colorado, on a section called the Maxwell Branch. The rail line had been created to transport milled lumber from the heavily wooded northern region of the Maxwell Land Grant. Ashley stepped off the train into a hastily built town of clapboard buildings and dirt streets but one which bustled with restaurants, feed stores, a blacksmith shop, and hotels. A race course, a dancing pavilion, and a baseball diamond provided entertainment. Catskill was thirty miles west of Raton on the southern edge of the Raton Mountains, just below the Colorado border, and it provided everything Ashley needed. Most of all, it had clean air and wide open spaces.

"There was no place for young men with health problems to stay except on remote ranches, often under very primitive conditions," Peggy noted of her father's first months in New Mexico.[17] Ashley took up residence on just such a ranch in the high country. As he recovered his health to become fit and robust, he became captivated by the land. The mountain scenery, the fresh air, the life at the ranch—all took hold of Ashley Pond Jr. During his months in Catskill, he took the first step toward becoming a rancher himself. He registered his Lazy A brand.

At about the same time, another idea kindled for Ashley. He began to think not only of having a ranch but also of incorporating it with a boys' school that would offer ranching activities to delicate young men such as he had been, giving them the opportunity to bolster their strength. He knew how difficult it had been to "keep scholastically abreast of his more rugged classmates." He envisioned a school where boys "could live under competent supervision, build up their health, and at the same time prepare for the leading colleges as thoroughly as in an Eastern school."[18]

Ashley took a step toward making his dream a reality in 1900 when he bought three adjoining ranches at the head of Shoemaker Canyon a few miles east of Watrous. His land totaled approximately 3,700 acres and was made up of properties the locals called the Streeter place, the Lynam place, and the Tipton place in Boone Valley. The Tipton acreage was a small part of a much larger ranch once owned by early settlers Enoch and Martha Tipton. When Enoch died, Martha was left with the 1,060 acres in Boone Valley, where, in 1883, her sons built her a large, two-story house using bricks fired on the property.

It apparently didn't take Ashley Pond long to meet his enterprising neighbor, Governor Hadley. By 1902 he was a partner with Hadley in a copper mine at Rociada, New Mexico, in which he owned a one-quarter interest. It was reported that "the new owners have ample means, and development will not stop for lack of funds."[19] It did, unfortunately, stop for lack of minerals. Despite the failed mining venture, the association with Hadley reaped rewards. That same year Ashley met Hadley's granddaughter, Hazel, while she and her brother were spending time at the ranch following the death of their father. Hazel was in an arroyo shooting target practice one afternoon when Ashley rode by. He stopped to compliment her marksmanship. He must have found other attributes to his liking, as well, because he soon approached her grandfather to ask for her hand. Peggy described in a poem that young woman who would become her mother.

> There is a picture I have of you that I love
> taken when you were sixteen, a picture in profile,
> a proud and delicate profile, abundant hair
> piled high on a small head,
> the head posed firmly,
> a velvet ribbon about the slender throat,
> determined chin, lips curved and not quite smiling,
> wide candid eyes.
> Oh very demure and made for lace and ruffles . . .[20]

The photograph of which Peggy wrote was taken the year Hazel met Ashley. They must have seemed the perfect combination, the young woman "made for lace and ruffles" and the attractive, athletic rancher full of enthusiastic dreams. Ashley and Hazel were married on January 27, 1903, in the Cathedral of St. John the Divine in New York. They left immediately for

Containing a dining room, kitchen, and staff quarters, this new building was destroyed the night of the Great Flood of 1904. The Pond family and the ranch school's teacher, nurse, and wrangler gathered on the porch before striking out through raging floodwaters to reach the barn on higher ground. Courtesy Los Alamos Historical Museum Archives.

a honeymoon in Europe. He was thirty, and she was seventeen.

Upon returning to New Mexico, the couple settled into a stone and adobe ranch house on the Streeter place. That first summer of their marriage might well have been an omen for Hazel as to the unsettled nature of life with Ashley. Hazel was pregnant by that June and also overwhelmed with planning for an extended visit by her father-in-law and Ashley's sister, Florence. And if that weren't enough, she and Ashley would be away for several days in June, visiting friends in Detroit and recruiting for the planned school.

At age seventy-five, Ashley Pond Sr.'s health had begun to fail, and it was hoped that a visit to the ranch would improve his condition. He had fallen and broken his hip that winter while stepping from a streetcar onto an icy Detroit sidewalk and never fully recovered. Florence herself must have needed the change of scenery at the ranch as much as her father, if for different reasons. She wrote to a friend in Michigan a few days after her arrival and confided, "It is such a relief to feel that I can be tired without interfering with any duties." For months she had attended her father during his recuperation, and the journey from Detroit to New Mexico by train was difficult with an invalid. She related, "Our journey was accomplished under as comfortable conditions as possible. Father seemed to suffer about the same degree of restlessness and pain as at home."

Ashley arranged to have the train stop at a crossing only a quarter of a mile from the ranch, saving his father and Florence the four-mile trip over a rough road from Watrous. Florence told Louise that "Ashley met us with a wagon containing a mattress on which Father was comfortably transferred." She also reported that "whenever the sun shines, he seems to be encouraged and to feel better. Things seem to be in fairly good shape, but Father is in a condition to worry over everything, and in depressed hours he finds so much to apprehend or deplore that I cannot yet tell whether the situation will be satisfactory, as regards his health." In view of her own outlook, Florence was enjoying herself, and she added, "I find the place most interesting and shall enjoy the life if all goes well. I have my bed on the porch as is the custom here, and find it delightful to sleep under the stars."[21]

Ashley Pond Sr. did finally tolerate, if not endorse, his son's plans for establishing a boys' school, and despite the hectic nature of the summer of 1903, the visit was a success. After the guests had returned to Detroit, Hazel could finally relax and await the birth of her first child.

"I was born in 1903, when New Mexico was still a territory," Peggy said, prompted to start at the beginning by a reporter sitting at her dining room table. Peggy was intensely proud to be a native New Mexican, never failing to point out that her younger brother and sister had the misfortune to be born somewhere else.

She sipped the Earl Grey tea she had poured for the two of them and looked out the window across her garden, beyond the Sangre de Cristos, to a place and time far beyond the stately adobe wall that surrounded her property on Camino Rancheros in Santa Fe. "The weather was fine," she said, almost as though she remembered it, so many times had she heard the story in childhood. "Mother had driven to Watrous in the buckboard for the nurse, supposedly arriving a month ahead of time."[22] She explained that her mother was young and strong and must have thought that a twenty-five-mile ride on a buckboard would do no harm, but her labor started that evening. Peggy recited the words she used once in a poem for her mother. "I remember that you bore your first child at eighteen in a New Mexico ranch house," she said in the gentle and precise voice that carefully delivered the nuance of every word. "And that it was a long labor and a hard one and your mother wasn't with you." The remembering voice possessed a softness that drew listeners into her personal and intimate realm. "The child was not the boy you had wanted but a girl, born a month too early."[23]

The reporter relaxed with the sound of Peggy's voice, having been a little intimidated earlier when he stepped onto her wisteria-covered porch to ring the bell. He had never met Peggy Pond Church, but he knew he was about to interview a woman in her early eighties, a woman revered by Santa Feans not only for her poetry but also for her character and her connections to the history of the state. The previous autumn she had been presented with the coveted Governor's Award for Excellence and Achievement in the Arts in the category of literature. The front door had opened, and she had greeted him with a smile before accompanying him through her adobe home to a room that was obviously the heart of the house. As she had guided him through the living room, he had learned even more about her. There was a sign that read "Gracias por no fumar." Endless shelves of books were filled with titles he wanted to stop and read. There were Navajo rugs on the floor and a baby grand piano dominating the room. As they sat at the bulky, wooden dining table, he studied a collection of smooth stones in the company of driftwood, arrowheads, and a shiny piece of weathered green glass, all arranged on a black lacquer tray. The room was a comfortable one, with a well-used desk, hanging pots of geraniums, and large windows that wrapped around one side to present a view that made the flagstone floor seem almost to merge with the mountains. From the kitchen, separated only by a countertop, the smell of fresh-baked bread added a final touch.

Peggy continued the story of her birth by explaining that her father had "kept the premature baby going by bedding her down in a basket lined with cotton batting in a closet with a tiny window and an oil stove."[24] As the story unfolded, she revealed more than just memories of events. There was wisdom in deep-set eyes, assurance in her bearing, and determination in spite of age. She wore her hair short, with a hint of upward curl at the neckline, and she dressed in the casual style always acceptable in Santa Fe. She was still a vital woman at eighty-one.

She spoke of her great-grandfather and how he had been a governor of Arkansas just after the Civil War, "during a period not much to anybody's credit," she added with a sly grin. "He came to New Mexico on the first train through the Raton Tunnel!"[25] She described his ranch, where he raised Clydesdales, and how her father had bought land nearby. "He was getting ready to start a ranch school for boys," she said of her father, "when a great flood in the fall of 1904 destroyed all his property except a two-story brick house which is still standing."[26] Memories flowed, and the reporter's afternoon passed too quickly.

Even with his father and sister visiting that summer of 1903, Ashley stayed busy with improvements to the Tipton place, planning to open his boys' school in the coming months. He had help from Albert Horton, a ranch hand who had come with him from Catskill. Albert had arrived in New Mexico about the same time as Ashley, looking for work as a wrangler, and with their common interest in horses, the two had become friends. Together, they worked to renovate the sturdy, two-story brick house standing on the property and then added an adobe house for the students and a larger adobe building with a dining room and kitchen as well as rooms for the staff. Eventually, Sarah Thorpe Tipton, a daughter-in-law of Martha Tipton, was hired as cook, and a young man named Daniel Scotten arrived from Detroit to teach.

Despite the demanding work, Albert somehow found time that summer to court Martha Tipton's granddaughter. Alice Gertrude Tipton, or Gertie, as she was called, had been born in the old brick house that Albert and Ashley were restoring, and she was destined to play an important role in Peggy's life. She and Albert were married in February of 1904, and Gertie enjoyed helping Hazel care for baby Peggy.[27]

When renovations were completed in Boone Valley at the end of the summer, Ashley and Hazel moved into the brick house from the Streeter place. Another ranch hand and a nurse were added to the staff, and the stage was set for the opening of the school. Unfortunately, the stage was also set for an event of a different kind the Great Flood of 1904, one of the worst disasters in New Mexico history. "That flood was probably the most exciting thing that ever happened in my life," Peggy reflected years later, "and I don't remember a thing about it!"[28] Peggy was less than a year old when the floodwaters ravaged the Pond home in Shoemaker Canyon.

The summer of 1904 had brought much-needed rain to New Mexico. Crops were good, the hay was in, and optimism was the predominant mood in the Mora River Valley as autumn began. By the end of September, however, the rains returned, not typical of the Indian summer usually experienced in northern New Mexico. An all-day rain soaked the countryside on September 28 and continued through the night. As the downpour went into a second day, some residents dug runoff trenches around their homes, but they still viewed the rains and mud as more of an inconvenience than a cause for alarm. Then the rains continued into a third day.[29]

Rivers and creeks began to rise along the eastern front of the Sangre de Cristo Mountains, which stretch from just north of Las Vegas to the Colorado border. The Mora River, the major concern for Watrous and the surrounding communities, has its headwaters near the mountain juncture of Taos, Colfax, and Mora counties. It flows south out of the high country and then turns eastward to be joined by the smaller Sapello River at Watrous. From there, the combined waters make their way through Shoemaker Canyon to meet the Canadian River thirty-four miles to the east. From the approximately 11,000-foot origin of the Mora River, the drop in elevation to the plains east of Watrous produces swift runoff.

In Boone Valley the night of September 30, Ashley Pond and Dan Scotten stood on the front porch of the old brick house and looked out at the Mora River, half a mile away. The yard in front of the house had turned into a shallow lake, and the reflection of the moon shimmered across its waters. They commented on the beauty of the scene, and then both went to bed around 9 p.m. Ashley joined his wife and ten-month-old baby while Dan walked to the adobe house on slightly higher ground, a hundred feet south of the main house.[30]

The two men, along with the other residents of the Watrous area, could not have imagined what awaited them that night. As one journalist put it almost eighty years later, "Before daybreak, there would be acts of unheralded heroics, of uncommon courage and of ultimate terror. Those who survived would forever have that night etched on their conscience."[31]

Sometime around 2 a.m., Dan awoke to hear Ashley shouting his name from outside. "What's up?" he called, peering out the window through the darkness and then hearing the roar of water. "Come out and you'll see!" Ashley yelled.[32] An upstream railroad embankment that was holding back the raging river had finally failed, and the water was rising rapidly, surrounding the brick house and both adobe buildings. The Mora River had become a torrent, filled beyond capacity by runoff from the tributaries that had collected water for three days. By the time Dan hurriedly dressed and stepped outside, he was joined by a dripping wet Hazel Pond holding Peggy wrapped in a blanket. Ashley had deposited his wife and child on the porch of the adobe building and headed back to the brick house. Dan later recounted in a letter to friends and family what happened after that.

"Not realizing the swiftness of the water, I jumped off the porch and made my way across to the brick house, and although the water was only above my knees then, I slipped and grabbed the air many times. Taking a quilt and something else from the arms of Mr. Pond, I started back to the adobe house, which was a little higher than the brick house, and the water, now up to my waist, was roaring past at an incredible rate. I barely grasped the porch of the adobe house and pulled my panting self up on the porch floor."[33]

Miss Sumner, the school nurse, had joined the others on the porch, and all three of them watched as Ashley and Miss Sumner's brother, a wrangler at the ranch, plunged into the churning waters, by then above their waists, and started for the adobe house. "We three, Mrs. Pond, Miss Sumner, and myself," Dan continued, "witnessed as well as we could in the black night their struggles to reach the adobe, and in fact their struggle for life. Several times Pond and Sumner were swept under the torrent . . . Both lost what they were carrying, and just before they grabbed our porch, a small pet dog dropped out of Pond's arms and looked like a black streak as it disappeared a second later."[34]

By the time Ashley and Sumner reached the adobe, the porch was six inches deep in water. "We went rushing through the house to the opposite side, looking toward the barn," Dan recounted. "Mr. Pond jumped into the rushing water, holding wife and baby, and I jumped in immediately after, holding tightly, arm in arm, Miss Sumner, who was rapidly becoming hysterical."[35] They all reached the safety of the barn, which sat on higher ground, but were scantily clad. The women were in nightgowns, and Ashley wore only his underwear and a pair of socks. At daybreak, the soaked and shivering group hitched up a wagon and started into town, the women covered mostly in straw and Ashley wearing an old horse blanket. If they dwelt on their troubles, their minds were soon changed as they entered what was left of the town of Watrous and passed a wagonload of dead bodies being taken into the small church. An area much larger than Shoemaker Canyon had been devastated by the storm.[36]

At least thirty people had lost their lives in the flood. Mr. and Mrs. J. E. Stephens of Watrous lost two of their three children. Separated from his family by the floodwaters, Felix Villareal finally reached his home the morning of October 1 to find that no trace of his house remained. He searched in vain for his wife and son as well as his mother-in-law and his wife's grandmother. Frank Aguilar lost his wife and three children. Half of the town of Watrous was destroyed, and in Mora, fifty homes were washed away and ten people were missing. Eight more had been lost along the Canadian River. The waters had taken a terrible toll, and they left such destruction in their path that help could not easily reach those who survived.[37]

Sixty miles of Santa Fe Railroad track were ripped apart, thirty bridges were swept away, and telegraph lines were down. Messages that would have normally traveled 133 miles by wire from Albuquerque to Las Vegas had to be routed to San Francisco and then back through Santa Fe to Las Vegas.

The first floodwaters flowed through towns on the evening of September 30, 1904, beginning their rampage of death and destruction. In this photo, buildings begin to fall along the Gallinas River, south of Watrous, New Mexico. Courtesy Citizen's Committee for Historic Preservation, Las Vegas, New Mexico.

"The most serious damage," the *Las Vegas Optic* reported, "was in Shoemaker Canyon which was swept from end to end throughout its nine miles. Five miles of track went out and the approaches to two great bridges were swept away." Railroad officials stated that "never in the history of the Santa Fe had any such flood disaster come to the system as in Shoemaker Canyon."[38] In view of such observations, the escape of the people from the Pond ranch seems all the more remarkable.

In the thirty-six hours following 6 p.m. on September 28, Las Vegas received between four and five inches of rain, and reports estimated that the downpour in the mountains was twice that. The storm that hit the region was part of a system that spanned from Flagstaff, Arizona, to Syracuse, Kansas. Other towns within that area received heavy rains and damage as well, but the storm released its major fury over the eastern slopes of the Sangre de Cristos.[39]

After drinking some hot coffee and borrowing clothes, Ashley and Dan drove back to the ranch and by late afternoon were able to wade through the mud to investigate. The adobe building that had held the dining room and kitchen was gone. Only the red roof could still be seen, supported by a couple of pillars. The roof and walls had caved in on the room that Dan Scotten had occupied, preserving some of his possessions. "After five hours work with a spade and hoe," Dan reported in his letter home, "I excavated about two-thirds of my belongings, and considered myself lucky."[40]

The Ponds lost everything in the flood except the brick house, the barn, and the animals and equipment it held. The hotel-size refrigerator that had stood in the school's kitchen was never seen again, and the Navajo rugs that decorated their home turned up in surrounding fields for years afterward. But as Dan Scotten pointed out in his letter home, Pond had another house and buildings on the other side of his ranch, so the family had a place to go. Others were not so fortunate. As the young Detroit man sat writing his letter that night, he reflected on the events of the past hours. "Many lives were lost in our valley and we don't know how many in the territory. We are cut off from the outside world, wires all down, . . . three weeks or a month before the first train from Trinidad reaches here. As I sit writing in the small hotel I can hear the moaning and wailing of a father and mother . . . whose three children were swept away. There are so many rugged and uncultivated heroes in this small town tonight who braved everything to jump into the maelstrom and pull out women and children. In such a contingency one learns to admire the brave characters that exist in this western neighborhood."[41]

Ashley's hard work and his dreams for a ranch school were washed away that night in the Mora floodwaters, and, in all likelihood, the incident represented failure in his father's eyes. So, in 1905, despite the lure of the "western neighborhood," Ashley Pond Jr. moved his family to Michigan in an attempt to please his ailing father and to leave behind his disappointment.

Chapter 3

The Michigan Years

". . . to run in the wind and sun and grow."

Mayblossom was a special horse. The morning sun streaming through the tall windows of the nursery made her paint gleam, and she had a real mane and tail. Mayblossom's sandy-haired owner was almost too small to climb onto the dappled gray rocking horse, but the stubborn little girl was not about to give up. She struggled until she sat proudly in the saddle, bouncing up and down with delight. Every now and then she leaned forward to pat the horse's neck with a chubby hand and offer lispy words of encouragement. "Fathter, Mayblothom, fathter!"

Peggy's early rides were confined to the upstairs playroom, but her developing imagination knew no such limits. Together, she and Mayblossom galloped across the open fields as she had seen her father do. They splashed along the shore of Three Mile Lake and went on wonderful adventures in the nearby woods. The little rocking horse was her first treasure, even before Wahb, the cherished teddy bear.

"How I loved Mayblossom," Peggy recalled, "and I wore her out, before my little sister was of an age to get astride her!"

The rocking horse was one of Peggy's earliest memories, among those "first streaks of consciousness" from her childhood years. For the attentive little girl, Michigan was a land of pure joy—"spring with its lilacs, summer with its heat, autumn with its odors of dead leaves and nuts, winter with its snow." There were "big boys from somewhere" who took her on their sled and coasted her down the hill. She had a swing in the trees, and she delighted in the smell of fresh wood shavings and the minnows that swarmed in the shallow waters of the lake. She learned the woods and played in a sloping meadow near her home. She was a child in love with nature, "the leaping fish, the golden cowslip, the blowing grass, and the asters on the autumn hill."

Sadly, there was another world besides the one she loved outdoors. Inside the house she was learning of displeasures, failures, jealousies, and

Peggy with her cherished teddy bear, Wahb, named for the bear in *The Biography of a Grizzly* by Ernest Thompson Seton, a popular book released in 1900. Wahb was passed down through the family to be loved by other generations of Pond and Church children. Courtesy Peggy Pond Church Estate.

The home of Ashley Pond Sr. stood at the corner of Woodward and Watson avenues in Detroit, Michigan. Courtesy of Ashley D. Pond and Family.

spankings. She was often referred to as an imp, only understanding years later that "the imp is what we try to suppress in all children, but the imp, the rebel, is part of the creative personality." She was a different child. A *difficult* child, her mother and father would have said. In reality, she was only sensitive and had needs they could not understand. Peggy's world in Michigan was one of opposites: the wonder and excitement of nature and the harsh reality of a family that was sometimes cold and full of discord.

Part of the discord resulted from her father's unhappiness at leaving New Mexico and working once again within a rigorous structure. When Ashley moved the family from Shoemaker Canyon to Michigan, he returned to his father's realm of austere formality and high expectations. Ashley Pond Sr. was an acknowledged leader of the Michigan bar during his distinguished career as an attorney. He had served as director of the Michigan Central Railroad and was chief counsel and advisor to Cornelius Vanderbilt on his eastern and midwestern railroads.[1] His record of professional success, however, did not transfer to his role as father and mentor to his family. He was referred to by his daughter, Florence, as Stone Ashley, a name she later gave to a great stone mansion she built in Tucson, perhaps because it was similarly cold and unyielding.

Ashley, Hazel, and year-old Peggy stayed with the elder Pond upon their arrival in Michigan, but they soon moved to nearby Bloomfield Hills, living there only long enough for a large, two-story country home to be built on the shores of nearby Three Mile Lake.[2] Ashley was well aware of his father's expectations and strongly felt the burden of the family name resting on his shoulders. Yielding to that responsibility, he accepted a position as vice president of the Auto-Commercial Company of Pontiac and attempted to settle into the kind of life his father envisioned.[3] He had returned to the scene of his unhappy childhood and resumed the role of dutiful son. Peggy commented on the shaping influence that Ashley Sr. had in his son's life. "I could imagine my father," she said, "surviving son of a wealthy and presumably doting father.[4] The great house on the corner of Woodward and Watson in Detroit, darkened with heavy draperies, filled to overflowing with its display of material possessions. [His] mother had died when he was seventeen, still in prep school. The dour old man left alone with his only son and daughter. The daughter who kept his house, to whom Emily Post was god." It was not a setting to Ashley's liking, but he tried to adapt.

Just more than a year after moving to Michigan, Hazel gave birth to a second daughter, Dorothy, born May 20, 1906. For two-year-old Peggy, life changed in a major way. "I have no recollection at all of her presence until she was able to toddle," said Peggy of her little sister, but "after that, until I was about six, many of my memories are connected with an intense jealousy of her because she was amiable and good-humored and everything that I seemed to have been told I was not but ought to be."[5] She was deeply wounded by her parents' reaction to the new baby. Evidence of her feelings of rejection still showed later in life when Peggy wrote her poem entitled "Sister."

> Until you came
> I had been the one and only;
> played with, recited rhymes to,
> scolded

She referred to herself as "the unloved elder sister," and lamented,

> When you came along it was evident
> you were the golden-haired true princess.[6]

Ashley doted on blonde-haired, blue-eyed Dorothy, and Hazel was obvious in her special affection for a son born two years later. Unintentional or not, they created a devastating situation in which Peggy felt herself to be the extra child. As a result, there were few meaningful times with her parents as Peggy grew up. The most lighthearted childhood memory she retained was of something that happened when she was very young. "I think how it is the moments of joy we remember through our lives," she wrote. "I remember a humorous game with father and mother and some pillow throwing when I was, perhaps, not more than three. Mother and father and child united in an interlude of pure fun." No other such instances of togetherness are recorded in her daily journals.

Another incident that Peggy recalled from childhood revealed just how much she wanted a closeness with her parents. "I was mortally afraid of crossing bridges," she admitted. "There was one footbridge I was especially afraid of where our nurse used to take us to walk. She was a devout Irish Catholic, and she gave me a holy card showing a guardian angel hovering protectively above a child crossing a tiny bridge over a black abyss. That picture was a great comfort to me. I used to sleep with it under my pillow and to rely on it for all the comfort my parents never gave me and which I so deeply craved."[7]

In 1906 a person who would make a lasting impression on Peggy reentered her life. Ashley persuaded Albert and Gertie Horton to come to Michigan. They accompanied a shipment of horses from the New Mexico ranch so that Ashley could "show what western horses were like." Albert remained to work for Pond for a few months, and Gertie again helped with three-year-old Peggy as well as seven-month-old Dorothy, by then known as Dottie. She was a natural with the children, and Peggy came to love and respect her. The warmth Peggy felt for Gertie remained even after she had grown up and lost touch with her. In 1976, when Peggy was researching her family history, she began to look for Gertie and found her living in Craig, Colorado, where she and Albert had homesteaded in 1908. Gertie recounted stories from both Watrous and Three Mile Lake and filled in gaps in Peggy's memory of her younger years. Despite her advancing age, Gertie's mind was sharp and full of details. "When we landed in Detroit," she recalled, "we had your grandfather's address—Woodward Avenue—and we went to his house. The butler took us in. We had lake trout for dinner. Oh, so good."[8]

On a chilly May evening in 1977, in the high country of Colorado, three elderly women sat around a kitchen table, finishing a good supper. Gertie, the woman who had once been Gertrude Tipton, born in the brick house in Boone Valley and married to Albert Horton, was ninety years old. Peggy, once a toddler in Gertie's care, had raised three sons and become a grandmother, but at that moment the years didn't matter very much. The important thing was the love the two women still felt for each other and for those shared days almost three quarters of a century before. Gertie's daughter, Iva, was nearing seventy herself but still doing the lambing and other chores on the ranch. She cleared the dishes as she listened intently.

In the glow of the wood-paneled room, Gertie's eyes sparkled as she talked of her youthful days in Michigan. "Your father met us at your grandfather's house and took us to Bloomfield Hills, about four miles from Pontiac, but we didn't live there more than a few months before we moved into that big, luxurious house at Three Mile Lake. The new house was four or five miles from Bloomfield Hills. Albert and I lived in the big house. We had a room on the east side, next to the nursery. Your mother's and dad's room was on the other side, but your mother took care of you at night."[9]

Peggy remembered no such nightly care. In fact she once said in a poem,

> *If I cried at night I can remember no one*
> *who came to comfort, but rather only to rebuke my nightmares.*
> *Who was it told me, 'Stop crying. You must not wake the baby?'"[10]*

She kept the thoughts to herself, not wanting to disrupt the flow of Gertie's story.

"Do you remember the woman who did the cooking?" Gertie asked. "She used to come out on Monday morning and stay till Saturday. She was a good cook. She made wonderful creamed codfish. I never ate anything like it. We all ate together." Gertie stopped for a moment, and her memories flowed in another direction. "I always thought your mother was a pretty woman," she said. "And she was a good mother. She wanted children to mind. Always wanted a boy."[11]

She got her boy, after you left to go to Colorado, Peggy reminded Gertie, but the older woman was already recalling other images.

"Your mother and dad were devoted. I can remember seeing them in the yard with arms around each other. Made me feel good." *Peggy nodded and smiled but knew secretly that the devotion hadn't lasted.*

"They had lots of company out at the lake," Gertie added.[12]

Those months must have been an exciting time for Gertie compared to the small town life she had known in Watrous, Peggy thought. Her mother had enjoyed the years in Michigan. Past the carefree childhood days on the Clyde, Hazel had never particularly liked the western scene. None of the women in the family had.

"My husband didn't want to go to Michigan," Gertie was saying. "Mr. Pond coaxed him."[13]

That was my father, Peggy thought, nodding in agreement. Always good at persuading people to do what he wanted. She watched Gertie closely as she related story after story, taking her life beyond the Michigan years and telling of her homesteading days with Albert in the mountains of Colorado. Gertie had experienced a hard life but had triumphed.[14] Words began to form in Peggy's mind.

> At night
> your face is still beautiful,
> You are not wrinkled
> nor stooped, nor scarcely shriveled.
> Your strong bones
> hold you erect still.
> Your eyes are the color of mountain water,
> hazel eyes, the same color, I remember
> as my mother's.[15]

One of the horses Albert brought from New Mexico was given to Peggy when she was five. His name was Jerry, and he was a tall horse for a child to ride. Peggy had to grab hold of his mane and walk up his left front leg to climb onto his back, but she was as determined with Jerry as she had been with Mayblossom. In addition to Jerry, other new experiences came into Peggy's life in her fifth year. A little brother, Ashley Pond III or "Laddie" as the family called him, was born August 4, 1908, at Three Mile Lake. At about the same time, Peggy was sent to the first of three kindergartens she would attend while living in Michigan. Although she had to leave home to attend, Peggy was happy at the convent school in Grosse Pointe. She recalled that she "was the littlest child there," and the nuns spoiled her. "One Sister gave me chocolates and ribbons for good conduct," she added.[16] What must the young Peggy Pond have thought when her teachers rewarded her conduct while her parents consistently found it a cause for criticism?

If the lesson of reward and punishment was a confusing one, there were other lessons that were far clearer, although for the sensitive child they were often a cause of sadness or disappointment. One such lesson laid the foundation for Peggy's sense of humor. When she and her siblings visited their grandfather's home in Detroit, they were cared for by a different nurse, "a strict woman, but loving." Their supper was served upstairs in the nursery, usually with some favorite food as a special treat. Hot biscuits were one such treat for Peggy. When April Fools' Day fell during one spring visit, the nurse prepared delicious hot biscuits for the children. When they bit into them, they found the biscuits were full of cotton. "At first I was puzzled and insulted," Peggy remembered. "Then the nurse explained about the April Fool, the tricks we were allowed to play on one another, the lies we were allowed to tell. We began to fool each other," Peggy said, taking no pleasure in the memory, for at the same time she thought of "the sense of power they each had felt when they fooled another; the delight in the permitted lie." The reality of it all set in. "How it hurts to feel we have been made a fool of, to experience the pain of ridicule," she observed, looking back at the incident.

She harbored bitterness at the recall of another such occasion in Michigan. "My father, the trickster, asked me if I wanted to see a tree toad. And promised me I should. Then kicked a tree on the street side and said, 'Now you have seen a tree toed.' It took me a few minutes to catch on. I was supposed to laugh and finally did, but my expectations had been greatly wounded."[17] With her serious outlook and such high expectations, Peggy would be easily wounded on many occasions. It was a problem she eventually identified but was never able to completely overcome. She once commented, "I have been gifted or cursed with an aesthetic sense. Always rebuked, especially by my father, for being sensitive."[18]

The love and respect of her father was something that Peggy wanted desperately, but she admitted that there were only "two moments of my life when I really felt close to him."[19] One evening in Michigan when she was seven

Peggy on Jerry, ca. 1910. Jerry was shipped from the New Mexico ranch to Michigan and given to Peggy as her first horse. Courtesy Los Alamos Historical Museum Archives..

or eight, she sat alone on the front porch after dark, listening to a whippoorwill. Her father came out on the porch. "He stood there for a long time listening, too, and I was surprised to think that grown-ups loved some of the same things that children did. I had a sort of intuition that he was infinitely lonely and somehow disappointed in the life he led."[20] The other memory was of a time when her father took her to the circus, just the two of them. "I felt we were both having fun in the same way," Peggy said. "He was not the parental authority that night but a gay companion. Afterward he took me, just like a grown-up lady, to a dinner at some sort of roadhouse, and I had a grown-up meal of frog's legs which impressed me enormously." Later, after they returned home, she glimpsed a different parental viewpoint. "I knew that my mother hadn't approved of the adventure at all, for she believed that children must always get to bed on time, and that my father was being a very irresponsible parent."[21]

The early steps in Peggy's journey took her through some difficult lessons, but not all of her memories of life in Michigan were hurtful. On an afternoon when she was perhaps five, she had been put to bed with a cold, but when the nurse's back was turned, she slipped away from her grandfather's "austere home." She was welcomed into "the relaxed home next door," where she remembered "lying on a warm white rug, before a warm fireplace, cutting out valentines with another little girl." Her nurse eventually discovered the escape and came to collect her, but not before Peggy had enjoyed part of a comforting afternoon. The companionship and the creative activities were the remedies she needed. And the work with her hands in creating pleasing cutouts and valentines may very well have been a prelude to creations with words that would eventually follow. In kindergarten, she enjoyed similar activities. "I learned to weave strips of colored paper into squares," she recalled, referring to such experiences as "raptures of creation and moments of discovery." There was, however, to be another experience of even greater significance. There was one activity that Peggy shared with her parents that would affect her life more than any other—Ashley and Hazel read poetry to their children. "My father used to read a lot and recite *A Child's Garden of Verses* out loud, and my mother had taken elocution lessons. I found I liked the sound of the words."

It was to be her lifelong joy to work with "the sound of words," skillfully crafting them into poems of observation and emotion. Indeed, poetry became the only outlet for her deepest feelings, which she could not seem to express any other way. Representative of that expression is a poem called "Five Years Old" in which she described the finest moments of her early childhood in Michigan, at the same time painting a picture of the beauty of childhood for us all.

> There was a field, I know, all warm with sun,
> Purple with asters blown through golden grass;
> And a stone wall where huckleberries grew,
> Broken in places so a child could pass.
> Beyond the wall the field became a hill
> That slyly steepened till a child must run,
> Arms flung against the wind, to finally spill
> With small brown feet and buttons half undone
> Into the laughing ripples of the lake;
> There to stand still as still and feel the sand
> Crinkle between bare toes, or wade knee-deep

Along the shore; to startle small green frogs
And little lazy turtles fast asleep . . . [22]

If the Watrous flood had signaled the end to Ashley's time in northeastern New Mexico, it was the death of his father that closed the door on the Michigan years. "My parents and I were in Bermuda in January 1910 when my grandfather died," Peggy recalled. Dottie and Laddie had remained in Michigan with the nurse, but six-year-old Peggy was considered the troublemaker of the three and could not be left at home. She had accompanied Ashley and Hazel on their extended vacation. At first they enjoyed the warmer weather that replaced the snowy winter they had left behind. They were drawn to the startlingly blue water and the stretches of white sand. Outings and picnics on the beach with her mother and father stood out in Peggy's memory, but she also reflected on what happened when her grandfather died. "They left me there with whooping cough while they hastened back to Detroit," she remembered. Two nuns looked after her while Ashley and Hazel traveled to the funeral, but despite being left in the company of strangers, Peggy wrote fondly of her childhood days in Bermuda. Her journals record autobiographical memories of "picnicking on the coral islands, whose surfaces rasped her bare feet and where she played hide-and-go-seek around the rock with the white-haired old gentleman whom they called Mark Twain."

The waves broke rhythmically against the white sand beach. Peggy played at the edge of the shallow, clear water while her mother watched nearby. She picked up an orange cockle and then a pink murex and ran to put them with the growing collection of pretty shells piled under the umbrella where her father dozed in a beach chair. Not that she knew the names of the shells at her age, but she appreciated the colors and the patterns, the textures and the smoothness. The tide was going out, and more of the beach would soon be exposed, so she hurried to the umbrella with her new treasures. As she was about to turn and run back to the surf, she noticed an old man sitting a bit farther up the beach. He appeared to be watching her. He had a droopy mustache and the whitest hair she had ever seen, sort of bushy at the sides. He sat in a chaise lounge with a plaid blanket covering his feet and legs. The weather was warm. Why was he all covered up like that, she wondered. His face was serious, almost frowning.

Was he really looking at her? He could have been looking past her, far into the distance. Peggy ran back to the water's edge, checking once to see if the man was still watching. He was! She darted behind a large rock near the shore and slowly peeked around the other side. His eyes were still on her, but they had softened. The frail old man leaned to the side of his chair to keep her in sight and smiled ever so slightly. Peggy giggled with delight and hid behind the rock once more. She ducked behind another rock and looked out again, fully into a game of hide-and-go-seek. The old man's smile widened. She forgot about picking up more shells.

In his last days, Mark Twain spent time in the warm sunshine of Bermuda. He died in April of 1910, shortly after returning home from the island. No one knows if he remembered watching a small child playing on the beach that day, but the small child remembered—all her life.[23]

The death of his father brought a freedom of choice for Ashley. There was no longer any pressure to remain in Michigan or to work at a job with status. He could pursue the life he loved, and that life was in the West. Almost immediately he began making plans to return, and, in so doing, he returned his daughter to the place where her destiny awaited as well.

For her younger sister and brother, the Michigan years were not a source of clear memories, but Peggy looked upon that time in her life as a valued experience, her introduction to nature. She summed up those years in the concluding lines of "Background," a poem she wrote in 1926.

> There was nothing else in the world for her to know
> Except to run in the wind and sun and grow.[24]

In view of the range of emotions that the young Peggy confronted in her first years and the feelings of low self-esteem that she had begun to experience, the conclusion to the poem is somewhat idyllic, perhaps one she might have wished to be true. In reality, she had barely begun her emotional struggle with life.

Dottie Pond, far right, celebrates her birthday at Three Mile Lake, Michigan, with her sister, Peggy, second from left, and two friends. Courtesy Los Alamos Historical Museum Archives.

Peggy has a good hold on little sister, Dottie, as Mom takes them for a ride in their Hupmobile Runabout, ca. 1909. Courtesy Los Alamos Historical Museum Archives.

Chapter 4

Pajarito Canyon
"It was a world to fill a child with wonder."

Freed from his Michigan bondage, Ashley Pond Jr. once again headed west, at first taking his wife and children to California where, as Peggy noted, he had "some classy friends living from his Detroit years."[1] They stayed for several weeks near San Diego at the Hotel del Coronado, where Hazel's grandfather was living.[2] It was a happy time for Peggy and, indeed, a rare time of contentment for the whole family. Years later she still talked about the hotel's "domed glass roof and the caged canaries singing around the edge." The family went for picnics beside the ocean, and Peggy learned to swim in the indoor saltwater plunge. She had developed into a slender, athletic child and "took to the water with ease." Her mother and father swam in the plunge daily, and her mother was "never happier than when exercising herself in the water." Hazel was delighted to be back in California, but her stay was to be short-lived. While in residence at the Coronado, Ashley saw an advertisement for land irrigated by artesian wells in New Mexico and impulsively bought a farm in Roswell.

The brief, happy stay in California ended, and the family moved to the rugged farming country of southeastern New Mexico in 1911. Hazel was *not* delighted to be in Roswell, especially in view of the fact that Ashley had promised her a farmhouse but managed to build only the garage. She found herself living in a place that was too hot in summer, bitterly cold in winter, and surrounded by barren hillsides. Nearby, telegraph wires hummed in the incessant winds. The setting and the living conditions did little for family harmony. Being back in the West was not a cure for the Pond family discord, but Peggy was away from it for most of the nearly two years they lived in Roswell. She was sent to a convent school in Albuquerque. She was unaware of the extent of her parents' problems until years later when she read an old Roswell newspaper and noted an item for September 4, 1913.

> Ashley Pond, a well known farmer on the Berrendo,
> has filed suit in the district court for divorce from
> his wife Hazel Hallett Pond.

"This was the first I realized that matters had come to such a pass," Peggy remarked, "and for a moment I felt as though my whole childhood were about to collapse within me. Obviously the divorce had never taken place, but the notice was certainly an indication to me of my mother's desperation and my father's blighted expectations of his irrigated farm."[3]

Hazel eventually had enough of the treeless farm and Ashley's promises. She took the children and went to Los Angeles to be near her mother. "I always thought this was so we could go to proper schools," Peggy said in reflection. After all, as a young child innocent of her parents' marital problems, Peggy had enjoyed her short time in Roswell. During the first summer there, she had been given a white horse named Sam, and she was free to explore the countryside. Her father told her that Sam was hers if she could keep him clean, but there was a river nearby and "Sam liked to roll!" Sam also liked to run away, and Peggy had trouble staying on since she had to ride bareback. Seeing Peggy fall off one afternoon, Ashley scornfully remarked, "You ought to know better than that how to ride." Not long after, a team of mules escaped from the corral, and Ashley commandeered the first available horse to go after them. That horse was Sam. Ashley didn't take time to saddle Sam; he simply jumped on bareback and took off. A few minutes later, Peggy noticed her father returning on foot. Having been convinced that the horse was "incorrigible," Ashley went to town the next day and bought Peggy her first saddle. She had no more trouble staying on.[4] Through the years, riding became one of her greatest pleasures.

In Los Angeles where she found herself at the Westlake School in the autumn of 1913, there was little opportunity for riding or exploring the outdoors she loved. She liked the school, but she missed the freedom she had known in New Mexico. By the end of the school year, however, Peggy and Dottie found themselves on a train, headed back to that freedom. Their father had sold the Roswell property and bought into a partnership with four Detroit friends attempting to establish a ranch resort in Pajarito Canyon, northwest of Santa Fe.

Hazel had stayed behind in Los Angeles to nurse five-year-old Laddie, who was down with whooping cough, so Peggy and her sister were met by their father at the train station in Santa Fe. The long trip was quite an adventure for two young girls, but an even greater adventure loomed ahead: the thirty-five miles from Santa Fe to Pajarito Canyon. After a night in the old DeVargas Hotel, the two girls piled into their father's vintage Hudson touring car. The canvas top was folded back, despite New Mexico's blazing sunshine, and the hood of the engine had been removed. Peggy further described the eccentricities of her father's car. "The running board on one side held two narrow spare tires, and on the other side was a rack with three big cans: one for gasoline, one for oil, and one for water. There were a couple of canvas bags hanging on the wind-screen and various picks and shovels here and there as well as a couple of long, narrow rolls of canvas stowed away, which he sometimes spread in front of the wheels when he had to cross a dry arroyo in order to avoid getting stuck in the sand." Equipped for almost anything, the trio headed west. "We drove down stony hills, across dry water courses, and came to the edge of a dark brown river," Peggy remembered. They had reached the "so-called town" of Buckman. "In 1914 there was nothing at Buckman but a log corral with chutes from which cattle could be loaded into the diminutive once-a-day train, an idle freight car or two, a few abandoned shacks, and a yellow box car that served as station and post office."

Named for lumberman Henry Buckman, the dubious town on the river was useful for one other thing besides loading freight. It had a bridge across the Rio Grande. Actually, it was the third bridge to occupy that site. The first two had washed away. In describing the bridge, Peggy noted, "I am not sure the word *built* is the right one to apply to its construction." It was a wood and rock assembly with weathered planks not much wider than the width of a car. "Mid-June of 1914 when I first encountered the bridge," she said, "the water was actually running a couple of inches deep over the planks at the center of the bridge. My father made his innocent little children take off their shoes and wade across it. Apparently he thought we were more amphibious than his car." Once on the other side and back in the Hudson, they continued on a road that climbed through black basalt cliffs to a realm of pine forests, mesas, and canyons—the Pajarito Plateau.[5]

Pajarito, Spanish for *little bird*, was the name given to the high plateau by the archaeologist Edgar L. Hewett, who explored the area and excavated ruins in the early 1900s. Ashley explained the geologic setting as he drove with his daughters toward the plateau. "I still remember the shivery feeling I had when he told me it had been built up by a succession of volcanic explosions," Peggy said. "This brought to my mind frightening visions of red hot cinders, torrents of lava that flowed like fire, suffocating clouds of ash like the last days of Pompeii which I had been told about in school." If she and her sister were frightened by such images, the fear left with the first sight of the ranch. "We sprang out of the car as though a spring had released us and ran instantly to the corral and barns without even bothering to pay attention

Peggy, Dottie, and Ashley in a rare moment of sibling accord on the sunporch at their grandmother Altie Hallett's home on South Westmoreland in Los Angeles, ca. 1913. Courtesy Los Alamos Historical Museum Archives.

Ashley Pond Jr. sits in his Hudson touring car, known as Ashley's Limo, ready to cross Buckman Bridge, ca.1914. Courtesy Los Alamos Historical Museum Archives.

to the tin-sided house which was to be our new home. It was late afternoon, and a swarthy, whiskered man named Felipe was milking a mild Jersey cow."[6] Felipe offered to let the girls try their hand at milking, the first of many new experiences they would have during the three summers and one winter they lived in Pajarito Canyon.

Peggy always wondered how her father had convinced her mother to return to ranching after the Roswell episode, especially after her first view of her Pajarito accommodations. Earlier in 1914 Hazel had left Peggy and Dottie in school in Los Angeles and returned to New Mexico with Laddie to help her husband restore the buildings and ready them for visitors. Her first look at the ranch Ashley intended to turn into an elite recreation club was ominous. There were corrals, scattered cabins, and a barn, but the dominating structure was a two-story building that would be their home. It was covered with corrugated iron and painted a dingy red. It had been the commissary for the lumber mill that had previously occupied the site. She saw no glass in the windows, and the door was hanging open on broken hinges. She stepped through the entry way and discovered a cow standing in the downstairs parlor.[7]

"Luckily my mother's greatest talent was for creating homes, and I must say," Peggy added with a smile, "my father provided her with some rare opportunities in his lifetime."[8] The old two-story house in Pajarito Canyon definitely represented one of them, but with the help of a Santa Fe architect, the building was turned into a picturesque home with white framed windows, a porch with pillars and white railings, and an upstairs balcony. Roses eventually grew on trellises, and nasturtiums bloomed in window boxes. Inside, a huge stone fireplace was flanked by shelves of books, and Navajo rugs accented new wood floors. The oak dining table and plush upholstered chairs from her grandfather's Detroit home assumed an honored role in the dining room. Even the old Estey upright piano had traveled by wagon from Roswell to take its rightful place.

The buildings in the canyon became known as the Pajarito Club. Guest cabins were added, a gazebo and tennis courts were built, and an orchard of mixed fruit trees and a vegetable garden were soon planted. The club was most probably the brainchild of Ashley Pond, but he needed financial help to make it happen. In 1913, he heard about the Ramon Vigil Land Grant being offered for sale. He fell in love with the land and talked some of his influential Detroit friends into the idea of a private ranch resort where they could ride, hunt, and fish while escaping the rigors of the business world. His

The Pajarito Club as seen from the north rim of Pajarito Canyon, ca. 1915. The Pond cabin, built by Ashley Pond and used as his office, is hidden by the large Ponderosa pine to the left of the photograph. Courtesy Los Alamos Historical Museum Archives.

The Pond home at the Pajarito Club in winter, ca. 1915. Courtesy Los Alamos Historical Museum Archives.

boyhood friends Roy Chapin and Henry Joy, by then automobile executives, joined him in the venture along with Detroit bankers Paul and David Grey. They purchased the 32,000-acre grant for $80,000, and Ashley volunteered to convert the existing buildings, make improvements, and run the ranch.

At the time the Detroit men purchased the Ramon Vigil Land Grant, the parcel of land already had a long and sometimes unscrupulous history, and Ashley's negotiations fit right in with the scheme of things. He was led to believe that he was getting the land at a bargain—$2.50 per acre. In reality, the bank agent had been authorized to sell for only $56,000. He intended to pocket the difference. The original land grant had been given to Pedro Sanchez by Viceroy Don Gaspar Domingo de Mendoza in 1742. It remained in the Sanchez family until 1851 when it was sold to Ramon Vigil for "a yoke of oxen, thirty-six ewes, one ram, and twenty dollars in cash." In 1879, when the Denver and Rio Grande Railroad came to the Rio Grande Valley and land speculation was rampant, a priest named Thomas Aquinas Hayes persuaded Vigil to sell the grant for $4000. Five years later the opportunistic Hayes sold it for $100,000. As Peggy noted, the priest was "apparently the only one to make any money out of it. Certainly my father and his Detroit friends never did."[9]

Ashley and his partners would eventually manage to avoid losing their original investment, but the plan for a ranch was ill-fated from the beginning. Ashley had bought the land during a wet year, when the stream in Pajarito Canyon was running full, but that was not the norm. "Apparently it didn't dawn on any of the men, least of all my day-dreaming father, till it was much too late, that there was hardly enough water on the whole grant, outside the Pajarito Canyon, to keep more than a few wild creatures and the little birds themselves alive."[10]

"My father was the kind of man who seemed to know everybody," Peggy explained. "He had influential connections. He was very well liked, outgoing, sociable, and had a wild imagination for possible projects which never quite came off."[11] In the summer of 1914, however, when Peggy and her siblings arrived to live in Pajarito Canyon, their father was enthusiastic and confident about his plans. He and Hazel were kept busy with improvements and entertaining guests, and "we were left pretty much to our own devices," Peggy recounted. She and Dottie and Laddie were free to explore the cliff dwellings in the canyon behind the corrals and look for petroglyphs carved in the smoke-blackened ceilings. They filled their pockets with fragments of pottery and collected arrowheads. "Life seemed to be a continual treasure hunt."[12]

"Between ten and thirteen it hadn't made much difference that I happened to be a girl," Peggy said.[13] She and Dottie played the same games as the boys and rode their horses just as well if not better. They occasionally had young visitors to play with, and there were other children at the Pajarito Club. One cabin had been converted to a one-room schoolhouse, and the Pond's governess, Ellen Purdue, taught the carpenter's three children as well as the three Ponds.[14] Miss Purdue took her young pupils on nature walks, gathered flowers and potsherds, and observed animals, but most of all, Peggy thought, "she kept us out of Mother's hair."

"I was at the time an ornery and athletic little girl, a dismay and stone of stumbling to my parents, a thorn in the flesh of my two younger siblings," Peggy admitted. She also described herself as shy and tongue-tied in the presence of the distinguished visitors who came to the Pajarito Club, but that may have been in part because of the frequent warning from her mother that children should be seen and not heard.[15] There were a good many visitors whom the young Peggy Pond might have found intimidating. Notable among the guests were John Curtis Underwood, author and poet from New York City; archaeologists Jesse Nusbaum and Sylvanus Morley; Riccardo Martin, a tenor with the Metropolitan Opera Company; William Hamby of the *Saturday Evening Post*; and Rose Dougan and Vera Von Blumenthal, the ladies of the famous Duchess Castle near the Tsankawi ruins.[16] Often, Peggy preferred to escape, as she put it, "on my own solitary explorations of ledges and hiding places and secret trails among the cliffs."[17] She thought of Pajarito Canyon as her "unlimited playground and focus of imagination and adventure."[18]

The window of Peggy's room faced east. She knelt and leaned on the sill to look out as she did most nights before going to bed, marveling at the stars shining "in untroubled light beyond the sky."[19] Earlier that evening, her mother had read to her and her sister and brother from a favorite book called The Friendly Skies. *On many warm summer nights in the canyon, their mother taught them about the constellations. They watched as night after night Scorpio and Lyra moved across the sky. They observed the Perseids and counted the falling meteors. The starry universe with its myths and legends came alive and became the counterpart to Peggy's daytime wanderings, when she would explore the sacred world of the Tewas and find their drawings on the rocks, communications from the past from people she would never know. She lamented that the canyon was theirs in a way it could never be hers, but nonetheless, she was discovering a*

cosmos and herself as a part of it. She thought back to the lessons learned in the convent schools. She knew about the Holy Lands, Jerusalem, and Mt. Sinai, but those places were far away. She couldn't build a relationship with them. In Pajarito Canyon, she lived in a world where people had formed their own cosmos. In that setting it was easy to connect myth to the world in which she lived, to make it a personal experience.[20]

Most days Peggy awoke before sunrise. She left her warm bed and crept down the stairs, careful not to wake anyone and have them disturb the spell of the early morning. Once outside, she ran through the woods where bluebells opened with the dawn and cobwebs shimmered with dew between the trees. She wrote of her impressions,

> *Such joy it is to be the first to bend*
> *the cool, sweet grass,*
> *to come so breathlessly*
> *on hidden birds. And strange it is to feel*
> *the self her mother knows is not so real*
> *as the half-fairy child who dances here.[21]*

Too soon a voice would break the silence, and Peggy would run back to the house and inside to breakfast.

Peggy's communication skills hadn't quite caught up with her ability to observe, but she began to have a desire to express her feelings. It was during the years in Pajarito Canyon that the first pull toward poetry took hold. She could never remember more than two lines of the first poem she attempted—"Oh bird so blue. Will you tell me true, / what makes you so happy today?"—but she felt good about the effort.[22] When she was given an assignment to write a poem during the next school term, she was eager to try again. For the first year in the canyon, Peggy and her siblings were tutored by Miss Purdue, but in the autumn of the second year, Hazel went with the children to San Diego so that they could attend a formal school. They were enrolled in the Francis Parker School, which offered a progressive education. Peggy attended seventh and eighth grades there and wrote her first real poem in 1916 as homework. She was twelve years old.

Ode to a Flower

Long have I watched o'er thee,
Cared for thee, tended thee
    Through bright spring hours.

Now has thou burst into bloom
Laden with sweet perfume,
    Queen of all flowers.

Soon wilt thou fade away,
Queen of a summer's day,
    Withered, forlorn.

But I shall plant the seed,
See to its every need,
    Till more flowers are born.[23]

Peggy's growing love of poetry was enhanced by her father, who often shared light and playful poetry with his children. "My mother had only one poem, Kipling's 'The Ballad of East and West,'" Peggy recalled, "but my father had reams and reams of Mother Goose and Edward Lear. He loved word play and punning, and occasionally composed rhymes himself." During her poetry readings in later years, Peggy was fond of including a little poem her father had penned.

Jiggle, jiggle little car,
How I wonder where we are.
From the roughness of the way
I should think near Santa Fe.

Then she would get a laugh from her listeners by adding, "I think you'll agree, it has hardly gone out of date."[24]

For Peggy, life in the canyon was good. She wandered and explored and rode her horse, Dolly, almost every day. There were always things to see or do. Edgar Hewett and his team were digging at nearby ruins in the summer, and Peggy watched them from a distance. She and Dottie were allowed to live part of the time in a log cabin all their own across the canyon, except for meals. And many afternoons were spent in favorite caves, where they built fires and roasted apples on pointed sticks. "The skins became burnt before the flesh was soft at all," Peggy reminisced, "but we swore to one another that nothing ever tasted better." The apple-roasting ventures led to some firsthand lessons. "The so-called smoke holes near the entrances to the caves never really worked successfully," Peggy said. "The trouble, we found out much later, was that they were really supposed to be ventilation holes, which was perhaps why our smoke kept blowing in instead of out! We quickly found out why the rounded ceilings of the caves were so black, making a fine blackboard for the former inhabitants to scratch their merry array of petroglyphs."[25]

On nights with a full moon, whiffenpoofs could be hunted. C. B. Ruggles, the guide and horse wrangler who worked at the Pajarito Club, told Peggy and Dottie how to catch one. "You first find a perfectly round pool," he explained. "Then you go there on the night of a full moon, taking with you a raft and an auger and a piece of cheese. You pole your raft to the exact middle of the pool, bore a hole through the top of the water with the auger, place the cheese on top of the hole and wait." Ruggles no doubt paused somewhere in his story to enjoy the wide-eyed look on the faces of two little girls. "Pretty soon the whiffenpoof comes up and eats the cheese which makes him so fat he can't get down the hole again, and there you have him." Whether Peggy and Dottie were really gullible enough to sneak through the moonlit canyon with a piece of cheese is not documented, but there was a small pool that sometimes filled with water near the ruins of Tshirege. In the canyon of 1915, it was dubbed the Whiffenpoof Pool, and the story made for a wonderful poem of the same name many years later.[26]

The house in the canyon had no running water or electricity. "We carried candles to light us to bed," Peggy pointed out in her many talks on Pajarito history, "and there were kerosene lamps with wicks to be trimmed and chimneys to be polished every day—if our mother could catch us." Peggy admitted that she and Dottie were more nuisance than help. And their "freckle-faced little brother" was only six. "For a long time he had been known as the lamb-pie by his mother, much to my sister's and my disgust," Peggy would add with a sibling's sly grin, even in her seventies. "By the time he was seven or eight he had grown out of that and liked to spend most of his time skinning rattlesnakes to make belts, which the dudes adored. It was a most unsavory occupation, especially on a hot midsummer day," she remembered, "and the rest of us tended to shun him as much as possible." In view of such activities and because her parents were often busy supervising helpers or escorting visitors, Peggy spent many hours in the canyon experiencing its solitude.[27]

Peggy Pond rode her horse, Dolly, throughout Pajarito Canyon in the summers of 1914 and 1915. The freedom she knew there, exploring ruins and experiencing nature, led her to claim that the years in the canyon were the most important of her life. Courtesy Los Alamos Historical Museum Archives.

⟨────⟩

Another one! Careful to avoid the unfriendly occupants, Peggy crawled on hands and knees around the outer edge of a large ant bed, looking for chips of turquoise among the tiny pieces of quartz and obsidian that the ants had piled into their hill. She picked up her latest prize and stood to add it to the others in her pocket, which also included the arrowhead she had discovered earlier. The arrowhead was black and shiny and perfect, a bird point less than an inch in length. It had been lying on the ground under a tree, having waited for centuries to be noticed, and now it was going into the collection she was making for the Pan-American Exposition that would be held in San Diego in the fall. Her mother would be taking her and her sister and brother there in September so that they could go to school. She brushed away the dirt on the knees of her pants and straightened her middy blouse before continuing on through Tshirege.

Within a few steps, Peggy stopped short and then detoured around a small rattlesnake guarding a dead bunny in the grass. The snake hadn't offered any warning and wasn't coiled, but she honored its territory just the same. Snakes had scared her when she first came to the Pajarito Plateau, but soon they became just another part of her surroundings. Before moving to the canyon, she had been taught English poetry and learned of cuckoos and primroses, skylarks and daffodils. Now she lived in a world of turkey buzzards and yuccas, skunks and scarlet penstemons. She learned that each animal had a kind of wisdom all its own. The canyon had belonged to them long before she came to share it.

She walked farther and stopped on the edge of a kiva, its roof caved in and filling with dust and weeds. She stooped to pick up a broken piece of pottery. On the inside it was painted with black stripes on a grayish background. The other side was decorated with two black lines and a row of dots. She turned the shard in her hand. Who had made this pottery, she wondered. What had they used it for? She never felt alone when she wandered Tshirege. In fact, it seemed crowded with invisible presences, as though she could almost hear the voices, as though the paths they had walked were still warm. But she was never frightened. Rather, she felt at home among the vanished people. The men who had held ceremonies in this kiva and the women who had shaped the pottery had disappeared, but she knew that the Indians of San Ildefonso and Santa Clara and Tesuque still worshipped the sun and the clouds and danced for the rain to come. Some things didn't die. Peggy's young mind was beginning to entertain large thoughts. The seasonal changes and the immensity of earth's processes—erosion, rock formation, rain, growing things—all were so vivid in the canyon. She was immersed in a dynamic world, becoming aware of rhythms other than human time.

She put the pottery shard in her pocket, too, and left the mesa. She untied Dolly and rode toward home. It would be sunset soon.[28]

For Peggy and her siblings, life in Pajarito Canyon was like living in a wonderland, but for Ashley and Hazel, the canyon world wasn't quite so idyllic. Almost from the beginning, Ashley was at odds with his Detroit partners. He thought of himself as the manager of the Pajarito Club, but the other four were never willing to make that designation official. Ashley wrote numerous letters, outlining his dreams for the club and describing the grandeur of the land, all the while asking the partners for money for improvements and expenses. "My father's idea of managing was to spend money on fixing up everything that needed fixing and quite a few things that didn't," Peggy said of the years in the canyon. "It wasn't long before he was spending almost a thousand dollars a month—which he expected the partners, to their evident consternation, to pay back." The partners themselves were never quite clear as to their vision for the Pajarito Club. They vacillated between making it a rugged hunting club or something more on the order of El Tovar on the south rim of the Grand Canyon. At one point, Chapin even thought the Pajarito region should become a national park and wrote letters to that effect to his friends in Washington. But despite the ideas flying through their heads, the reality of the situation was that the four Detroit men had high-powered jobs with expectations to fulfill and little time to vacation at a hunting club in the mountains of New Mexico. Only two of the partners ever visited the property. Their major connection with the project was to write checks to cover what they saw as Ashley Pond's extravagances. As Henry Joy put it in 1916 in a letter to one of the other partners, "Mr. Pond, while he is the nicest fellow in the world and with the nicest family, and would help materially in making the ranch attractive and cheerful to the visitors, has not the business talent and managerial capacity to conduct the affairs of such a club as we hope to develop along efficient, economical lines." They knew Ashley well enough to understand that his "dreams usually tended to outrun what they thought of as any man's practical good sense," Peggy explained. "Practical good sense to them was synonymous with knowing how to make proper use of money, and this was an attribute with which the Fates had not seen fit to endow my father."[29]

An example of Ashley's managerial style is evident in a 1914 telegram sent to his partners.

> Wire authority to purchase two hundred head of
> cattle. Grass growing rapidly on flats and must have
> cattle to save it, otherwise will suffer great loss. Also
> have authority to purchase water pumping outfit
> to water cattle and barn in which to store grain.
> Can buy three hundred tons feed cheap if we had
> eighteen miles of good gravel road which I have had
> experience in building. Could market milk with
> small loss.[30]

That was not what the Detroit partners had in mind. "What they wanted was a nice couple to live on the place and keep it open for visitors," Peggy said. In addition to the growing animosity between Ashley and his partners, his wife was becoming disenchanted as well. "My mother didn't want to be a part of that nice couple," Peggy added. Hazel knew the hard work demanded by ranch life. She had lived on a working ranch before marrying Ashley. After two years in Pajarito Canyon, she decided that ranching was not to be in her future. If she was going to stay in New Mexico, it would be in a proper house in Santa Fe with a housekeeping allowance. She already had money set aside for the children's education. Her father-in-law, knowing his son's shortcomings, had left Hazel shares of stock in a large Detroit cemetery to be used solely for school tuition.[31]

By the early summer of 1916, Ashley was tired of arguing with his partners. He gave up the idea of the recreation club and sought a new direction, one that would allow him to stay on the Pajarito Plateau. He went into partnership with Harold Brook, owner of a ranch on a nearby mesa. Ashley intended to return to his dream of establishing a boys' school.

Life in the canyon had come to an end for Peggy, but she would always look on those two years as "the most important of my life." When Edgar L. Hewett wrote his classic *Pajarito Plateau and its Ancient People*, he challenged his readers to sense an unseen world, to restore to the mesas, canyons, and ruins the human spirits that had lived there through the centuries. He called for a creative imagination. "Unless the stones come to life," Hewett said, "the voices of the past are inaudible."[32] Even at such an early age, Peggy was equal to that challenge. She had entered that unseen world and heard the voices, and from them she had learned that nothing lasts forever.

"I remember how we children sat in the back seat of the car as we were driven down Pajarito Canyon for the last time, singing over and over with quavery voices, 'When you come to the end of a perfect day'. . . We looked back as long as we could see."[33]

Chapter 5

A Ranch School for Boys
"Hio! we sing of the mountains!"

"My father wanted a ranch. My mother wanted flower gardens." With the move from Pajarito Canyon, Peggy's parents each got what they wanted, at least temporarily. In the fall of 1916, Ashley bought a home in Santa Fe on East Palace Avenue, giving Hazel the city life she preferred. For himself, he turned to the partnership with his friend Harold Brook, who had established his Los Alamos Ranch in 1907.

To supplement their income, Brook and his wife, Cassy, had taken on some of the managerial duties at the Pajarito Club in its last months. It was during that time, presumably, that Ashley sold Brook on the idea of starting a boys' school. In the beginning, Brook was agreeable to Ashley's plan, but the two men soon had a falling out. As a result, Ashley bought Los Alamos Ranch outright, and the Brooks left the plateau. Ashley wasted no time in readying the ranch for students. By May of 1917, he had completed a two-story log structure, affectionately known as the Big House, to provide classrooms and lodging for students and staff. It also held a dining area and a common room with a large center fireplace. Ashley hired A. J. Connell, a forest ranger with experience in the Boy Scout program, to manage the school. In the fall of 1917, Los Alamos Ranch School welcomed its first student.[1] The following year, Connell brought in a young Yale graduate named Fayette Curtis as the first headmaster.

Nature-loving Peggy and horse-loving Dottie longed to attend their father's school, but that was not to be. Instead, they were sent to boarding schools for almost all of their remaining education. Laddie, on the other hand, entered the Ranch School at age ten. Peggy always saw an irony in the fact that her brother was the only one of the three Pond children who "never developed the fascination with horses and trail-riding which had so motivated my father."[2]

Peggy and Dottie returned to the Francis Parker School in San Diego for another year, so neither of them spent much time in the family's Santa Fe home until the summer of 1917. The setting was vastly different from their beloved home in the canyon, although there *was* a cow on the lawn. "My father was a sensual man and loved good food," Peggy recalled. "Garden fresh food. Milk from the Jersey cow, fruit, raspberries, strawberries with whipped cream. Pancakes, griddle cakes we called them, with maple syrup or honey." A honeycomb on the table was a part of each morning's breakfast, but, if some segments of life on Palace Avenue were good, others were not. Ashley was often away, dealing with the organization of the Ranch School, which left Hazel in charge of the house and the children. When Ashley returned home at intervals, he and Hazel spent much of their time arguing, which invariably led to Ashley loosing his temper. Ashley's self-image had taken a beating with the failure of the Pajarito Club and the loss of respect from his lifelong friends, compounding the already low self-esteem created by his controlling and judgmental father. In his insecurity, Ashley dominated the only people he could—his children. He frequently battered Peggy's self-worth with cutting remarks at a time when she was fragile and struggling to establish her identity. She was soon torn between loving him and fearing him. In the best moments, she idolized her father; at other times she was aware only of the side of him she could not even like. She shared his sensitivity and his passion for the land, but she often fled to her mother for protection from his tirades.

Peggy was at an awkward stage when she arrived home for the summer of 1917. She was thirteen years old, a child striving to be an adult one moment and fighting against it the next. Her maturing side had begun to notice relationships between boys and girls at school, between men and women when she was at home. Peggy compared herself with her mother, who charmed every male who visited their home, and in that comparison she found herself lacking. She thought of herself as plain and unattractive. She had hated being a wallflower at the dances and social events at the Francis Parker School, which was coeducational, but she didn't have the knack of "chattering about nothing" to her male classmates. She wanted desperately to have a boyfriend like all the other girls seemed to have, but when she became attracted to a sensitive and delicate boy in her class, the girls teased her about having a crush on him. Peggy still escaped often into a make-believe world. She spent hours reading the legends of King Arthur and the fairy books of Andrew Lang. "I flung myself obsessively into my fantasy life," she admitted, "resisting maturity." It was easier to imagine herself in a carefree landscape of Arthur Rackham trees than to cope with reality.[3]

Peggy's teenage mood swings were too much for her mother. Hazel's patience ran out. She sent Peggy to the Ranch School to spend a few weeks with her father. By serendipity, Peggy found herself in just the situation she needed, one in which she could fulfill both sides of her being, the fantasy self and the young woman seeking acceptance. While staying on the plateau, she met Aileen Baehrens, a woman who would greatly influence Peggy's development and become a lifelong friend.

Aileen was a young widow with a four-year-old son. She had been hired as matron and hostess for the Ranch School, but she was expected to do more than keep health records and entertain visitors. She sewed, cooked, saw to the interior decorating of the school, nursed the sick, and cared for the younger children of the employees.[4] Although born in New Mexico, Aileen had lived more than half of her life in France. Her experiences and education had given her the manners and charm of the Old World, and those qualities, along with her beauty, made an impression on all who met her, most especially the children.[5]

Aileen was the first person to treat Peggy as an adult, an equal rather than the incorrigible child her parents thought her to be. Peggy responded instantly to Aileen's attention, which eased her toward adulthood, but she still clung to the fantasy world as a private retreat. Much to her delight, she observed that Aileen could be a part of that world, too. Aileen was of Spanish-American and Celtic descent, raised on legends and folk tales, and she wasn't too dignified to enter the world of the children living on the plateau. She played with them during magical, fun-filled afternoons.

Aileen danced in a circle of excited children, her summer dress reflecting the bright sunlight. The little ones held hands and laughed gaily, caught up in their carefree game. Peggy couldn't turn her eyes away from Aileen when the young woman started to sing and broke the circle to lead the line of children skipping through the meadow. The scent of the damp grass was her perfume, and the vivid purple and gold of wild asters and dandelions stood out like an artist's colors against a dozen shades of green. Aileen's smile and enthusiasm were contagious, as though she cast a spell. She was a radiantly feminine being. Even Mr. Connell had called her the beautiful housekeeper, and there was never a shortage of gentlemen admirers. Peggy had always thought of herself as a tomboy, but watching Aileen she saw for the first time another possibility. Aileen was different from all the rest of the adults. She was a grown up, but she still knew how to have fun. She wasn't afraid of what people would think if she waded in puddles or raced cloud shadows across a field or went on treasure hunts. She read fairy tales to the children and

believed every word. To Peggy and the others, she was a goddess, and they were her children and her playmates.

Peggy wrote a pair of poems in 1926 in tribute to Aileen, saying of her,

> You were the goosegirl of our storybooks,
> Hair flying to the wind, and white bare feet,
> Swift to run on the grass and through the brooks
> And underneath the vines and hand in hand
> With children treading over rippled sand."[6]

So important was Peggy's fantasy realm that it inspired poems for years, even after she was married.

During her summer weeks at the Ranch School, Peggy also watched the relationship between Aileen and her son, Deric. She saw an "almost divine representation" of motherhood, an image that stood in contrast to the way she felt toward her own mother. It was this contrast that finalized the widening gulf between Peggy and Hazel, leading to the "mother fixation" that would affect her for the rest of her life. Peggy admitted many years later that she could never find "the reconciling symbol between the two figures."

Peggy experienced other contrasts that summer as well. Her world of imagination was foreign to the world of regimen surrounding her at Los Alamos. The Ranch School ran on rules and principles "to which everything feminine seemed anathema." Because of that, she turned even more strongly to fantasy, "for out of it poetry grows." Nevertheless, a conflict between the two worlds was destined to cause inner turmoil for Peggy as she matured and took on responsibilities. Even though she identified the connection to both realms within her personality, she struggled to justify time spent away from a daily routine in pursuit of poetry. The fantasy world would always be at odds with her rational side.

The next years brought a series of transitions. Peggy had always attended private schools, but in the fall of 1917, she found herself enrolled at Santa Fe High School. This change was precipitated by America's entry into World War I and the adjustments and decisions the war brought about for the Pond family. Planning to volunteer for pilot training, Ashley tried to enlist in the army but was turned down because of his age. Undeterred, he handed over the reins of the Ranch School to A. J. Connell and joined the Red Cross. He was soon serving in France as a canteen worker near the front lines, so close that he came under fire during the American attack at St. Mihiel in Lorraine.[7] In Santa Fe, Hazel kept the girls with her for the first year of the war, with Laddie attending the Ranch School close by. For her own contributions, she planted a victory garden and promoted patriotism by organizing a Girl Scout troop for Peggy and her friends. It was the first troop west of the Mississippi. The girls participated in the usual hiking and camping activities, but they also sold vegetables from their mothers' victory gardens and helped with the fruit harvest in nearby orchards. They even went door to door selling victory bonds. Though Peggy enjoyed her friendships with those other "first" girl scouts— Anita Rose, Katherine "Peaches" Van Stone, Frances Andrews, Kathleen Rolls, Frances Wilson, Florence Earnest, and Constance Walter—her involvement in scouting was to last for only one year.[8]

With the optimism brought about by Allied victories in the summer of 1918, Ashley and Hazel decided to send Peggy away to school again. She entered the Hillside School in Norwalk, Connecticut, for the fall term. Away from home and isolated by a lack of friends once more, Peggy turned more strongly to her poetry. She had continued to write since her first efforts in Pajarito Canyon, but it was at Hillside that she began to earn recognition as a poet. She submitted a verse titled "A Tale of Spring"— about a wood nymph and a water sprite—to the St. Nicholas League and won the League's silver badge. She was proud and excited about the award, but it apparently did little to boost her self image. She still harshly compared herself with others.

In January of 1919, Peggy transferred to Wabanaki School in Greenwich, Connecticut, where she was pleased to find another girl from home. She made friends with Gay Young-Hunter of Taos. Even though Gay was a year her junior, Peggy immediately idolized her as she had Aileen, admiring her poise and femininity. Gay was a "child of adoring and artist parents," Peggy wrote years later in her journal. That summer, Peggy visited Gay in Taos and was immersed in a world of art and dance, music and culture. Gay's parents were both from English families of privilege, and she herself had been born in a pre-Tudor, moated manor house in England. Her father was an accomplished portrait painter whose work was compared favorably with the paintings of his family friend John Singer Sargent. Young-Hunter had paintings in the Tate Gallery in London and the Luxembourg Museum in Paris. Gay's mother

Peggy and her Santa Fe friends visit the Los Alamos Ranch School, ca. 1917. From left to right are Anita Rose, Olive Allen, Kathleen Rolls, Rosemary Horgan, Florence Earnest, Josephine McManus, Helen May, and Peggy Pond. Courtesy Los Alamos Historical Museum Archives.

was also a portrait artist as well as a painter of fine landscapes. The family had moved to the United States when Gay was quite young and alternated between homes in New York and New Mexico. Peggy was also impressed with Mrs. Young-Hunter's "visions," an ability that had evidently passed to her daughter as well, since Gay had shared some of her own visualizations while at school. Peggy reflected on that Taos visit in her journal. "What incentive did I have," she recalled, "to adjust to my own commonplace life?" In the fall, she and Gay went their separate ways, but Gay had nonetheless shown Peggy another example of a persona she admired but could not, in her own eyes, equal. Despite parting to attend different schools, the two remained friends throughout their lives.

With the fall term of 1919, Peggy headed west to board at the Marlborough School in Los Angeles, but the following year she returned to New England. She enrolled again at Hillside, and at the end of the spring term, Peggy made a decision that would set her on a new course of self-discovery. She didn't return to Santa Fe for her summer vacation but instead chose to attend Camp Aloha in Fairlee, Vermont. It was to be an experience that would finally change the way Peggy looked at herself. "Perhaps it was not till Aloha," she observed, "that I really felt loved and valued."

A column of smoke rose into the night sky from the campfire that burned near the lake, sending its reflection shimmering across the dark water. Peggy walked toward the shore with her friends. When she saw the Aloha Honor Girls standing in a semicircle behind the fire, her pace quickened. Next year's Honor Girls were about to be announced. It was a ceremony that took place every year as summer drew to a close. Each of the current Honor Girls held a flaming torch aloft. The dancing lights revealed glistening eyes and solemn faces that couldn't hide the regret of a special time coming to an end. The campers arranged themselves around the fire, and excited murmurs passed through the crowd until Mrs. Gulick, the camp founder, stepped to the center of the circle. In a short speech she gave each year, she reminded them of what it meant to be an Honor Girl and explained that handing down the torches from old to new meant entrusting the ideals of Camp Aloha. The Honor Girls began to sing, and at the end of each of their eleven refrains, Mrs. Gulick called the name of a new Honor Girl. "Dorothy White . . . Elizabeth Mann . . . Peggy Morgan." Peggy's heart beat faster for a moment as she heard her own first name called, but then, it was someone else. The older girls continued to sing after each name, building the suspense. Another refrain, and then, "Peggy Pond." Her breath caught in her throat. Slowly, a huge smile spread across her face. Before she could truly comprehend the moment, she and the other new Honor Girls were being carried off by the enthusiastic crowd and wildly congratulated.

A few days later, Peggy wondered where the summer had gone as she packed her belongings to return to school. The weeks at camp had been the most fun she'd ever had. Besides the sports and outdoor activities, she had written for the camp newspaper, the weekly Scamp Spirit. *Some of her poems were published there, and another one, "Aloha Twilight," had become a camp song. She had been the center for the basketball team, and when the Aloha girls had played the team from a nearby camp, the newspaper had reported, "Hanoum played a splendid game, but Peggy Pond got the jump every time." How proud she was to read those words! But the swimming, canoeing, and camping—her fun-filled summer—had come to an end.*

Peggy boarded the train in the late afternoon. She sat by the window, holding the gold felt letter "A" she had received as an Honor Girl. She would sew it on her camp uniform for the next year, where it would represent the ideals of Camp Aloha, but for Peggy, it meant far more. It represented the first time her submerged self had been recognized. On the trip back to Hillside, she clutched the letter in her hand all night.[9]

Sixteen-year-old Peggy Pond and another camper enjoy a ride in the summer of 1920 above Lake Morey at Camp Aloha, Fairlee, Vermont. Courtesy Los Alamos Historical Museum Archives.

Writing in her journal in 1974, Peggy revisited that moment of acceptance at Camp Aloha as she examined thoughts of her adolescence. In her younger years, such acknowledgements were few and far between, especially within the family. "Neither Mother nor Father acknowledged the 'me' I felt to be important," she wrote, but she admitted that at home her inner self was "jealously guarded, hidden deeply within under the shaggy-banged, impatient, willful exterior."   From a very early age, her relationship with the family was strained. Despite being away at boarding schools so much of the time, Peggy once observed that she never remembered feeling homesick.

In her last year at Hillside, Peggy expanded her writing. She penned a short story titled "Gorgeous Things" and entered it in *The Atlantic* short story contest. To her surprise, the entry won second place and an award of $50![10] The achievement took her to a higher rung in her climb toward self-esteem, but she was also working to improve her image in another way. She had always enjoyed school, but in her senior year at Hillside she experienced a drive to excel academically. As the college boards approached, the drive turned to stress. Peggy began to show signs of severe nervous depression. The school provided special counseling and even arranged for a masseuse to help her relax. It took a dedicated effort from her teachers and the school's administrators to get her through the tests, but they succeeded. Peggy was admitted to Smith College in Northampton, Massachusetts, for the autumn term of 1922.

At Smith, Peggy continued to feel the "need to surpass in some way—to get good grades, to be accepted," though she did learn to relax somewhat and enjoy her surroundings and the opportunities. She was elected to class office and was treasurer of the athletic association. "I was mostly so happy," she said, "with several close friends, budding into someone, away from family and boarding school restrictions, enthralled with Walter de la Mare's poetry." She loved shopping on a street near the campus. She bought "clothes and books and prints and tea things." And when she was on campus, she relished the academic atmosphere. "I remember how I loved that library with its high arched windows looking out on the stately trees—cathedral-like in its stateliness, especially the twilight hours when I loved to study at the long tables." She delighted in having access to "all those wonderful books," and new experiences and friendships filled her nonacademic hours. She spent Thanksgiving with the Gulicks in Boston and was their guest the next year for a white Christmas at Camp Aloha. Peggy was finally becoming comfortable with her individuality and thriving away from home.

When at school, Peggy may not have been homesick in the literal sense, but she did often miss New Mexico. She carried with her at all times a copy of Alice Corbin's *Red Earth*, reading the poems about the Southwest until the book fell apart. She also wrote poems about her native state. Her words described the beauty of the Truchas Peaks and fragrant grasses on the mesa, revealing her longing for the landscape of New Mexico. Then, while home for the summer after her freshman year, Peggy met a young man who could give her just the thing to satisfy that longing. He could fulfill her dream of returning to the Pajarito Plateau.

Fermor Spencer Church had just completed his second year as a master at the Los Alamos Ranch School when he met Peggy. He would have been a good prospect in spite of his place of residence. He was a graduate of Harvard and had grown up in Connecticut, where his father was a pharmacist and owned a store in South Norwalk. Ferm was at first attracted to Peggy because she was familiar with New England, but they had other things in common as well. Ferm was in love with New Mexico and the outdoor life, and, as Peggy discovered one summer afternoon at the Ranch School, they both loved classical music. "I visited the so-young schoolmaster upstairs in his small room on the top floor of the Big House," she said, looking back. Ferm had

In his master's quarters on the top floor of the Big House at Los Alamos Ranch School, Fermor Church courted Peggy Pond by playing classical phonograph records for her. Courtesy Los Alamos Historical Museum Archives.

Ponce de Leon, a German shepherd, offers his help as Ferm courts Peggy at the Los Alamos Ranch School, ca. 1924. Courtesy Los Alamos Historical Museum Archives.

played a record of *Wagner's Fire* Music on his small gramophone, and Peggy commented, reflecting on that afternoon, "It was this bond of music that won me to him, like a kind of spell."

Peggy was engaged by the end of the summer, but she completed one more year at Smith before returning home to marry Ferm.

Looking forward to a week-long stay at Camp May, Peggy and Fermor Church are packed and ready to leave for their honeymoon, June 27, 1924. Courtesy Los Alamos Historical Museum Archives.

Chapter 6

Life on the Pajarito Plateau

"In those first years, I had glamorous ideas of ranch life."

To say the least, Peggy's married life began in a somewhat nontraditional way. First of all, for a betrothal gift Ferm gave her a Colt revolver. It was no doubt a practical thought on his part, considering that he would be taking his bride to live on an isolated ranch, but Peggy had obviously hoped for something with a bit more sentiment. "It was very plain to me / I couldn't hit a six foot tree," she penned, referring to the hours of shooting practice with her husband-to-be. "But just the same, I wish my love / had given me a soft-winged dove."[1]

"We got married on June 26, 1924, without preliminaries," Peggy explained. She had planned to return to Smith College for her junior year, but she began to feel that she'd had enough of being away at school. She wanted to be in New Mexico. She and Ferm had talked about a honeymoon at Camp May in the mountains above the Ranch School, but it had to be scheduled well ahead of time. No such plans had been made for that summer, but then, suddenly, Camp May became available for a week. That prompted a quick decision and a very hurried chain of events. "We hustled down to the courthouse and got a license," Peggy recalled. She borrowed a veil from Margaret Kelly, longtime friend and neighbor of her parents, who also served as her matron of honor. "I think I wore the white dress I'd worn for my high school graduation," she said, trying to remember years later. "My mother lent me my wedding ring." Her brother gave her away, since her father was in Europe at the time, and she and Ferm were married in her parents' house on East Palace Avenue on the same day they made their decision.[2]

Then, there was the other less-than-ideal situation. She and Ferm spent their wedding night in her old bedroom on the second floor of her parents' house, coming downstairs the next morning to face an assortment of jests. Surely things will improve, Peggy must have thought as she and Ferm left for a week of camping at the Ranch School retreat.

"We spent a week of our honeymoon romantically at Camp May," Peggy explained whenever she gave talks about her early days as a Ranch School wife. "At least we expected it was going to be romantic. In those days there was nothing there but a one-room log cabin with a galvanized metal roof in which the lightest hailstorm pounded like the charge of the Light Brigade." She and

Ferm carried water in canvas buckets from a nearby spring and fought with a miserable, old wood stove that "smoked and smoldered." The accommodations also included "a pair of creaking cots that had a chronic habit of collapsing at the most inauspicious moments." If that weren't enough, "a hoard of pack rats scrabbled over the roof at night, stealing whatever we left loose."[3]

To further complicate matters, Peggy was not a veteran camper. Her only experiences had been overnight trips with her Girl Scout troop and some outings to the Pecos Wilderness with friends. She and her mother had occasionally stayed there in a cabin near Cowles with some girlfriends, but "to be with Ferm was not like being with a girl companion. There was this absence of being able to talk—Ferm content not to, as always, and I inarticulate and shy." The beauty of the surroundings inspired poetry and daydreams that she longed to share but which she found impossible. "Still, in memory, the delights of that week linger," she wrote years later, remembering especially a "picnic on the west-facing slope of Pajarito Mountain and Ferm's love of the horses and his competency in caring for them."

Their days on the mountain were filled with a mixture of wonder and humor. "The aspens glimmered and whispered on the slope, our horses munched the long grass, birds sang at dawn. We took picnics every day, riding to the edge of the Valle Grande and up Pajarito Mountain." Peggy often reminisced in her talks about those early summer days in 1924, but then she would playfully contrast the pleasant memories by admitting that "the bride was woefully unskilled at cooking camp food." She referred to an "anomalous hunk of meat the groom had provided to last the whole week." It was tough the first few days and "rather green at the end." Whatever she tried to do to it only made it worse. Their best meals were breakfast, which Ferm cooked, and "the sandwiches for lunch with fool-proof ingredients like fried egg or marmalade and peanut butter." Peggy always said that "it was just as well for the groom that the bride didn't have to do much cooking that first year, since all she could boast about when she married was her skill at making gingerbread."[4] Like the other masters, Ferm, along with Peggy, ate in the dining hall with the boys.

After their week in the mountains, the honeymoon ended and the realities of marriage set in. Peggy soon realized that her lack of cooking skills was not the only obstacle she faced in married life. If the accommodations at Camp May had been lacking, the comforts offered by their living quarters at the Ranch School were not much better.

Their apartment was in a small, slab-sided construction known as the Pyramid because of its peaked roof. Ferm and Peggy combined their meager possessions to furnish the limited living space. "We had a tiny sitting room with an old spool day bed, covered by a Chimayo blanket, and an upright Estey piano," Peggy remembered. "There wasn't room for much else besides a chair or two and the little folding tea table I had in college, along with a fragile Japanese tea set painted black with silver dragons that was my special treasure." Water for tea had to be heated on a two-burner oil stove in the bathroom, which was equipped with only cold running water and shared with the other resident of the Pyramid, the school's secretary.[5] On the wall—"wherever could there have been wall space?" she wondered—were hung her little woodcut of some boats and her framed picture of an elf in the autumn woods.

In addition to their sitting room, there was a small dressing room that adjoined a screened sleeping porch. Peggy and Ferm, like everyone else at the school, slept outside on a porch year round. The winter of 1924–25 was a cold one, and there were only canvas shades that rolled down to cover the screens and offer protection from the weather. "I remember well how I sometimes used to wake up in the morning to find my face frozen to the eiderdown, though under the covers, *lots of covers*, I was always warm."[6]

Conveniences in the Pyramid didn't extend as far as hot baths. For that, she and Ferm used the guest bathroom upstairs in the Big House. "I usually took mine in the afternoon when the boys were out riding," Peggy recalled. She never forgot one such afternoon when she lay in the tub, "dreamily munching an apple," she added, "as contentedly as Eve. The door opened and in walked Mr. Connell, our fastidious director, escorting two lady visitors. Of course, they burst out even faster than they had burst in, but not before Mr. Connell, who never forgot his manners, had time to politely say, 'Excuse me.'"[7]

The apartment offered few luxuries, but the lack of comforts in her living conditions bothered Peggy less than the loneliness she encountered in those first months as a new wife. Ferm followed a rigorous routine of responsibilities to the school. He was busy all day with classes and many evenings with student activities, and his demanding schedule left Peggy alone in their small quarters much of the time. That summer, while Ferm had duties at the school's summer camp, Peggy returned to Santa Fe for a visit with her parents, but in August she and Ferm finally managed some time together. They took a trip to Denver in a car borrowed from Peggy's mother. On the way through western Colorado, they stopped at Mesa Verde National Park to visit Aileen, who had by then married the archaeologist Jesse Nusbaum. It was a good trip through the kind of beautiful scenery she and Ferm both loved, but the carefree days of traveling and enjoying friends didn't last long enough.

Peggy returned to her isolation, and to add to her discomfort, she was beginning to feel nauseated much of the time, a fact soon attributed to her being pregnant. Following the doctor's orders, she took daily walks, but afterward she would return to the confinement of the Pyramid to read or play the piano or listen to music. She poured over the *Ladies' Home Journal*, the *Atlantic Monthly*, and the Sears Roebuck mail order catalog. She played Chopin preludes on the old Estey or delved into the small collection of Caruso Red Seal Victor records for the wind-up phonograph. When she tired of being alone, she sought out Genevieve Ranger, the school's nurse, and spilled out her uneasiness about her pregnancy. Peggy's sister-in-law, who was also a nurse, sent her a book on childbirth, but neither the book nor Miss Ranger's reassurances completely alleviated her concerns about motherhood and giving birth. "I tried to talk to my husband, but found I could not, as I had talked and laughed with my college roommate. He was uncommunicative," she said of Ferm, "and I was totally a lost child." In her uncertainty and loneliness, she began to wonder if she had married too soon and for the wrong reasons.

In the lonely hours when Ferm was away and before the baby was born, Peggy reflected on her married life. Had she done the right thing in leaving college to marry? She thought back to the day of her wedding, when she had "hung back at the door between the kitchen and the living room, terrified, in my borrowed veil . . . with my mother at my shoulder." Hazel had sensed her daughter's fear and resistance. She told Peggy that she needn't go through with it even then if she didn't really wish to. It was a moment of recognition between the two, perhaps one of the few times Hazel understood and sympathized with her daughter. Peggy wrestled with her fears and doubts in that moment. She suddenly realized that she was about to marry a man she "did not love in any way." She wondered if she even knew what it was to love. "But something deep within me felt, nevertheless, his essential nature," she admitted. "He was someone I could lean on whose calm and stability was like a quiet harbor into which I sailed after the turbulence of my parental home, the dissatisfied mother, the turbulent father." In her reflection, Peggy knew there was another fact to confront as well. Ferm's calm and stability were not her only reasons for marrying him. "Did I do wrong," she thought, "to marry for self interest, on account of my desire to abide in that landscape with its tremendous beauty?"

In her first months of marriage, Peggy felt unfulfilled. She had always held an image in her heart of the imaginary knight that most girls envision, and Ferm was falling woefully short. There was an absence of communication between them. Ferm did not share her world of books, imagination, or humor, and the marriage was not turning out as she had hoped. "Is it because I married the landscape instead of Ferm?" she would candidly ask herself.

"Women have seen men lose their hearts to landscape," Peggy wrote almost sixty years later in a poem about her ranching ancestors, but it is not only men who lose their hearts to the land or feel it "summon something like music" to their blood.[8] No one knew that more than she. "It's the land that wants to be said," she would acknowledge after a lifetime of expressing her feelings for it in poetry.[9] In retrospect, Peggy would not have been the poet she ultimately became if not for her intense bonding with the land, but in 1925 the shaping force of that land had placed her in a difficult situation. She was once again living on the Pajarito Plateau, but she was married to a man, albeit a good one, who was very different from her own nature. There was a baby on the way, and she would have to adapt to motherhood and raising a child when she hadn't even succeeded in charting her own life. She had escaped the turmoil of her family home, but she had not yet escaped the turmoil of her inner self. Having grown up in a family that was not close, she had little experience with relationships. Would she be able to overcome a lack of outward expression in dealing with her husband and child? The unknown answer was a constant worry.

The young couple continued to live in the Pyramid for a while after the baby came, "which naturally was required to be a boy," Peggy always said with a sly smile, referring to a Ranch School myth that A. J. Connell required his masters to father only sons.[10] Theodore Spencer Church was born April 26, 1925, and the already crowded living space in the Pyramid shrank even more. With a gift of money from her parents, Peggy and Ferm began construction on a house of their own.

Like almost all of the other buildings on the ranch at the time, the new home was a log structure. Ferm designed the house himself, taking into account the size and height of the pines available for constructing the walls. "We had no central heating for the first two or three years," Peggy said. "The house was warmed by an ancestral kind of space heater, a very good term," she added, "for most of the heat went off into space as quickly as it could." There was also a circulating stove in the baby's room. Peggy described it as "one of those cozy-sounding pieces of equipment that the Sears Roebuck catalog used to advertise as quite sufficient to heat a four- or five-room house. The heat was supposed to go out into the little hall at the center of the house and spread around, but somehow it never seemed to do much spreading, except up to the ceiling, where it loitered while the cold collected around our disappointed feet." The most comfortable room in the house was the kitchen, where there was a big Majestic range, but as Peggy never failed to point out, "Majestic is a trade name, not an adjective!"[11]

Miss Ranger taught Peggy a bit about cooking and provided her with some recipes, but learning to prepare them on a wood-burning stove was another matter. The range was quite attractive with its black enamel and nickel trim and had round lids and warming ovens up above. Peggy must have developed a rapport with the stove, for she spoke of it fondly years afterward, saying that "though the pine wood sooted up the grates like anything and I always loathed cleaning them, I loved the feel and presence of a live fire." There was also an icebox which sat on the back porch and had to be filled two or three times a week with chunks of ice that were cut in winter from a nearby pond and stored in an ice house.[12]

After Ted was born and could be left with a nurse, Peggy set about improving her circumstances by riding some of the nearby trails, pursuing her writing, and seeking out her few female neighbors to escape the male-dominated world in which she lived, but she still chafed at the strict regimen of the school. Because of that attitude, Peggy frequently found herself crosswise with A. J. Connell. He was opposed to females at the Ranch School, being of the opinion that his young charges needed to be separated from the influence of women. He preferred that his masters remain single. In the first seven years of the school's existence, only one master, Henry Ruhl, had been married, and he and his wife had lived at the school for only two months before Ruhl was caught in a snowstorm and died while on a hunting trip. Peggy was breaking ground and going against the Irish stubbornness of A. J. Connell at the same time. Her husband was expected to continue his full-time dedication to his students despite his choice to marry and start a family. Consequently, Peggy usually found herself alone on her explorations.

"At Los Alamos I had a horse of my own from the beginning," Peggy explained, "and a beautiful worn and supple old eastern saddle that had belonged to my great-grandfather when he ranched in Colfax and Mora counties. The saddle had been passed on to my mother, who would never officially give up the title to it, though she let me ride it for more than twenty years."[13] A mare named Daisy was her first horse at the Ranch School, and, as Peggy put it, "she was a stubborn creature who liked to lead me a cock-eyed chase with ears laid back and an occasional flippant show of her heels." She would run around the corral several times before letting Peggy catch her. "It

Peggy Church watches her father, Ashley Pond Jr., hold his grandson Ted on the sleeping porch at the Church cottage, ca. 1925. Courtesy Los Alamos Historical Museum Archives.

seems to me," Peggy commented, "that half my afternoon riding time was spent stalking her with the bridle in my left hand, held coyly behind my back . . . and my right hand enticingly cupped in the hope she'd think I carried a palmful of oats." Peggy smiled as she commented, "Games people play with horses!" Daisy always knew. However, Daisy was a good trail horse, which was important in view of Peggy's often unaccompanied rides.

A warm breeze blew that morning. The snow that remained in the shaded areas under the pines and junipers was slowly melting, sending off rivulets that glistened in the spring sunshine, and the first flowers were opening. With Miss Ranger's help, Peggy had learned the names of many of the flowers on the plateau. Peggy looked for her special favorites, the pasque flowers. They had a tendency to grow in the mat of pine needles under the trees. As she rode north from the Ranch School toward Guaje Canyon, Peggy entered a clearing and saw the fresh furrows of a homesteader's field. Mr. Gonzales was plowing, readying his land for the crop of frijoles he would plant soon. She rode on, entering another forested area. Eventually the trees thinned, and the soil of the trail changed to pumice deposits spewed out long ago from a nearby volcano. She glimpsed the Rio Grande in its valley 2000 feet below.

The land where tall, ancient pines grew today had once been a landscape of seething red rivers of molten rock and thick ash fall. She loved the geology of the plateau, and she was learning more about it from Ferm. He knew about such things and shared them with her when they could find time for outings together. That morning, though, she rode alone. She had to admit that the solitude was good for her poetic moods. Many times her afternoons on horseback inspired poems that would take form when she returned home. A startled deer dashed through the trees as she rode along the mesa's edge. Soon she saw the ruins of a pueblo. Five kivas lay ahead, carved in the rock by a forgotten people. Even then, so long ago, she knew the river below had looked to them as it did to her. Earth's changes were mostly subtle and centuries in the making.

The people who had lived here were unaware of the ocean that had once covered this place or the volcanic eruptions that had laid igneous rock over sediments, but the earth knew. "Thus yesterday reaches backward and forward forever and disappears like the sky," she thought. Words began to come quickly. "Yesterday, riding to Guaje," she penciled in the little notebook she always carried. "At a cliff's edge I saw a ruined city / whose name is now forgotten. / Not even high-flying birds remember these walls." The first few lines took shape. "I heard the wind on a mesa beyond / stride furiously from the mountain." Lost in the past, she failed to see the swift clouds that encroached on the present until they blocked the sun. She looked up to see the advancing rain.[14]

Fermor Church leads a trail ride at Camp Aloha in the Vermont mountains in the summer of 1926. He and Peggy worked as camp counselors while on a trip east for Ferm's five-year reunion at Harvard and the commencement at Smith College, which would have been Peggy's graduating class. Courtesy Los Alamos Historical Museum Archives.

In 1926, Peggy and Ferm spent their summer in the East. Ferm attended his five-year reunion at Harvard, and Peggy visited friends at the Smith commencement that would have been her own had she stayed in school. From there they took Ted to visit Ferm's mother in Washington, Connecticut, and left him with his grandmother while they worked for several weeks as counselors at Camp Aloha. It was during their time at Aloha that the first outward signs of Peggy's emotional stress appeared. She was depressed and suffered panic attacks accompanied by periods of weakness and sudden fits of crying. The strain in her marriage and the anxiety of motherhood had been building for some time, and the addition of the demanding camp schedule proved too much. As well, she undoubtedly compared her previous times at Aloha with that summer of 1926. Even if unconsciously, she must have confronted that emerging young girl of promise she had once been. Peggy fulfilled her duties at the camp, but the symptoms she experienced foreshadowed darker days to come.

By the time she and Ferm and the baby returned to the Ranch School in the fall, Peggy had managed to pull herself together. Plans were under way for adding a second story to their log house, and she was writing again after the hectic summer. However, many of the poems reflected the troubled spirit still within her and even reverted at times to the fairy realm of childhood. In the poem "Bridal," she wrote of a young woman beckoned by nature. She lamented in "To Certain Ones Who Do Not Understand" that "All of her days go similarly by" but added that, still, she "lives more poignantly than you can guess." The young woman in the poem speaks of "sun-touched hills" and "moving light on wind-hushed grass and trees" as though they make up for the days dragging on in similarity. "She becomes part of earth with every spring / and bears earth's blossoming as if her own," the poem says, but the words are unconvincing. The poem introduces the reader to a woman with an unfulfilled dream. In "Bondage," Peggy admits, "I am held back from flight by such small things," a patch badly needed, new strings for the baby's bib, dishes to wash. "I'll have to stay. I cannot run away," she concludes. "And so I'll sing and mend a toy and sigh / And make believe I'll go another day."

In still another poem finished that year, she did, in some sense, escape. She returned to thoughts of childhood to write a tribute to Aileen Baehrens Nusbaum. Whether this loving and beautifully written poem, "Children Remember Knowing Aphrodite," was sparked by the visit with Aileen at Mesa Verde or came from wistful longing for a simpler time, it represented the last of her writing attraction to the make-believe world. Thereafter, Peggy's poetry took on a more realistic tone, and she tried to approach life on a positive note. One such step in that direction was a set of poems written at the request of artist and family friend Gustave Baumann of Santa Fe. The poems were called the New Mexico Santos Poems, and they were created to go along with a set of woodblock prints on which Baumann was working in 1927–28. The imagined publication of prints and poems never became a reality, but it did offer Peggy a chance for her first involvement with the Santa Fe colony, a close group of writers and artists who gave support to each other's creative efforts.

In two other ways, 1928 was a landmark year for Peggy. She gave birth to her second son, Allen Bartlit Church, on June 22 in Santa Fe, and in the autumn, a woman from Pennsylvania named Edith Warner moved into the little house beside Otowi Bridge, where the road to Los Alamos crosses the Rio Grande. Though Peggy didn't see it when she first met Edith and described her as "a prim little figure . . . wearing a blouse and skirt that looked as though they might have come out of a missionary barrel," Edith was a woman who had an extraordinary impact on all who met her, and she would ultimately figure strongly in Peggy's life.

Fermor Church designed and built this log cottage for his family in 1925. His design matched the log and stone style of other buildings at the Los Alamos Ranch School. Courtesy Los Alamos Historical Museum Archives.

Peggy with Allen and Ted and their German shepherd, Ponce de Leon, at Los Alamos Ranch School, ca. 1930. Courtesy Los Alamos Historical Museum Archives.

On the Pajarito Plateau of the mid-1920s, Peggy had limited options for visiting friends. Santa Fe was thirty-five miles away, and reaching it meant driving a precarious dirt road with switchbacks and navigating a railroad trestle with the car straddling the rails as they crossed the Rio Grande. Aside from the small Ranch School community and the seasonal homesteaders, her nearest neighbors were Frank and Connie Smithwick. They were managers of a 320-acre spread about five miles to the southwest. Frank and Connie had come to the plateau in 1921 with their three sons and a young man named Alex Ross who was in their care. Anchor Ranch, complete with a beautiful seven-room adobe and surrounding gardens, soon became a gathering place for locals—John and Martha Boyd from Frijoles Canyon, the Mathers who lived in Water Canyon, and the families from the Ranch School.

On an Indian summer morning in 1925, Peggy felt like getting away. She needed the companionship of another woman, a touch of gentleness, and maybe a bit of local gossip. As she sometimes did when such a mood set in, she packed some sandwiches in her saddlebags and rode over to spend time with Connie. It was a typically fine autumn day, with only a hint of coolness in the air, and the gold leaves of the turning aspens shimmered against a bright blue sky.

Pleased to have some company, Connie welcomed Peggy into her rustic sitting room for a cup of tea. They had talked for only a few minutes when a stranger entered the room. Connie introduced the woman as Edith Warner. She explained that Miss Warner was from Pennsylvania and would be staying at Anchor Ranch for a while to help with Alex. With the customary view of westerners meeting a tenderfoot from the East, Peggy noted that Edith was too shy, too thin, and looked totally out of place in her new environment. What she learned later explained that first impression. Edith was one of five daughters of a Baptist minister, and she had been in poor health before coming to the West in 1921 to seek fresh air and sunshine. Connie had met Edith while she was staying with the Boyds at their Frijoles guest ranch. Edith had fallen in love with New Mexico and wanted to find some way to remain, so, in benefit to both, Connie had invited Edith to Anchor Ranch to work as a governess for Alex. Edith contributed almost nothing to the afternoon's conversation except a few sentiments about western wildflowers, which she apparently liked very much. In the large room she seemed small and insignificant, the image of a scared coyote, though she was thirty-three years old and should have acquired more self-assurance by then. Peggy would eventually look back on that day as a lesson in how wrong an impression can be when made on outward appearances.[15]

"It was just as well that a log house in the wilderness presented a good many special problems that helped keep my feet on the ground and my wits from wandering too much of the time among the stars," Peggy said of her first decade as a Ranch School wife. Her home was the farthest north in the row of log and stone structures that housed some of the masters and staff. Only a stand of young pines stood between the Church home and Pueblo Canyon to the north. Because of the location, Peggy and Ferm sometimes felt that they had the mountains and mesa all to themselves. "I don't know whether it was my good fortune or my bad," Peggy said, "to have been so enchanted with the great dramas of cloud and light that we looked down on every season from our windows. Perhaps they made me too often dissatisfied with the routine of daily life and with the mere mortals that I lived among and that I rather hated to admit I was." Peggy yearned to get out of the house, to walk, to ride, to touch the open spaces, and after the first couple of years of married life, she was able to spend time doing just that by hiring full-time maids. Sometimes it was a girl from a ranch hand's family, or at other times she hired girls from the village of Peñasco or nearby pueblos. She taught them to cook, "far better than I could," she admitted, and they cleaned house and looked after the little ones, giving Peggy time for her writing. The arrangement helped her cope with the continuing problem of depression, though she still relapsed occasionally. During those times she would be sick in bed, but as she once said, she seemed "to have written a good deal of poetry while being sick in bed or on it!" She believed that such an escape was sometimes the only way for a housewife with even the slightest kind of creative gift, but she was torn also between the urge that drew her to create and the demands—or supposed demands—of reality. "I remember how envious I used to be of my poet friend," she once said, "whose wife kept his house and guarded him from all frustrating interruptions. If only the poet in me had such a wife, I used to lament."[16]

By the end of the decade, life had settled into routines and occasional much-needed escapes. Peggy and Ferm had good friends in Lawrence Hitchcock, the school's headmaster,[17] and in Henry Bosworth, who was hired

Church Family, ca. 1930. Courtesy Joan Pond.

first as the school's secretary and later taught math. There were often rounds of bridge with "Hitch" and "Bos," and on several holidays they traveled together, exploring the Southwest. They went on pack trips and adventures to Lee's Ferry and Cameron in Arizona, and they spent a Christmas together in Guaymas, Mexico. After her first flight in an airplane in 1929, Peggy's adventurous spirit led her to take flying lessons for a short time. Her father loved flying, so Peggy may have been inspired by him, but it was also the era of those dynamic women pilots like Katherine Stinson and Amelia Earhart who served as role models for so many women.[18] Peggy was still enraptured by the experience years afterward, recalling her lessons and the times when she "wrote ecstatically about flying, back in the days when Anne Lindbergh was in the news!" She took lessons until the owner of the plane crashed it and was killed. That brought the realization that "the mother of two small children had better practice keeping her feet on the ground."

After the second boy arrived, the house was enlarged. She and Ferm finished an upstairs room, "covered with slabs on the outside to match the logs." Their home in the pines offered the comforts needed for the family, but for Peggy it was still very often a lonely place. Frustration continued because Ferm had to be at the school so much of the time, leaving "so little opportunity to sit by our own fireside." Their home was definitely a realm of opposites. Both she and Ferm loved the beauty of their surroundings, but they could not seem to share it in the same emotional way. "The years that were filled with the presence of the moon," Peggy called that period in their lives. "The moon that seemed to be mistress of shadow—the shadow of the ponderosa pines on the white snow." Many times she and Ferm stood in awe of the winter beauty of their world of untrodden snow in the silence of the night, but in the face of such wonder, Peggy had to put her feelings into *words*. Ferm felt no such need. There remained a serious lack of communication between them. She expressed their difficulties best poetically: "he was a stone, she was the rippling water."

Chapter 7

The Difficult Years
"I wish to be other than I am."

Peggy's third son, Hugh Whitney Church, was born in February of 1932, but the months leading up to his birth had been a struggle. Ferm was away for several weeks that summer, tutoring two of his students at their home on the Banded Peak Ranch in Colorado. Peggy fought nausea and a lingering nasal infection, and Teddy and Allen took turns being sick with scarlet fever and whooping cough. As a result of the illnesses, Peggy decided to stay in Santa Fe through the cold winter of her pregnancy. She rented a small house on Acequia Madre to be near a doctor, but there were other advantages as well. The time in Santa Fe provided a respite from the isolation of the plateau and the problems with her marriage.

In Santa Fe, there were opportunities to spend time with old friends, and among them was Aileen Nusbaum, who had returned that year from Mesa Verde when her husband Jesse was appointed director of the fledgling Laboratory of Anthropology. Peggy and Aileen immediately renewed their closeness, and Aileen became the natural choice to be Hugh's godmother. Aileen's nurturing warmth that Peggy remembered from childhood was a welcome comfort in those months.

Peggy became better acquainted that winter with the writers and artists of the Santa Fe colony, in particular poet and author Haniel Long, who would become not only a mentor but an intimate and guiding friend. She met Haniel and his wife, Alice, through Jane and Gustave Baumann, long-time friends of her family. "No one could be very tongue-tied in the presence of Jane and Gus," Peggy said of this vibrant Santa Fe couple, but she was generally shy around the other artists and writers she met. At a picnic at the San Felipe Feast Day in 1931, she had been introduced to Alice Corbin Henderson, whose book *Red Earth* Peggy had worshipped during her college days, but Peggy's shyness kept her from saying anything to the woman she so admired! Ironically, Peggy had managed to gather enough courage two years before that to approach Mary Austin for an appraisal of her poetry. In the autumn of 1929, Peggy wrote to the self-styled grand dame of the Santa Fe literary enclave, asking for advice about her poems. Austin had a far-reaching reputation as a respected writer and poet, but a local reputation as a cantankerous, out-spoken critic of just about everything. She was kind to Peggy in regard to her technique but was hard on the content. By the time Peggy wrote for Austin's opinion, she had already published poems in *The Atlantic, Poetry, Parents Magazine, Scribner's, The Southwest Scene,* and *Literary Digest,* and one of her poems was included in Henderson's *The Turquoise Trail: An Anthology of New Mexico Poetry.* She was gaining recognition, but Austin told Peggy, in her usual blunt manner, "You write very well, but you don't have anything to say." With Peggy's shaky self-confidence and the uncertainty in her life, it is a wonder that she ever produced another poem, but balancing Austin's harsh critique was a burning desire to write, even if she never achieved acclaim as a poet.[1] Thus, Peggy continued, but the years ahead would not be easy ones. Experiences awaited that would cause her to confront her deepest insecurities.

When Peggy returned to Los Alamos with her third son, it became obvious that the Churches had once again outgrown their home. Plans were quickly under way for an addition to the log house. Friend and Santa Fe architect John Gaw Meem designed a living room with stone walls and a large fireplace to complement their rustic dwelling and add needed space.[2] As though construction and a new baby were not enough of a challenge that summer, Peggy invited guests for July. Dorothy McKibbin and her ten-month-old son, Kevin, came for a two-week stay. Dorothy was a Smith College graduate, and though she was six years older than Peggy, they shared common experiences from Northampton life. Dorothy had moved to New Mexico only the month before and may have met Peggy in her first days back in Santa Fe, but it is also possible that the two crossed paths briefly in 1926 when Dorothy spent a year as a patient at Sunmount Sanitorium in Santa Fe, where she battled tuberculosis. Whichever the case, Peggy was "starved for female companionship" at the Ranch School and was delighted to have a woman visiting, especially one who shared many of her interests and sensitivities. Though not of Peggy's caliber as a poet, Dorothy also wrote poetry. Both women had young sons, and Dorothy loved New Mexico, so much so that she had taken a chance on moving to Santa Fe as a young widow with no employment. She was confident that she would find a job and be able to stay in the place where she wanted to live and raise her son.[3]

Dorothy's husband had died of Hodgkin's disease seven months earlier, and Peggy was possibly the first person to whom she talked about the devastating loss, the long weeks of his illness, and the strength she found to care for him through the bleak days. Their conversations can be glimpsed through four poems that Peggy wrote late in 1932, all bearing inscriptions to Dorothy or DMcK or, in one case, simply "For D." They reveal a world of peace and loveliness shared by the two young women during their summer visit. Peggy and Dorothy walked among the pines and aspens and found solace in the meadows of the plateau. Dorothy relaxed, perhaps for the first time since Joseph McKibbin's death. It was a time of emotional awareness, of healing and renewal, "when life is something more than being incarnate and human, and death is an interval that is not important," Peggy wrote.[4]

As Dorothy talked of her husband and her marriage, Peggy reflected on her own situation. In spite of Dorothy's sadness, she had an aura of brightness about her—

> she yields her face to the sun;
> her love, like the evening star,
> shines clear for everyone.
> Love is a light in her.[5]

That was an image Peggy could not see in herself. In another poem, she wrote of the love that gave Dorothy the strength to face her husband's death, saying,

> It was over.
> And I wept when you told me this.
> I did not weep for you. You needed no tears,
> you who were alone as a tree is alone and beautiful in the wind
> on the wind-stripped slope of a mountain.
> I only wept for myself, I who have everything.
> What do I know of love, I wept.
> What do I know of it?[6]

At the end of the two weeks, Dorothy returned with her son to their Santa Fe apartment at El Zaguán and soon found work at the Spanish and Indian Trading Company as a bookkeeper. She was ready to take the first positive steps in establishing her new life and regaining control of her happiness, while Peggy remained precariously balanced between her love for the plateau and her discontentment with herself and her marriage.

The summer ended, autumn trees turned gold, and the first snows of winter arrived in northern New Mexico, bringing with them the usual ailments of the season. In early February, Ashley Pond fell ill with a particularly bad case of influenza. Within two weeks his symptoms indicated a subacute stage of encephalitis. The disease lingered for several more weeks, and finally, in late April, he and Hazel traveled to southern California to seek more advanced medical attention. Peggy made arrangements to join them, but by the time she arrived in Pasadena, Ashley's condition had worsened rather than improved as they had hoped. He was suffering from encephalomalacia. The only thing Peggy could do was watch helplessly as her father deteriorated. He was losing the fight. "Hero and warrior," she thought as she watched the figure on the white sheets grow thinner day after day,

> you
> were rider of stallions,
> rescuer from floods,
> fire fighter and
> first nurse of my infancy.[7]

She had wanted so desperately for him to notice her. "I rode wild horses to please you," she admitted in "Portrait of My Father." She recognized, too, that other side of Ashley Pond, calling him a "wistful child" but observing, "How could we help loving you." One afternoon she went to the hospital wearing a bright summer dress, and as she entered her father's room, he looked up and said, "What a pretty girl you are." The compliment stunned her. "He had never before told me he thought me pretty," Peggy wrote in her journal. "His conviction was that it would have produced conceit. Beauty in women was supposed to be a snare, a deceit, a trap, stifling goodness of character. The manly virtues were the ones to be admired. Athletic prowess, courage, ability. And so I strove to be a boy as much as I could." Those few words of praise gave Peggy a glimpse of what they might have shared, but it came too late.

Ashley Pond Jr. died on June 21, 1933. The loss proved too much for the young woman already juggling a family, an unhappy marriage, and her passion for writing. Peggy fell into a severe depression. She would lie on the sleeping porch much of the day, experiencing "terrible sinking feelings," and at night she would awake in terror and reach out to Ferm. Five months after her father's death, she suffered a nervous breakdown. A housekeeper was hired to look after Ferm and the boys, and Peggy was sent to a hospital in New Haven, Connecticut. By the time she began treatment, her strength was nearly spent. As always, she recounted the struggle in her journal. "'Tired, so tired,' I'd say. 'Depressed,' they'd say. But I did not know what depression meant, this nameless fear, this sucking away of my energies, so that I could not read nor write nor even look at letters."

The Connecticut hospital was chosen by the family so that Peggy could be near her brother and sister. Ashley III, who was finishing his last year in medical school at Yale, was an intern at New Haven, and Dottie was married to a dentist and living nearby in Stony Creek. It was also a setting in which Peggy had spent happy days in her youth, and it proved to be a good place to recuperate. In addition to the New England environment and the treatment she received, another factor contributed to her recovery. That factor was a deepening friendship with her mentor, Haniel Long. She had begun to know him better as they worked together compiling her first volume of poetry, *Foretaste*, earlier that year. After several weeks in the hospital, Peggy received a note from Haniel in which he referred to his own breakdown years earlier. He told her that the distress she was experiencing could lead to a new beginning in her life. "Clean everything out and get started all over," he advised. "Take all the time you need. It is vital. You will never have to do it again. But every person of imagination and feeling has to do it once to be any good." He signed his short letter, "Deep love and confidence, Haniel."[8] Peggy was impressed that he would take the time to show his concern, but after she wrote to him in turn, his next letter was even more surprising. He began by talking about a poem they had shared but then took up an entirely different topic.

> You are with me in thought a good deal, and I
> am always concerned about you and at times
> apprehensive. When you come back I hope that
> there will no longer be unnecessary barriers between
> us, that we can find words for things behind the
> uninstructive reality of the days . . .
> You have come to me in love dreams twice. I
> tell you that because I want you to know that you
> are dear to me, but I realize too that it is something
> I would have no right to tell you if I did not believe
> that love is a path of non-pursuit and has nothing
> to do with the cult of pleasure. You doubtless know
> Blake's lines —

Peggy on cross-country skis in Stony Creek, Connecticut, winter 1934.
Courtesy Los Alamos Historical Museum Archives.

> *I will go down to self-annihilation and eternal death*
> *Lest the last judgment find me unannihilate*
> *And I be besieged and given into the hands of my*
> *own selfhood.*

One chief result of my own breakdown was that it at least showed me the way to break the chains of self . . . I had to fight very hard, because the ego in me at first prevailed and wanted to die. Gradually its desire changed to a sacrificial death . . .

Tell me how I can help. Believe in my love for you. You are so beautiful it is impossible not to love you, and if you can now shift to another plane of being you will find all problems vanish that now baffle you, and you will fulfill your nature in a most beautiful life, as beloved to all about you as a shade tree in the desert.[9]

The words both astonished and flattered Peggy, who had always thought herself plain, and the quote from Blake touched something deep. It was destined to become a cornerstone in her recovery and the redesign of her life. Blake's lines came from *Milton*, a work of prophecy that defines the spiritual journey. In this narrative poem, John Milton teaches Blake about his poetic role, and by parallel, in presenting the words to Peggy, Haniel attempted to do the same, to awaken her to her poetic path through life. A key point in *Milton* is that to initiate a spiritual journey one must confront one's errors in life and lovingly accept the journey.[10] Peggy began to understand that she must target her self-doubt, develop better relationships, and let life happen to her rather than try to always design and control it.

After more than two months in the hospital, Peggy went to stay with her sister, planning also to visit friends in the area. Her weeks in the East brought about a recovery, but they also brought something that she never expected. While staying with Dottie in Stony Creek, Peggy went out one evening for a casual dinner with the husband of a friend who was away on a cruise. His name was Bill Barker, and like Ferm, he was a teacher at a private boys' school.[11] At dinner, Peggy found Bill to be expressive, tender, and passionate about their shared interests. They talked freely about Peggy's recent illness and the causes, and Bill was open about a similar difficult period in his life and the help he was

Walks with her sister, Dottie, in the brisk winter air of Connecticut helped Peggy recuperate after being hospitalized for a breakdown in 1933. Courtesy Los Alamos Historical Museum Archives.

finding through analysis. As they were leaving the restaurant, they clasped hands "in a moment of human sympathy." It quickly turned to something more. They went to his apartment. "I trembled to think of what might be going to happen," Peggy confided to her journal. "I lay on a sofa in front of an open fire . . . and struggled within myself to know whether I would accept the adventure or reject it out of prudishness. And how Blake's lines that Haniel had sent me in the hospital ran in my head." At that moment, she interpreted "selfhood" as her ego that had always clung to security and pride. She had to decide if she could take a risk and react to the love she was suddenly feeling. "In some strange way," Peggy said, "the lines from Blake gave me the courage to abandon my straight-laced and conventional self, and a whole different self took over which accepted what was happening and entered into the experience completely." There followed a sequence of nights throughout the next two weeks in which Peggy and Bill shared much more than "physical compatibility." They talked and laughed and cried. They knew the joy of sharing their love of poetry and literature.[12] Bill was a sensitive and philosophical man, and Peggy had fallen in love.

At the end of their two weeks, Peggy and Bill acknowledged a desire to spend their lives together. When he saw her off on the train to New Mexico, it was with the understanding that she would ask Ferm for a divorce and return to the East as soon as possible. In a completely unexpected turn of events, Peggy arrived home to find that Ferm had fallen for the housekeeper who had taken care of him and the children in Peggy's absence. The woman was unhappily married and thought she wanted to leave her husband for Ferm. At first glance, the situation seemed destined to resolve itself, but, of course, nothing is ever that simple.

Through the years Peggy had become very close to her Aunt Florence, whom the family affectionately called Tante. Peggy and Dottie had spent time with Tante as they grew up, and recently Tante had generously given Peggy an allowance to pay for maids and child care so that she could have time for her writing. Her aunt had been highly supportive of Peggy's poetry, even sending some of her niece's early work to her cousin Florence Converse, who was an editor for *The Atlantic*, thus getting Peggy's foot in the door at that major magazine.[13] Peggy knew she had to tell Tante about the impending divorce, but she couldn't bring herself to put that kind of news in a letter. She and Ferm waited until his Easter vacation in the spring of 1934 to drive to Tucson and tell her in person.

Like her brother, Ashley, Tante had a bit of wanderlust about her. She had traveled widely after her father's death, and while in northern Italy she became enthralled with the stone villas and the structured gardens of Tuscany. She wanted such a home for herself. It wasn't, however, to be in Italy. Tante had invested her inheritance wisely and had the means to live just about anywhere she chose. When Peggy and Ferm visited her, she had just bought 320 acres east of Tucson, and construction was under way for the grand two-story, seventeen-room granite mansion that would become Stone Ashley.[14] The house was to be situated in such a way as to enjoy sweeping views of both the Santa Catalina Mountains to the north and the Rincon Mountains to the east. Florence Pond was a woman of solitude and privacy, and Stone Ashley was designed to give her both, although she allowed use of the gardens for charitable gatherings on occasion. During World War II, she opened her swimming pool every Tuesday to the young servicemen at Davis-Monthan Air Force Base, but she was not one for lavish entertaining, as the home would suggest.[15]

In her seclusion, Florence was an avid reader, particularly attentive to books on mysticism and psychology. When Peggy and Ferm visited at Easter, she was reading *The Secret of the Golden Flower*, a European title that had become immediately popular in erudite circles in the United States with its first American publication. Whether by chance or destiny, it was a

Peggy and Ferm look over her aunt's desert mansion for the first time in 1934. The Italianate home named Stone Ashley, built on 320 acres east of Tucson, was still under construction during their Easter visit. Courtesy Los Alamos Historical Museum Archives.

book that would change the course of Peggy's life and finally open doors to communication between her and Ferm.

Ferm was the first to begin reading the book during the spring visit with Tante. *The Secret of the Golden Flower* held an ancient Taoist text that presented a guide to the integration of personality. It offered a process of coordinating separate personality elements into a balanced whole, helping produce behavior compatible with one's environment. It also included a commentary by the famous psychologist Carl Jung that linked the Eastern insights to his psychological research. The preface described the book as providing "the secret of the powers of growth latent in the psyche."[16] Ferm was impressed with the philosophy and mentioned it to Peggy. Soon they were reading the book together. She later commented, "It was the first book we read in real accord." The book's message somehow made it possible for Peggy and Ferm to step back from their problems and see them from a different point of view. It opened a better understanding of their motivations, and they gained a "shared revelation that consciousness grows out of the unconscious, like islands emerging from the sea." The book suggested that "by understanding the unconscious we free ourselves from its domination," and it taught that consciousness is often filled with compulsive intentions, a thought that was not a stranger to Peggy. She had always tried to force life to go in the direction she thought it ought to go, but by examining the ego and self according to Taoist philosophy, she saw the importance of accepting reality, of trying to see things as they are rather than the way she wanted them to be. In reading the book together, she and Ferm discussed their individual growth needs, the ones they could work on together and others that needed to be addressed as individuals.

During their week in Tucson, Peggy and Ferm seriously discussed the possibility of continuing their marriage, "to stick it out," as Peggy put it, "and work out one's destiny within the marriage instead of escaping from the burden into something that seemed nearer the heart's desire." They returned home, never having told Tante of their real reason for visiting that Easter. Ferm resumed his teaching, and his brief affair ended somewhat painlessly, the housekeeper deciding to remain with her husband. Peggy, on the other hand, struggled with her decision. She lived in Santa Fe, apart from Ferm, and they exchanged letters in an attempt to establish communication, heal wounds, and set a new course in their relationship.

A part of Peggy still wanted to marry Bill, but having returned to her familiar surroundings and security, she realized that another part of her was afraid. She confronted an instinctive knowledge as well. "I could not give up my children, nor Ferm whom I did not love, but who loved me in spite of his involvement." Ferm no longer wanted to break the marriage. In her pain and confusion, Peggy turned to Haniel, remembering that "he had been the one to give me the key to open the unknown door." He counseled her not to leave. "You are making your first explorations on a plane that is new to you," he told her. According to Haniel, an experience such as she and Bill had shared was "a gift of the gods" and that to possess it for themselves at the expense of others would be wrong. He convinced her that her experience was not unique and that she should look at it as a kind of initiation. "Somehow," she recalled, "Haniel made me aware of what was going on."

Haniel sent Peggy for further counseling to his good friend Erna Fergusson, another writer Peggy greatly admired. Erna and Peggy's mother were friends, so Peggy was already acquainted with her and was comfortable talking to her. As an unmarried woman, Erna spoke of "what a woman's independent life could be." She gave Peggy a copy of Esther Harding's *The Way of All Women*. "From Esther Harding," Peggy said, "I learned that a woman will carry into any new marriage the unsolved problems of her former one." Peggy was beginning to see more clearly her own inadequacies and inexperience in love, insights that were turning her away from the relationship she thought she wanted with Bill. Harding's book also made her aware of the possibility of independence and individuation within marriage. It gave different possibilities for relationships between men and women. Haniel's words continued to ring in Peggy's ears— *Love is a path of non-pursuit and has nothing to do with the cult of pleasure.* Haniel had given her something else to think about in a poem he wrote for her.

> Be very quiet. Do not act
> Until you know that love is acting in you,
> That it is not your selfhood that is acting.[17]

"But how are we to know that love is acting?" Peggy had asked him, but at once she knew the answer. "Only, I suppose, when we have managed to put ourselves aside."

Peggy wrote to Bill and broke off the relationship. Though she believed she was doing the right thing in staying with Ferm and keeping the family together, she was still very much in love with Bill. She immersed herself in her poetry and turned her thoughts to publishing another book. Gradually she and Ferm made progress in communicating and reestablishing the bounds of their marriage, but their lives had been altered.

The room was still. Too still. Too quiet. Teddy and Allen were outside playing, and Hugh was finally down for his nap. She sat at the table and looked through the window to the east. It was a time of day she dreaded, a time when her thoughts were her only companions. How could she escape the pain? She opened the notebook that was never far away and wrote.

> *There was nothing I could do for my beloved,*
> *and so I put my arms around a child who was crying,*
> *and kissed one who was hungry for my kiss,*
> *and spoke to another who was lonely.[18]*

Of the changes Peggy and Ferm worked on individually and together, one of the most important involved his understanding and support of Peggy's need to write and to have her own space for writing. With Hitchcock's help, Ferm built a one-room cabin on the south rim of Pueblo Canyon, about half a mile east of their log house. The "poem cabin," as Peggy called it, was made of rough boards and a corrugated metal roof, slanted slightly to allow the snow to melt off. It was furnished with a simple table and chair, a bunk, and a small pot-bellied wood stove. A north window looked out on the peaceful realm of the canyon. The retreat was far from lavish, but it was just what Peggy needed. In the next months she wrote poems for a second book as well as a children's story about a recalcitrant burro named Tomasito. *The Burro of Angelitos* was published by Suttonhouse Ltd. in 1936 and won a Julia Ellsworth Ford Foundation award for children's literature. The story of the lazy, little burro earned high acclaim when it was said to have the sophistication of "The Pope's Mule" by Daudet and the unusual charm of John Steinbeck's *Tortilla Flats*.[19] The poems she wrote in the little cabin found praise in a second volume published by the Santa Fe Writers' Editions. In 1936, they released *Familiar Journey*.

While working with Haniel to face her emotional problems and to produce *Familiar Journey*, Peggy's relationship with her mentor deepened. Haniel Long had been in Santa Fe almost five years since resigning his professorship at Carnegie Tech in 1929. The poor air quality surrounding Pittsburgh's steel mills had driven him to look for a healthier environment. Through the years he tried moving to several locations, but none had suited his needs. Then his poet friend and fellow Harvard graduate Witter Bynner invited Haniel and Alice to visit in Santa Fe. Alice, also a poet and artist, loved the setting, and Haniel was immediately comfortable in what he described as "a very different kind of life from any I have ever known, a much older one, in many ways a better one."[20] When Haniel eventually suffered a breakdown in Pittsburgh from the stress of trying to balance his writing with his teaching, the Longs moved to New Mexico. Though his best writing was yet to come, Haniel had begun to make a name for himself with *Poems* (1920) and *Notes for a New Mythology* (1926). He had no trouble adjusting to Santa Fe.

Bynner introduced him to other writers who had migrated to the inspirational atmosphere of New Mexico, among them Alice Corbin Henderson, Mary Austin, Frieda Lawrence, and Spud Johnson, as well as natives like Erna Fergusson and Fray Angelico Chavez. There was a host of

The poem cabin sat on the south rim of Pueblo Canyon and gave Peggy the privacy and seclusion she needed for writing, ca. 1935. Courtesy Peggy Pond Church Estate.

fledgling authors in the Santa Fe area seeking to make themselves known, and Haniel was soon looked upon as a leader in their growing colony. Unlike Mary Austin, who saw herself as the center of the Santa Fe literary world but was not especially revered by her contemporaries, Haniel Long was admired and respected for his intellect and the gentleness with which he approached life. He was introspective and a romantic, and his concern with feelings and with nature showed clearly in his poetry and writing. As Lawrence Clark Powell observed in an article in *Westways* years later, Haniel was "magnetic to both men and women." He and Witter Bynner were known to have been lovers in their younger days, and he viewed relationships with women as "a mystical source of meditation and creation."[21] Haniel enjoyed several close relationships with women despite being happily married and devoted to his wife, Alice, whom he wed in 1913. He had a philosophy of life that in many ways rivaled the openness of the 1960s. It was also a philosophy that seemed contradictory to his upbringing. Haniel was born in 1888 to missionary parents serving in Rangoon, Burma. He was given a traditional education at Phillips Exeter Academy and Harvard, and many of his writings revealed a classic and religious tradition, in particular *A Letter to St. Augustine after re-reading his confessions* and his most enduring effort, *Interlinear to Cabeza de Vaca*. The seemingly conflicting sides of his persona made Haniel Long, as

Powell put it, a man of "great sensitivity and highly independent vision."[22]

Peggy was drawn to Haniel's sensitivity, but she also learned from his independence. In many ways they were kindred spirits. In Haniel's description of his first encounter with New Mexico, his obvious admiration for the land and its inhabitants made clear the basis for their eventual friendship. On a trip from Los Angeles to the East, Haniel's train was delayed for two hours near Laguna Pueblo. He wrote of his impressions:

> "I stepped down into the freshness and vastness of
> the diminutive piñon forest and as I walked about
> among the blue-green odorous trees, I felt like a
> giant, for over their heads was the horizon of the
> mountains. On a near-by hill was the ancient town,
> the first pueblo I had ever seen. I was pleased that the
> houses could be so unpretentious, built simply of the
> earth and leaving nothing to be improved upon."[23]

Haniel and Peggy had become acquainted when they participated in the annual Poets' Roundups begun by Alice Corbin in Santa Fe in 1930. The roundups were planned as fundraisers for the New Mexico Association on Indian Affairs, and in the course of their nine-year existence, they became much-enjoyed sources of literary frolic and aid to Indian welfare. Held in the private gardens of Santa Fe residents, local and visiting poets in western attire would bolt from cardboard chutes, as at a rodeo, and recite their verses for the gathering of admirers. The atmosphere was marked by spontaneity and enhanced by guitar-playing musicians performing traditional southwestern songs.[24] The popular Santa Fe event spawned another literary endeavor in 1932 when Alice Corbin and Haniel Long founded the cooperative publishing venture known as the Santa Fe Writers' Editions. They were joined by other writers, most from the Santa Fe and Taos colonies, who were finding it difficult to have their work accepted by the large publishing houses in the East. Haniel believed that the growth of American literature could be enhanced by regional publishing. Most of the authors assumed financial responsibility for the printing of their own books and turned back a small portion of their profits to an endowment fund that would aid in the publishing of, as Haniel put it, "good books that otherwise might not see the light of day." The writers also pooled their lists of prospective buyers. The only thing lacking in the beginning of this good idea was a press.

In the summer of 1933, Walter L. Goodwin arrived in Santa Fe, persuaded by Haniel Long to move his Rydal Press from Pennsylvania to New Mexico. Having worked for Lippincott, Goodwin brought with him publishing experience as well as his small private press, which he set up in a large frame building on a ranch in Tesuque. Local writer Raymond Otis was recruited for his business skills, and with the addition of this last important element, the cooperative was off and running.

In working with the Poets' Roundup and the authors of the Writers' Editions, Peggy not only became acquainted with Haniel Long and Alice Corbin but also met a score of writers and poets who were considered members of the close-knit colony that included names destined to be well-known literary figures: Witter Bynner, Mary Austin, Spud Johnson, Lynn Riggs, John Gould Fletcher, Eugene Manlove Rhodes, Fray Angelico Chavez, Stanley Vestal, Elizabeth Shepley Sergeant, and many others. Though not all of them were published by the Santa Fe Writers' Editions, they formed a vital support system. A letter from Bynner (known to his friends as Hal), written in response to two poems read by Peggy at the 1938 Poets' Roundup, exemplifies the communication shared within the colony.

> Nov 18, 1937
> "You extraordinary girl of a Peggy! You often have surprised me with rare turns in your poetry but never so much as in the two poems, "Omens" and "Horses in the Moonlight." They seem to me to reach higher by far than anything you have done hitherto,—moving and real and auspicious."
>
> Yours heartily,
> Hal[25]

Peggy was also collecting admirers from outside the local ranks, as can be seen in the poignant request of an Atlanta gentleman.

> I have just finished rereading your poem "The Humming Birds Coming" again and as usual it

has charmed me. It says so much to me that I
would love to own a copy of it in the author's own
handwriting so that I can frame it and hang it over
my desk to read every day.
> Thanking you in advance, I am,
> Very sincerely yours,
> Ralph Baruette[26]

Though these compliments must have produced warm feelings
in Peggy and bolstered confidence, Haniel was still the major influence
in her development as a poet in those years. He made suggestions
concerning the selection of poems for *Foretaste* and *Familiar Journey*, but
his contribution to her esteem as the books were prepared for publication
was the most important element, as seen in his evaluation of the poems
for her second book.

> The new condensation makes the manuscript more
> impressive. On me it has made a deep impression
> all along, as I told you. It is a fuller picture of a
> Being, a Life, than any I know in contemporary
> letters. The three aspects of our sentience—
> environment, personality, racial memory—are in
> a really wonderful balance. Nearly always we poets
> take one of the three and drop the other two—we
> naturally go farther with the one we take than
> we could with all three—perhaps we don't feel all
> three (I know that I am rarely conscious of racial
> memory—environment in human terms occupies
> me almost exclusively). The triple harmony you
> have woven here makes a music as sane and sound
> as it is lyric.[27]

As Peggy continued her struggle for stability, Haniel saw it as part of
his duty as a mentor to help her with more than her poetry. He and Peggy
communicated often and began to share things beyond their commentaries
on each other's poems. They exchanged pages from their journals that revealed
insights and feelings that could not be as easily spoken, and they wrote poems
to each other. Their close friendship was bordering on something more, yet

Haniel was still focused on helping a friend make a difficult passage. At one point, he even called Bill in Connecticut in an attempt to smooth the situation and help Peggy recover.

To understand Haniel's approach to his relationship with Peggy and his sincere love for her, one must be aware of the unique character of Haniel Long. In a paper written in 1964, the noted scholar John R. Slater of the University of Rochester said of Long, "He is always a dreamer trying to be also a human helper in a superficial world." Dr. Slater credited him with being at his best when "recognizing uniqueness in others." He also noted, "In men and women, young and old, Haniel Long sometimes perceived hidden beauty beneath masks."[28] In Peggy's case, Haniel did exactly that. Peggy held back a part of herself, finding it difficult to reveal her thoughts and feelings unless they were written in poems. She had thought of herself as plain and unattractive since childhood, and she had all too often combined those negatives to believe that she was unlovable. Only with Bill had she managed to discard that idea, which may have been the single most difficult issue in deciding not to return to him.

Haniel grasped all of that and more in his time spent with Peggy. He talked frankly about the differences in her relationships with Ferm and Bill. He was blunt, telling her finally, "I do not see that you are making much progress in killing the egocentric." He then attempted to alter her viewpoint. "If you could read your journal with fresh eyes you would see what I saw, that no one individual is particularly important to you just now, only love is." Haniel convinced her that it was necessary to understand love before she could understand the choices she must make in her life. Commenting further on the journal entries, Haniel admitted, "My agony on some of the pages was terrible, it was so like my own nature, it was so emphatically the other half, as you say."

The dilemma Peggy faced was something Haniel had experienced years before, but his solution had led him in a direction not taken by many. "We must accept our nature," he concluded, and he came to resist the "widespread and primal belief that love must be single." He was an admitted experimenter where his own life was concerned, but despite the fact that he had affairs, at least two of them homosexual, he never entertained thoughts of leaving his marriage. He was devoted to his wife and apparently viewed an affair as "only a phase," adding, "With me there cannot be disloyalty." He clearly did not define loyalty in the common way.[29]

Perhaps Haniel best identified his views of life in his book *A Letter to*

St. Augustine after re-reading his confessions. In writing to the fourth century bishop, he reveals,

> I find in you a man simple as a child, who loves the
> world for what it is. You accept your body, your
> senses, your instincts; you see the comeliness of
> others, feel bodily sympathy with them. You feel
> the charm of social life, are friendly and taste the
> sweetness of friendship. Above all, you perceive
> that these are God's gifts to us; we may have them,
> we may flourish in a marvelous world, if only we
> remain human, become more and more human.
> You are more than a man of letters, or pamphleteer,
> or advocate . . . you are a poet.

When reading Haniel's description of St. Augustine, one becomes aware that he is explaining his own motivations and the model by which he patterns his life. "Courtesy costs nothing; sympathy is better than detachment," he continues.

> You reveal an aspect of your nature which draws me
> to you and disarms me—an aspect of which I need
> not beware when I find it in myself or in others. It
> implies no inordinate preferences for the world's
> goods, but rather a passion for justice, a sense of
> quiet nothing can assuage till all of us treat one
> another in human fashion. Human is a word we
> use today for the attitudes of mind and heart we
> consider best. When we speak of a person as really
> human, we mean that the spirit of that person saves
> the finest elements of life. We should not need to
> keep re-examining the law and the prophets; what
> our religion requires of us is constant goodwill
> directed by thoughtfulness."[30]

Haniel believed that feeling was the only true source of values, and he trusted and allowed his own feelings to establish his values, whether or not they conformed with the accepted views of his day. So it was with these values, guided by emotions, that he approached his relationship with Peggy, continuing in his own way the counseling that had begun in Connecticut. The result was a closeness that helped Peggy shape her self-concept as a human being as well as a poet. Years later, she acknowledged that "it was Haniel who saved my marriage," but the passage he helped her make was a painful, if illuminating, one.

The past night's rain had left the ground damp. Water still dripped from the canales of the flat-roofed adobe houses along the old streets of Santa Fe. An eager trickle ran through the narrow channel of the Acequia Madre. It was early morning, and Peggy walked along under aging cottonwoods that sheltered the unpaved road. A lizard warming itself on a crumbling adobe wall watched her warily as she passed. She loved the early morning. Only the sound of birds broke the quiet. It was always a time to gather her thoughts. This morning those thoughts were of Haniel as she made her way toward his house. Just nights before she had walked the same route with a burning need to see him, only to falter and stop, full of despair, beside a street lamp near his home. She had looked up at a wide-ringed moon and the shimmering mountains, beseeching them for peace but dropping her gaze so that a passerby might not see that she was crying. Nearby poplars had swayed in the wind, and lightning had flashed in the distance. She wrote later of the grief she had felt that night in the storm, "thinking of the one I could no longer love and how I had wounded him, / weeping because I could no longer love him, / weeping." She had needed Haniel's comfort, but the hour was late. Too late. "And I passed the house of my brother, oh more than my brother." She had turned away, thinking, "Why should I lay the weight of my heavy heart upon my brother?" Then came the poem that he had written for her that same night. She unfolded the copy of his poem as she walked and read the words again.

> *I go out to the garden and walk in the lightning,*
> *glad that the storm is here at last,*
> *glad that you have been suppressed and waiting*
> *and that the fire of your fears and needs*
> *playing in the clouded beauty of your words,*

at last illuminates you to my heart,
and I need never wrestle with you again,
never separate you from myself again.
Because one loves Mozart and roses
is one not to love Wagner and violets
and lilies and Debussy?

My dear, my dear,
that is all they mean, your fears and needs:
be reconciled.

 He had paced in his garden as she had paced the streets nearby, and he had acknowledged that her poem was straight out of his emotions the night of the storm. It was almost frightening how they so often experienced the same feelings. She remembered her hesitation, the decision to not disturb him. "But if I had opened the door I would have found him walking there," she ended her own poem, "walking in his garden under the petals of lightning, holding my heart upon his heart." The closeness she felt, the need, was increasing.[31]

Haniel recognized a restlessness in Peggy, an independence that he saw in all "developed women" and knew to be at the source of their struggles. He was ahead of his time in his view that women should be treated as equals. "Developed women," he said, "are as clear-headed as men and know what they are after. They are after developed men. And they are going to pieces because they cannot get them." He also believed in the duality of human beings, that men and women had a mixture of both male and female qualities and that they should be in touch with both aspects of their personalities. To reach the goal of equality, he thought, "sympathetic understanding talk" was necessary. It was understanding talk that he pursued. Peggy could speak openly in her journals and reveal her inner self in poetry, but she had trouble communicating one on one.

 On a day in June of 1934, Peggy and Haniel drove high into the Jemez Mountains. They parked the car and walked along a trail through the pines. Recalling that afternoon in his journal, Haniel remembered that "her silence was deeper than ever, but it was a silence she wanted him to enter." They stopped beside a stream. He admitted afterward that "he could not honestly say he had no idea such things would come to pass, but what he consciously went there for was a long and uninterrupted talk on the fundamental issues facing her." A time had come, however, when talk was no longer necessary. He had succeeded in making her feel worthy, feel capable of love, and they savored the victory.

Both knew that their time of sharing and the tenderness of the days after could not last, but those days completed an enlightenment, a vital part of Peggy's self-discovery. "As for you and me," Haniel said, "let it go at this, that we are the unity which we are, and forever each other's in more than one way and one fashion, always sure of each other . . . identified through the lightning and the unceasing calm of tides."

Peggy redirected her efforts to raising her children and building a new relationship with Ferm, while continuing to grow as an individual. Her quest for self-realization was a long way from over, but she had taken a significant step in the journey. For Haniel, there were moments of despair and sensuality unfulfilled, but "they are to be expected," he wrote, ever trying to understand his own evolution. He felt a keen satisfaction at having aided her achievements. "She is out of the chrysalis," he noted in his journal, "and if I ever see her slipping back into it I know I can save her because she herself has given me the blessed keys. And perhaps she will be articulate in beauty past our generation's comprehension."[32]

"I will never love anyone more beautiful than you," Peggy wrote in "More Than Mortal," a grateful tribute to Haniel. During the two years following her father's death, she wrote the poems for her second book, *Familiar Journey*, poetry that gave evidence of what she had learned from the experiences of those difficult years. The title poem, "The Sister's Song," was secretly dedicated to Haniel, and the poems in the book were written about the three men in her life, with some of the best poems, Peggy admitted, being about Ferm.[33].

The promotional circular for the book revealed a new outlook in Peggy. Her struggles had been carried on in her poetry, presenting, as she put it, "a human experience not just personal to me." She was asked by a friend why she called the book *Familiar Journey*. "I ask you in turn," Peggy responded, "what else I could have called it? For love is not something that belongs to any one of us, but a road we travel, a ritual journey, an ancient pilgrimage." Added to that was Haniel's comment on the journey itself, one that is "between the inward and the outward world which is familiar to all who let life happen to them as landscape happens on a highway, instead of trying to select from life only what seems appropriate to the individual ego."[34]

Peggy's "inward and outward" world evolved within the rocky years of 1933 and 1934, but the road was still not a smooth one. In the summer of 1935, the school's business manager Fred Rousseau and his wife, Edna, looked after Ted, Allen, and Hugh so that Peggy and Ferm could get away for some time alone. They explored Yellowstone and continued on to Berkeley for a visit with Peggy's college roommate Kate Stratton and her husband, Malcolm. By the time the travelers arrived on the Stratton's doorstep, it was clear that the time away had not helped the situation as much as they had hoped. Kate had presumably been forewarned of the marital situation, and after witnessing a heated argument between Peggy and Ferm within the first minutes of their arrival, she was ready with a suggestion. She recommended counseling with Dr. Elizabeth Whitney, a noted psychologist in the Bay Area. Peggy and Ferm agreed to meet with Dr. Whitney and ultimately worked with her during several sessions while visiting the Strattons. Their joint counseling was beneficial, but Peggy soon took it a step further. She began working individually with Dr. Whitney to analyze her motivations and understand her inner self. When she and Ferm returned to New Mexico, Peggy found an analyst in Santa Fe to continue what she had begun in Berkeley. Those first sessions in self-analysis were the beginning of a lifelong commitment.

The following year, the family traveled east so that Ferm could attend the Harvard Tercentenary in September. The best part of the trip for Ted and Allen was attending Camp Mishe Mokwa on Lake Winnipesaukee in New Hampshire, a summer camp where their father had spent time as a boy. For Peggy, the high point was attending a presentation by Dr. Carl Jung. The renowned psychologist spoke at a symposium held in conjunction with the Tercentenary celebration. Jung's talk concerned the psychological factors that determine human behavior. His work on the awareness of the unconscious interested Peggy greatly. It was not a concept new to her, but she was seeing it from a different angle. "I had had hints of this," Peggy said, "through reading Mary Austin's *Everyman's Genius*."[35] The book approached the topic through Austin's interest in parapsychology. "Mary became aware of the 'cosmic' world much as I did," Peggy realized, "through her contact and immersion in the natural world." In elements of the natural world, Peggy identified adaptation and growth needs, and she equated those concepts to adaptation in humans, both to inner and outer realities. After Jung's speech at Harvard, Peggy began to record her dreams, waking in the early morning hours to write down as much as she could remember. She became more and more involved with Jungian analysis and also studied other philosophers and writers. As she read, she kept notebooks with lists of questions, definitions, related information, and page references from works by Thomas Merton, Meister Eckhart, Rabindranath Tagore, Shakespeare, Dante, Blake, Colette, and a host of others, both classical and contemporary. Peggy had entered not only a phase of self-exploration but also of self-education.

After the poem cabin was built in the fall of 1935, Peggy spent hours at a time there, inspired by the view of Pueblo Canyon out her window. In the cold months, she would light a fire in the tiny wood stove and sit at the table or lie on her bunk, watching the snowflakes drift silently downward to disappear far below. In her private world surrounded by tall pines and evergreens draped in white, she wrote.

> Here is ground juniper the which to find
> we followed where November snowfall, quietly
> cherished,
> lay unravished by sun or wind in steepest canyon
> shadowed by rock walls
>
> and by the laced fingers of a thousand fir trees
> all day weaving sun and wind into silence,
> all day spreading an impenetrable web of twilight
> over that canyon.[36]

In the isolated cabin, the secluded hours were both productive and healing.

Companionship also aided Peggy's recovery. When she wasn't writing, she would sometimes take the boys to visit Edith Warner at Otowi Bridge. In 1928 the shy Easterner whom Peggy had met at Connie Smithwick's ranch had done the unimaginable and taken on the job of guarding the Ranch School freight at Otowi crossing. After it was unloaded from the Denver and Rio Grande train, the freight was stored in a boxcar until it could be picked up by someone from the school. She had only to make sure that no one broke in to steal anything, which meant living in a small, unfurnished house near the narrow gauge tracks. She rented the little house from Julian and Maria Martinez, the famous potters of nearby San Ildefonso Pueblo. For most people who had known Edith from her first months in New Mexico, she seemed the least likely person for the job, one that required a good deal of self-sufficiency in living alone at the bridge. Connie Smithwick remembered Edith lamenting, "I can't even boil water." In her case it was true because she had to first build a fire in a wood stove, and, as Connie put it, "that became an art." Slowly, while Edith had lived at Anchor Ranch, the Smithwicks taught her needed skills, the most important being, as it turned out, how to bake a "never-fail chocolate cake." Connie and Frank helped Edith search the Sears Roebuck catalogue for the bare necessities with which she could live at the bridge. "I will always remember the first night at Otowi," Connie told Peggy years later. "After Frank and I had helped Edith unbox all the crates from Sears, . . . I had blessed candles for each room and holy water to dedicate and bless her venture. And her first night we decided was to be spent there alone! That was the beginning!" An irate Genevieve Ranger had called Connie to berate her "for encouraging and allowing Edith—all so inexperienced—to go sit by the side of the road in that sand heap." Connie added, "I just couldn't convince her it was the thing for Edith to do."[37] But Connie had been right. Edith settled in beautifully.

Edith's friends from the plateau were not the only ones to worry about her being alone in the little house. The Indians at San Ildefonso thought of her needs, too. She hadn't lived at the bridge very long when Atilano Montoya, one of the pueblo's elders, came to help with some of the chores and make improvements around the place. He began to work there daily, and eventually, after he had built a fireplace in the corner of the living room to add warmth to her home, Edith "suggested that he come and live there" instead of traveling back and forth.[38] And so Tilano, as he was called, became her companion and her helpmate as well as a friend to all who stopped at the bridge to visit.

Edith was soon running a small store from her home, selling a few canned goods, tobacco, candy, pop, and gasoline to make extra money, and eventually she opened a tearoom that served fresh bread and her destined-to-be-famous chocolate cake. When Peggy and the boys would stop in at Edith's, she would give them slices of the cake and a bottle of pop, and Tilano would take the boys outside with him. They loved swimming at the edge of the river or making sand castles or helping Tilano get water from the well. The bucket was attached to a rope and pulley that hung under a small roof above the well, and Tilano would lower it very slowly, all the while explaining that he had to be careful not to knock spiders off the walls of the well or disturb the frogs that lived in the water below. Then he would hold the wide-eyed boys over the rock sides of the well so they could see the shimmering water.[39] Tilano

Tilano cleans the muddy feet of Allen Church after a fun time wading in the river at Edith's place, ca. 1933. Courtesy Peggy Pond Church Estate.

was in his early sixties by then. His only child had died along with his wife in childbirth many years before, so he delighted in Peggy's sons and the children who came for visits from the pueblo.

While Tilano watched the boys, Peggy would talk to Edith, sharing news, spilling out problems, or sometimes reading a new poem. She realized from the first visits that her initial reaction to Edith had been very wrong. Edith possessed a quiet spirit and a vision of life that touched people in a gentle way. Edith was more a listener than a counselor, but, despite the fact that she sometimes said very little during the visits, Peggy would feel soothed by Edith's calming ways. With Edith, there was always unspoken communication. Because of Peggy's responsibilities at home and the rough road leading from the Ranch School, visits with Edith at the bridge were less frequent than she would have liked, but they were always meaningful.

Though life for Peggy at the Ranch School was not always easy, it was the good times that were remembered years after. Despite keeping up with three energetic boys, Peggy found time for activities and friends. She had a flower garden in which she loved to work, and evenings frequently found other masters gathered at her house, listening to Ferm's collection of classical records.

Oscar Steege, who eventually became the headmaster at Mooreland Hill School in Connecticut, remembered the importance of such leisure hours. "Many times I think of those wonderful evenings of music by the fire at the Church's! Lying on the floor, holding a scotch and soda, and munching tasty cheese and crackers! Seemed at the time all that anyone would ever need for peace and contentment!"[40]

In many ways, the Ranch School was a close-knit community, but because Peggy wanted Ferm home with the family occasionally or to accompany her on a ride or picnic now and then, she was almost constantly at odds with A. J. Connell, who expected one hundred percent dedication from his masters. In one of her outraged moments, Peggy wrote a poem that made clear her thoughts on Connell's philosophy concerning females at the Ranch School.

> No bitches may disturb the peace
> among our canine population.
> No restless mare may here abide
> to cause our geldings mild vexation.
> And if ourselves should choose a wife,
> why wives may come and they may sit

Peggy and Benigna, her favorite horse at the Los Alamos Ranch School. Courtesy Los Alamos Historical Museum Archives.

in little harmless hennish groups
apart from us and chat and knit.[41]

A return volley may have been fired when Connell adopted a scruffy
little terrier and named it Peggy! But on other occasions Peggy redeemed
herself with Connell, particularly by working with the students on their
musical productions. Being a talented pianist, she accompanied the boys for
their Gilbert and Sullivan operettas. In the weeks leading up to the programs,
the young men would gather around Peggy's piano for practice sessions. The
all-male casts were sometimes supplemented by masters who were more
willing to take the female roles. One can only imagine how Peggy managed to
keep a straight face while watching two very robust men such as her husband
and Oscar Steege singing the female leads. The operettas were popular events,
attended by invited guests from the Española Valley and Santa Fe, and they
lent an atmosphere of excitement to the years in which they were presented.

Peggy worked also with the younger students on the mesa, the children
of the Ranch School staff who attended the local elementary school. She
taught them traditional songs and prepared them for caroling at Christmas. It
was a special time of year for her and the other residents of the little mountain
community. One might almost say magical.

Children's voices filled the cold night air. They were singing "Silent Night"
in Spanish. As Peggy stood with them, she thought of the first afternoon these
children had gathered around her old Estey piano to learn their Christmas songs
for caroling. She had typed out copies of the Spanish words for them to memorize
but soon discovered that the children of the ranch staff only "spoke" Spanish. They
couldn't read it! Only English was allowed in their school, even on the playground.
In spite of that, the little ones had learned the song anyway, just by listening, and
now they sang it in the moonlight, joined by a few parents who walked with them
to each of the houses scattered among the pines.

As the children sang, Peggy looked out over the wide expanse of the lower
farm fields to the east. There were no streetlights, only the moon and stars. She could
see the twinkling lights of the villages across the valley—Pojoaque, Nambé, even
Truchas in the far distance. She imagined that she saw the luminarias, the piñon
kindling fires that guided the Santo Niño, the Christ child, on that special night.

The Ranch School boys had gone home for the holidays, and the families of the masters and ranch workers had the snow-covered mesa all to themselves. A large Christmas tree awaited beside the huge stone fireplace in Fuller Lodge, and the hanging Navajo rugs shared their walls with garlands of evergreens for the festivities. A. J. Connell always supplied a gift for each child, along with stockings filled with candies, nuts, and fruit, and Ferm was, at that moment, dressing as Santa Claus to hand out the presents.

Tomorrow her own children would open more gifts. Wearing new coats and mittens they would be out on their sleds by midmorning. Also under their tree would be cakes and jellies from the wives of the other masters and the little bundle of pitch pine tied with a red ribbon that Edith and Tilano sent each year. In the afternoon, she and Ferm would visit with friends to say thank you and admire one another's decorations. As they walked through the snow, they would look for the tracks of a passing deer or of rabbits or birds. It would all be over too soon, but for that moment, standing under the stars in the clear night sky over the Pajarito Plateau, the world was a serene and beautiful place.

Peggy's life in the male-dominated world of the Ranch School changed for the better in 1935. Master Cecil Wirth courted and married Virginia Davis, a teacher at the Brownmoor School for Girls in Santa Fe. The young couple moved into Spruce Cottage, and Peggy found in Virginia a kindred spirit. Virginia's father was a mine superintendent in Dawson, New Mexico, and she had grown up in mining camps throughout Wyoming and Colorado. She rode horses and camped and had been a Girl Scout. Her upbringing was somewhat like Peggy's; she had even gone to college in the East, attending Mt. Holyoke in Massachusetts. And she was soon raising two young boys. With the birth of the second one, Peggy wrote to Virginia in St. Vincent's Hospital, accusing, "You're just an old copy-cat. What are you trying to do? Have as many sons as the Churches? Hope you weren't disappointed it didn't turn out a gal. Or was the old school spirit too much for you after all?"[42] As Peggy and Ferm looked at their sons and saw future Los Alamos boys attending the school their grandfather had founded, so Cecil and Virginia must have expected that their sons John and Tim would wear the Ranch School uniform one day, too. The school's reputation was growing, and life held good things for the two families who became close friends on the mesa. As Peggy wrote in her poem, "Letter to Virginia," in 1944, "The days were luminous. The vines were sweet above the porches. / Thunder did not appall us; the mountains hung with rainbows." For a time "the ripe world" did flower around them, but in looking back, "Time split like a dried seed." In her poem, Peggy asked, "Do you remember those days, Virginia, / When we were young and Time was innocent?"[43] The idyllic setting of those years and the innocence of their lives were not to last.

In the summer of 1938, Peggy received devastating and unexpected news from Massachusetts. Bill Barker had died of a heart attack. It had been just more than four years since her affair with him, and the news of his death touched still painful places. As she mourned his loss for a second time, she must have reflected on the fact that had she left Ferm and torn apart her family, it would have been for such a short time. Bill's sister wrote to tell her the news. Bill had gone to his farm in New Hampshire and had collapsed while taking a walk in his fields. She shared details of his last months, telling Peggy that Bill had become involved again with analysis and had reached a wonderful state of contentment and peace. All Peggy could do was write a last poem to him and move on.

> Now you are dead. What is there more to say?
> In this last grief all little griefs are crowned.[44]

Despite the personal trauma involving Bill's death, Peggy held to a steady course and continued working on her marriage. In the fall, Ferm took a leave of absence to do some special work in geology at Stanford University. While in Palo Alto for the academic year, Peggy and Ferm were introduced by friends to religious studies that became a turning point in their lives. Peggy credited their experiences and responses to the studies as "one of the sources of unity" that developed between the two of them. Dr. Henry B. Sharman, a New Testament scholar, had designed a method of examining the records of the life of Jesus that used a Socratic approach to group discussion, encouraging individual discovery through thoughtful inquiry into the gospels. The outcome of the Sharman method was individual insight, arrived at by questioning and listening to shared observations. Sharman seminars were available throughout North America, and Peggy and Ferm traveled to Pine Lodge at Capitan, New Mexico, more than once to participate in the following years and attended an international gathering at Minnesing, Canada, in the summer of 1941.

The Church family, ca. 1936, standing in front of the stone addition to their original log cottage. From left to right are Hugh, Allen, Ted, Peggy, and Fermor. Courtesy Los Alamos Historical Museum Archives.

The seminars and studies brought them closer together and were a logical complement to Peggy's ongoing analysis.

Peggy's journal pages from the late 1930s reflected a mixture of emotional states, including dreams written down for analysis and reactions to the disturbing signs of growing political unrest. She listened to radio broadcasts each night for news of the world situation and recorded the dire events in Europe alongside those at home. She and Ferm were reading Tolstoy's *War and Peace* to each other. Life on the plateau was normal, but it was tinged with uncertainty. Then, on a day in late spring of 1940, Peggy noted the fall of France in her journal. It was obvious that the United States couldn't avoid joining the war effort for long, but she and Ferm and the others on the plateau couldn't have imagined the effect that entry into the war would have on their lives.

Peggy's poetry from those years took on a new tone, revealed by titles such as "Comments on a Troubled Era," "For a Son in High School," "Epitaph for Man," and "Omens." With a war on the horizon, one of Peggy's greatest worries involved having a son in his late teens.

> Fashioned out of these years of growth, of careful nurture,
> the father's watchfulness, the mother's affection;
> the life in you tenderly guided to its becoming,
> the hope unfolded, the anxious moments outwitted.
> And to what purpose?[45]

At the Ranch School, life went on as usual for a time, but the inhabitants had begun a slow downward spiral into destiny. Peggy recorded in her journal a family outing to Polvadera, a visit to Mother Mather in Water Canyon, Ferm's summer days at Camp Hamilton, and Ted being away at a work camp in West Virginia during the summer of 1941. Classes at the Ranch School began as usual in the autumn, and the aspen leaves turned gold and fell from the trees. Gray winter clouds brought the first snow. And in December the Japanese bombed Pearl Harbor. The war had started, but even then life on the plateau did not change greatly, though there were signs of things to come. The first serious adjustment came with the loss of the school's headmaster. Lawrence Hitchcock was called up from reserve status to active duty and promoted to lieutenant colonel. His vacancy was to be the first of many.

Another opening in the teaching staff was created in a very different and unforeseen way. In the summer of 1942, Cecil Wirth was diagnosed with cancer. He was only thirty-two years old. It was a tremendous shock to all who knew him. Cecil and Virginia and their boys left the Ranch School and went to New York, where he would begin treatment. With Hitch and Cecil gone and other masters enlisting, Ferm took over as acting headmaster, but he had a difficult time "piecing together a faculty." For Peggy and Ferm, yet another change became necessary. With Ted in his last year at Los Alamos and planning to attend college, the decision was made to sell their log house to the Ranch School and move into smaller accommodations to save money. With Allen enrolled as a student and living in the Big House, only space for three was needed. Peggy, Ferm, and ten-year-old Hugh moved into Spruce

Cottage, but their stay was far shorter than anticipated. Soon Peggy observed in her daily writings the presence of "Army men swarming all over our mesa." A. J. Connell had received the first hint of a possible government takeover as early as August, but it did not become final until just before Christmas. On November 23, Peggy wrote to her mother, who was living in Taos.

> Dearest Mother —
>
> It looks as though the worst were coming to the worst rapidly. This is confidential because we don't know any details yet, and I wanted to get off a line to you this morning, so if I phone and say "the die is cast," you'll know what's up!
>
> Albuquerque headquarters phoned yesterday and told Los Alamos to have its board of directors and attorney on hand this morning, as a man was flying out from Washington with papers . . . Ferm says his present plan (if they permit it) is to skip Christmas holidays and finish the term in mid-January when it so happens that special college board exams are being held. He is going to see if he can get his graduating boys (Ted among them) into college in February! The Army still hasn't said what they're planning to use it for. Anyway, it's evident this chapter in our lives is rapidly closing.[46]

On December 7, 1942, a telegram from Secretary of War Henry Stimson was read to the community at Los Alamos. The decision had been made. The government was condemning the Ranch School as well as the properties of other ranchers and homesteaders on the Pajarito Plateau.

The plan to delay the takeover until after the holiday was accepted, and on January 28, 1943, four students, among them Theodore Spencer Church, became the last young men to graduate from Los Alamos Ranch School. On February 8, 1943, the last personnel from the school made their way down the mountain, and the top secret Manhattan Project took full charge of the campus. The effort to build an atomic bomb was under way.

Chapter 8

Uprooted!
"We felt as the people in the ruins must have felt . . ."

Just after Christmas 1942, Peggy and her youngest son, Hugh, left the Pajarito Plateau for Taos. The moment was so wrenching that years later Hugh couldn't even remember how they got to his uncle's home. He assumed that his mother drove them there, because his father stayed behind, along with other staff members, to see the students through their remaining coursework. An entire semester had to be completed within the few weeks that remained before the government takeover. The ending was described as "profoundly upsetting to those who had to close up the school and leave their homes, their community, and their way of life," but those words can't possibly account for the emotions felt as the last of the masters and students drove down the winding road from the Ranch School for the final time in early February, exchanging their idyllic world for one of war and uncertainty.

As with many of the families who left the plateau, the Churches dealt with separation not only from their home but also from each other as Ted left for Harvard and Allen transferred to the very different atmosphere of the Webb School in Claremont, California. Ten-year-old Hugh was left behind in a life suddenly devoid of dreams, devastated by the prospect of never becoming a Los Alamos Ranch School student. For Peggy and Ferm, the loss of their livelihood and their home on the plateau was overwhelming. A bond Peggy had known since the age of ten had been broken, and for Ferm, who had come to the Pajarito country in 1921 as a young man fresh out of college, the displacement was just as painful. He harbored a deep love of the mountains and the school he had helped to shape for more than two decades. It was a traumatic time, but in retrospect, the shared pain of their loss was another step in the process of building a stronger marriage.

In Taos Peggy, Ferm, and Hugh moved into a rented house near her brother's home, and a difficult winter dragged on. Ferm looked to private schools for a teaching assignment when he wasn't in Santa Fe working with Connell and Rousseau, the business manager, to organize the Ranch School's financial and academic records in order to place them in the state archive.[1] Hugh attended Taos Elementary School and spent his afternoons and weekends riding Adobe, the horse brought for him from Los Alamos. Despite having work and activities that occupied their time, each of them felt as though they were in exile, and Ted and Allen were missed by all. A pervading sadness filled the first letters sent to Ted in his freshman year at Harvard.

Light snow fell past the window. Peggy sat at the dining room table in front of her typewriter, searching for inspiration to begin a letter to her son. Through the snow she watched Ferm prop open the wooden doors of the garage and then roll the carcass of an old bicycle into the light. He turned the bike upside down, balancing it on the seat and handlebars. With an oil can in one hand and a screwdriver in the other, he began to work on the chain. Peggy's attention returned to her typewriter and the sheet of personalized writing paper lying beside it. She marked out the old address, inserted the sheet, and typed Box 21, Taos, New Mexico.

February 15, 1943

Dearest Pooh:—

*Which one of us owes which one a letter? Well, I've
heard about your schedule, and it doesn't seem to leave
much time for writing letters, so don't unless you pine
to communicate.*

It was the mother who pined to communicate as she thought of the boy who had acquired the nickname of Pooh, now grown to a tall young man who was on his own more than two thousand miles from home.

*Father is going to go to work on your bike this
morning and see about getting it fixed up and crated
on to you. I thought you might need it where you are.
That's the reason I've been saving it so hard for you all
these years.*

She summoned her humor to counter the longing for better times by suggesting to Ted that he should put himself on an allowance to cover clothes and incidental expenses.

*You shouldn't have to go around wearing gunny sacks
for pants! Of course, if you really like it I've got a couple
of old bags here I could send on to you.*

Peggy stared again at the snow, thinking of what to write next. News of the family would be welcome.

> *Well, your Uncle Ash has sailed for 'furrin' parts. Of course, no one knows what parts. The only thing Lou knows is that it will probably be two months before she gets to hear anything from him.*

A large, gray tabby jumped onto Peggy's lap. Mr. Hyde was a warm and welcome interruption of sad thoughts, and he was in need of attention. There was never a shortage of pets in the Church household, but Hyde was a special one. He had grown up with the boys, a rough and tumble companion. She scratched the purring cat behind his ears before returning to her letter.

> *Taos is very nice now. Thanks to you the furnace is working fine. We'd have probably burned up or exploded by now if you hadn't shown us how to get that ash pit door closed! Hugh has a good time with his horse. Adobe is a nice animal. I've ridden him several times when Hugh had a cold and am growing quite fond of him. Our garage is full of hay.*

Thinking that Ted might be homesick and missing the Ranch School, Peggy added an encouragement to visit one of the former masters.

> *Why don't you see if Charlie Jenney is still at the Belmont Hill School, and if he is look him up in one of your idle moments.*
>
> *Father came up Saturday night and is going back today. We must wander downtown now and see if we can locate a crate for you.[2]*

> *Love,*
> *Mother*

The winter months passed, but the melting snow and the budding of spring failed to improve anyone's spirits that year. In early April, the news came that Cecil Wirth had died. The loss of their dear friend, and one so young, was yet another stunning blow. Peggy was devastated for Virginia and the two boys who would grow up without their father. A few weeks later, she and Ferm joined others from the Ranch School for a memorial service at A. J. Connell's house in Santa Fe. Late in the day, Cecil's ashes were scattered near Los Alamos, as near as one could get in 1943, and on that afternoon, Peggy and Virginia found time to sit under a pine tree and remember. So many changes had come so quickly, and the two friends needed those moments together, time to reflect and to console each other. In the evening, they went to supper in the familiar surroundings of Edith Warner's tearoom, a place that had always offered comfort.[3] In those few hours, embraced by the warmth of a piñon fire and the love that filled the house by the river, they were able to return home one last time.

For Peggy and Ferm, Cecil's passing made raw again a wound that had barely begun to heal. Perhaps a move from New Mexico, away from the memories that were still so close, would be something to consider. Ferm began to look for work in Arizona and California.

In June Ted entered the navy as an apprentice seaman assigned to the V-12 program at the Massachusetts Institute of Technology. Though Peggy had dreaded hearing that news, she had known he would enlist sooner or later. Just two months earlier, she had written to let him know she understood and to offer a bit of motherly advice. "Your letter of March 3rd received today sounded a touch gloomy! Well, it's a gloomy world. Most of the time I manage to keep my chin above water, but there are times when the waves go over my head. The fellows your age seem to be having the toughest break." She knew Ted was struggling with his uncertain future. "Once you know for sure what the armed forces want to do about you, it probably won't be so bad." She tried to balance her anxiety with realism. "I can't say I relish the thought of having you go off to war," she told her son, "but that seems to be what's on the menu for today. You'll get some kind of an education, though it may not be the one you'd planned on. If you can make up your mind to make the most of whatever happens, you'll come out all right." Then, as always, she tried to lighten the mood. "Granny and Lou and I are planning an extensive garden. It looks as though everyone's greatest problem this coming year will be how to get enough to eat. I'm glad I have that cookbook that tells me how to cook a wolf!"[4]

The search for a new job for Ferm ended in Carpinteria, California, and by early summer Peggy was sorting through possessions and packing. "I'm getting rid of as many things as possible," she wrote to Ted, "and everything we leave except the household furnishings will have to be stored in the room off the garage, and perhaps eventually shipped out to California if we should locate there permanently." Ted was having his own dilemma with possessions he couldn't take with him to his navy assignment. "Don't send anything home collect till after July 1st," Peggy warned him, "as I just haven't got enough money in the bank to pay for anything but the groceries till then."[5] Times were rough with Ferm out of work and almost everything being rationed. Traveling was becoming more and more complicated for civilians, but she knew the times were hard for everyone. The shortages and difficulties simply became a way of life. "I'm enclosing the number one ration book, too, though you didn't ask for it," she added. "If you find you don't have to have it, send it back!"[6]

In California Ferm was taking a position at yet another school affected by the war. There had been a private school for boys on Catalina Island when the war broke out, but the faculty and students were forced by the government to evacuate the island, as it was deemed unsafe to be that far from shore. Curtis Cate, the headmaster of the Santa Barbara School, invited Keith Vosburg, the headmaster of the Catalina Island school, to bring his boys to the campus in Carpinteria. The schools combined and became known as the Cate and Vosburg School.[7]

In the fall of 1943, Ferm, Peggy, and Hugh took up residence on the upper floor of the school's dormitory after their long drive from New Mexico. On arriving, one of the immediate tasks was a sad one. In her first letter from Carpinteria, Peggy wrote to tell Ted that "we lost our dear Mr. Hyde" on the trip. After driving until past midnight across the California desert, they had stopped in a tourist camp at a small place called Cabazon. While there, Hyde managed to get away. He had most likely had enough of being cooped up in a car for four days. The trio, and cat, had reached Gallup the first day by driving at "the furious rate of almost forty miles an hour."[8] Thereafter, they had taken advantage of the trip west to camp among Navajo hogans and in the pines around Flagstaff, with detours for short visits to the Grand Canyon, Prescott, and the Hassayampa Hills. They stayed in Cabazon until one o'clock the next afternoon, searching for Hyde, but it was no use. After leaving their name and address with the local postmistress, they continued on, stopping in Claremont to visit Allen before proceeding to Carpinteria.

Allen was already familiar with his father's new school. He had been allowed to attend summer school there on a supported scholarship to study Latin. On his bicycle, he had explored the small town in his free time after class and the completion of his assigned daily chore—feeding the school's pigs! In a family fond of nicknames, such an opportunity was not to be passed up. The affectionate name of "Pig Allen" hung on for quite some time!

Carpinteria was typical of southern California coastal settings. "This is a very beautiful location," Peggy wrote to Ted. The school looked down across a valley to the ocean from a mesa top and was bordered by mountains on the other side. "Really truly mountains," Peggy was happy to say. The mornings she described as foggy and the days as cool. There was no heating, "only little gas stoves that plug in here and there," but none in the bathroom. It was almost as though she were back with the inconveniences of her log home that first year at the Ranch School, only the new climate would not be nearly as cold in the winter.

Their apartment consisted of four small rooms and a study for Ferm down the hallway at the other end of the dormitory. Peggy reported that the living room was "especially small and ugly," but she spread a Chimayo blanket over the couch to add color and a touch of home. Above the fireplace she hung their big, new oil painting of the Taos mountains "by Mr. Berninghaus," and with that, she added, "it really looks quite pleasant."

They settled in, and five days later she wrote excited notes to the boys. "Guess who got off the train at the Carpinteria depot yesterday afternoon—or rather who was thrown off the front end of the train in a crate before the train had stopped moving? None other than our old pal Mr. Hyde!" A postcard had arrived a couple of days earlier from the postmistress at Cabazon. "She said Mr. H. had appeared in her back yard on the fourteenth. We last saw him on the eighth, so he had been at large in the desert for six days," Peggy marveled. There was no freight office in the small town, so the postmistress had asked a friend to take Hyde into the nearby town of Banning and hand him over to the American Express people, who saw him onto the train. "He apparently took two days to come some 250 miles," Peggy reported, describing him as "noticably thin and dingy of fur, but apparently quite proud and pleased with himself." As she wrote her letter, Hyde was "asleep in the most comfortable chair."

The first weeks in Carpinteria in the new landscape and climate were a bit like a vacation rather than day-to-day reality. Though they couldn't explore and go sightseeing on their ration of three gallons of gas a week, the ocean was close enough to enjoy a swim and a walk along the beach. Soon, however, news from home began to trickle in, and they felt cut off from life as they had known it and from the landscape they loved so much. They began to like the school and their life in the dormitory less and less. It wasn't that Cate was a bad school, for it had a fine reputation. It was just different. The students were often rowdy and noisy, and on weekends there was shouting and whistling and loud music and seniors coming in around midnight. Compared with what they had known at Los Alamos, it seemed undisciplined and unstructured. Before long, Peggy and Ferm started to entertain thoughts of reopening the Ranch School in a new location.

There was very little news of Los Alamos with the tight secrecy in place, but Edith Warner did write several times to say that "they" were paving the road from Española and that "they" came down to her place often for dinner. From Taos, Peggy had occasional news of her brother, who was in the medical corps and setting up hospital units along the Burma Road. Then in the second week of February 1944, shocking news arrived from Santa Fe. A. J. Connell was dead.

"Perhaps you will have heard this sad news already," Peggy wrote to her older sons. "Sounds as if it must have been heart failure," she told Ted and Allen, but in her own thoughts it was most likely a different kind of heart problem. "Whatever the doctors may have called it," she said, "we who knew him well must always feel, I think, that what he died of was a broken heart." Peggy understood, perhaps better than others, that the Ranch School had been Connell's life. She had sparred with the demanding headmaster and disagreed with him on more occasions than not, but in writing the news to Ted, her deeper feelings showed through.

> You can't help knowing that I differed from him
> in many ways. Yet when most annoyed at some
> of his oddities—the ones, of course, which most
> interfered with *my* comfort and convenience!—I
> always realized that he was a really great man. He
> was more of an influence in my life than my own
> father, and I shouldn't wonder if you boys wouldn't
> feel that he was as much a father to you as your
> own. I wish I knew of any other school that stood
> as firmly as Los Alamos for the real decencies
> of manhood. I hope you are as grateful for your
> training there as I am. We were all extraordinarily

blessed to have lived so long in such surroundings. The way of life was good, better than anything I have ever seen elsewhere, better than anything we're likely to find in this age of cheap mechanical entertainment. I can't help thinking that somehow those of us who care must see that the ideal Los Alamos stood for does not die. Somehow we must try to build it up again. I keep remembering that after his first attempt was flooded out, my father kept his vision alive for fifteen years until he was able to put it into effect. Perhaps we should look forward with the same faith and determination.

By February Ferm was corresponding with Hitchcock and Rousseau about the possibilities for reestablishing the school. He and Peggy both yearned to return to New Mexico, but they realized that it would not be an easy task to find a place for a ranch school, staff it, and then recruit enough students with the war going on.

When summer came, Peggy and Ferm packed up to leave Carpinteria, but they went in separate directions for the first month. Ferm and Hugh picked up Allen in Claremont and drove home to Taos, while Peggy stayed in California to work with a noted Jungian analyst, a rare opportunity in America at that time. In the 1940s, there were only three cities in the United States with analysts who had actually studied with Carl Jung, and Los Angeles was one of them. Not knowing when she might have another chance, Peggy rented a room and began sessions with Hilde Kirsch, who, with her husband, James, would eventually found the C. G. Jung Institute of Los Angeles. Throughout her time in California, Peggy had been having dreams filled with self-doubt, neglected children, and resistance to Ferm. Even though there had been improvement in the marriage, there were issues that needed more work, and Peggy knew she had further to go in her quest for self-understanding. Still, she was dismayed when Kirsch bluntly told her that she had a "mother fixation." To identify with her mother was the last thing Peggy wanted to do, even though a previous analyst had also hinted at that as a cause of some of Peggy's trouble, but with Kirsch's direct words, she could no longer deny that such an identification was at the root of her problems with Ferm. "My marriage had been disturbed from the beginning because I felt that Ferm— indeed he told me so—identified me with my mother. I could never feel adequate in my own way," she admitted, dealing with all those "collective expectations." Kirsch provided even more food for thought when she pointed out that Peggy allowed her feminine, fanciful side to live only in her poetry. "You seem so afraid of what you are," she observed.

Peggy left Los Angeles with difficult issues to face as well as the serious work ahead to help Ferm set up the Los Alamos School in Taos. She had admitted to Ted months earlier that she and Ferm had never had aspirations of running a school or of Ferm being a headmaster, but, she added, "there doesn't seem to be anyone else to do it!—and we don't want to let a good cause die." Those words were written with cautious optimism in February as she and Ferm planned for a new school, still not knowing at that time if they could get the necessary backing to make their plan a reality. "Hurry up and get the war over, will you," she told Ted, "so you can come back and help us if we do!"

Staffing the school would be difficult, but the greatest stumbling block was money. In the spring, Ferm consulted Hitchcock and others about acquiring funds from the Los Alamos Foundation, the controlling entity for the Ranch School's assets. Recent action by the foundation had provided pensions for a few long-term administrators and masters from the school, but the main mission was to support education. With that in mind, funds were allocated to the restart effort in Taos. Not many months before, money had been made available to former Ranch School master Tommy Waring to move his Waring School for younger boys from Santa Fe to less-crowded quarters in Pojoaque. Thus, the foundation had hopes for two schools to carry on the Los Alamos educational traditions.[9]

By the time Peggy got to New Mexico, Ferm had rented the buildings and grounds of the Sagebrush Inn south of Taos for the new campus, and he had found an old adobe home for sale in Ranchos de Taos, a rural community not far from the school. The house needed work, but its character suited Peggy's sense of tradition perfectly. She and the boys set to work on the house at the same time Ferm and those same two boys began making needed improvements at the school site. Hugh and Allen helped build corrals and a tennis court and renovated an existing adobe building for a tack room at the Sagebrush Inn, and when they weren't working for their father, Peggy had them planting trees, lending a hand with construction of a wooden garage, and building a fence on their new property. Those were the major outside chores, but inside a more tedious task awaited them.

Helen Blumenschein drew this pen-and-ink sketch of the Church house in Ranchos de Taos. Helen was a good friend to Peggy from her first days in Taos, helping her meet people and later enjoying hikes and picnics together. Courtesy Corina Santistevan.

She said, raising a fastidious brow,
Your floors are made of dirt!

Indeed, the floors of the Ranchos house were dirt, but so were the floors of many old northern New Mexico adobe homes built before the twentieth century. It was not a disgrace, as Peggy's out-of-state visitor implied, but a part of the traditional architecture of early Hispanic colonists who began settling New Mexico in the seventeenth century. They brought with them the wooden forms for making adobes from the mud of the new land, and to their homes made of the sun-dried bricks they added such embellishments as carved corbels and posts along shaded portals and lush flower gardens in interior courtyards. They imported not only remnants of their Spanish-Moorish background but also a gracious style of living that reflected their roots. For Peggy, the Ranchos house embodied all of that.

> *Yes, made of dirt, I said,*
> *of earth mixed well with straw*
> *that once was a sunned field*
> *mellowed and rotted to pliability*
> *by the skilled chemistry of rain.*

The heritage that made New Mexico unique found its way into many of Peggy's poems. In the late summer of 1944, that much-loved heritage slipped easily into some lines about her dirt floors. She was pleased with her "new" Taos home, but as anyone who has lived in an adobe with dirt floors will tell you, the upkeep is not the pleasing element. The walls of an adobe must be remudded with regularity, and the floors require a special treatment to keep them sealed to prevent erosion and wear. The floors in the Ranchos house had not known such attention. They were worn, and the dirt was thin in places.

> *An old man, laughing, mixed it,*
> *stirred dirt and water to an almost fluid*
> *boggy consistency, carried it in pails*
> *indoors. An old woman laid it*
> *deftly smooth between four white walls,*
> *kneaded and leveled it and smoothed it,*
> *with only a skilled eye to measure it,*
> *only two good firm hands to marry it*
> *to the hard ribs of earth beneath.*

The rebuilding of the floors had to begin immediately, before furniture could be moved in. In addition to her own efforts, she had a ready, if less-than-willing, pair of helpers. Two strong young sons! Thinking of the long days on hands and knees, she built her poem as she and the boys rebuilt the floor.

> *She washed it often*
> *with water and a grimy piece of*
> *sheep's wool, pressed it harder, firmer . . .*

Buckets of mud mixed with straw were hauled in and smoothed and leveled into the thinning sections. The settlers of earlier centuries had applied animal blood to the drying floor as a sealant, giving their floors a rich red color, but Peggy's floors were sealed with multiple applications of linseed oil and turpentine.

Hugh, Peggy, and Ferm pose in the doorway of their home in Ranchos de Taos, an old, traditional adobe they purchased from Dr. Gertrude Light. Courtesy Peggy Pond Church Estate.

*It took many days of coating the floor and waiting for the oil and spirits to season
and dry.*

> *Yes, they are made of dirt,*
> *my floors. They say the Lord God*
> *formed man of the same stuff.*
> *I walk upon them*
> *reverently, most often without shoes,*
> *feeling the holy oneness of all living.*

*After a while the furnishings were moved into the restored rooms, and they were
occupied. Visitors could be entertained, but only those with knowledge of the old
Southwest understood—and appreciated.*

> *My visitor's lifted eyebrows*
> *frowned still, spurning still the humble*
> *dust-colored texture of my floors.*
> *I think her ashes*
> *will rest in a cold urn, well mausoleumed,*
> *for centuries after mine have joined the living*
> *passionate texture of earth . . .* [10]

In getting the school stocked and ready, one item was necessary above
all others for the success of a ranch school: horses! The government had
commandeered the Los Alamos Ranch School horses the year before and
used them for mounted security patrols in the first months of the Manhattan
Project, but the horse patrols were eventually cut back. In mid-summer of
1944, Ferm Church and Tommy Waring bought back some of the school's
stock, and in August Ferm, Allen, Hugh, and former master Manuel Diaz,
drove a dozen of the horses to Taos from Pojoaque. Hugh Church, a twelve-
year-old that summer, remembered sixty years later the route they took. For
him, the excitement of the horse drive marked his first official task as a student
at the new Los Alamos School in Taos, something that he had thought the
previous year he would never be. He and the other drovers took the horses
on the high road through Chimayó and Truchas and into Peñasco, where

they put up their herd for the night in a forest ranger's pasture. The next day, Hugh recalled, "We deviated from the highway and went over the pass west of U.S. Hill and down Miranda Canyon into Ranchos."[11] The entire journey led them through a historical adventure in northern New Mexico, but in the last miles they retraced a route that men and horses had traveled for almost three centuries—a northern extension of *El Camino Real*, the Royal Road that once connected Mexico City with the early settlements in the Rio Grande Valley. It was a passage not only for settlers and livestock but for a language and a culture. Fermor Church, Manuel Diaz, and the two boys were most likely among the last drovers to bring horses over that route into Taos.[12]

With the arrival of the horses, school could begin, but in spite of the hard work to ready the campus and recruit students, the horses outnumbered the boys. Recruitment with a war going on had been difficult. The year began with eight boys ranging in age from twelve to seventeen. They came from as far away as San Francisco and Kansas City to join Hugh and Allen Church and another New Mexican, Michael Baca of Santa Fe. Christie Luhnow, who had attended the Los Alamos Ranch School in 1941–43, returned for his fourth year. The low enrollment was a disappointment, but the boys found an outstanding staff awaiting them nonetheless. Fermor Church, the headmaster, had a Harvard degree and taught Latin and mathematics. Manuel Diaz, who had taught the final year at Los Alamos, held a master's degree from the University of Chicago and taught Spanish and science. John J. Cape, assigned to classes in history and mathematics, had been a lecturer in economics at Boston University before joining the staff. Cape served also as the school's business manager.[13] Rounding out the teaching staff was Ruth Hatcher of Taos. She was a graduate of the University of Oklahoma and taught English. Though basic coursework was emphasized, the arts were not neglected. Oscar Berninghaus was the art advisor for the school, which gave students the unique opportunity to work with one of the founders of the famed Taos Society of Artists. Audrey Diaz filled the position of school nurse, and Helen Kentnor, owner of the Sagebrush Inn, served as the school's matron.

The eight students lived and studied in the beautiful, traditional adobe inn, built in the style of a three-story pueblo, but in keeping with the educational philosophy of the Los Alamos Ranch School, many of the learning experiences came from outside the classroom. Some of them were to be gained from Oscar Berninghaus. Due to the small enrollment, Berninghaus was able to invite the boys into his studio, located as it was in one room of his home. "I recall one trip we made to his studio," said Allen Church, looking back on his year in Taos. "He demonstrated the steps involved in doing a stone lithograph." Berninghaus was a master at the process. "It was interesting," Allen still recalled years later, "to see the role that a wax marker, water, and ink could play in transferring an image from stone to paper."

Another part of the curriculum taught the boys to care for their assigned horses and the associated equipment. They went on Saturday rides in the nearby mountains and took longer camping trips to learn outdoor cooking and survival skills. In all of their pursuits, the students were surrounded and inspired by the grandeur of Taos Mountain and the vast plains extending westward, but regardless of the unique beauty of the terrain, something was lacking. The environment that had been so much a part of the Los Alamos

Master John Cape relaxes in front of the fire at the Sagebrush Inn with five of the students at the Los Alamos School in Taos. To Cape's left are Allen Church and Ben Hatcher, with Peter Butler by the hearth. Hugh Church is the chess player to the left, and the young man on the right unfortunately remains unidentified after so many years. Courtesy Los Alamos Historical Museum Archives.

Ranch School couldn't be duplicated. The heart of the program was missing. Coupled with low enrollment, the school's problems became insurmountable. Despite the planning and hard work put into resurrecting the school, it wasn't to be. After a year of classes and a summer camp, the school closed for the final time. Two young men, Allen Church and Christie Luhnow, received the only diplomas from the Los Alamos School in Taos.

Once again Ferm was out of a job, but after living in Taos for a year, he and Peggy had come to like their new home and hoped to stay. The small town offered beautiful scenery and an atmosphere alive with New Mexico's history and culture. In 1924, when she was a new wife at the Ranch School, Peggy had written, "Perhaps I shall take root here like the pines."[14] She had done that, establishing her home and her identity in oneness with the Pajarito Plateau. Could she do it again, send down roots into another part of New Mexico? She began to make a start of it. She wrote to a friend: "We've been lucky ourselves, to be able to go on living in New Mexico and to have the country we love still at our back door. We own a beautiful, old adobe that looks out over the old church at Ranchos, very old, very simple, with enough modern improvements to make it very livable. We hope we won't have to move away, though so far we haven't figured out the necessary means of livelihood." But that, too, fell into place. Ferm found short stints of work with the Harwood Foundation, the Kit Carson Electric Cooperative, and the Philmont Scout Ranch before finally hiring on with the engineering firm of Tynes & Loftin.

In mid-July of 1945, Peggy recorded early one morning in her journal a disturbing dream she had had in the night. She saw whirlpools and whirlwinds, "a great cosmic power unleased that men could not deal with." When the news of the bombing of Hiroshima and Nagasaki was released and New Mexicans finally knew that the fireball in the predawn sky of July 16 near Alamogordo was more than an ammunition dump exploding, Peggy remembered the dream. Curious, she went to her journal and thumbed through the pages, stopping on the entry for July 16. The dream had occurred three hours before the test bomb exploded at Trinity.

Like every other American, Peggy was grateful that the war was over, but it was also a time of great introspection for her. The war had ended with the dropping of the atomic bombs developed at Los Alamos. She examined her feelings both in her poetry and through her Jungian analysis. There was much to reconcile—the loss of her beloved Pajarito Plateau and a post-war world that was still in crisis. The emotional disturbances of the war years led Peggy to some deep insights, and she translated those into what is considered by many to be her finest poetry.

Reviewing Peggy's third volume of poems for the *Saturday Review of Literature* in 1946, William Rose Benét remarked, "Mrs. Church's poetry is distinctly of this time, the work of a fine human being, concerned with the terror of the hour." He noted that "in the present book she has grown, it seems to me, far beyond her earlier work." *Ultimatum for Man* was well reviewed even though the first press run was small, a fact that was criticized by John E. Baker of the *Santa Fe New Mexican*. "It is a sorry commentary on the state of poetry and poetic appreciation that even a fine and honest volume of verse (and there aren't many such) prints in terms of only a few hundred copies," Baker wrote. "Here is writing which uses the poetic form to express thoughts which cannot be expressed otherwise." He added, "Mrs. Church has produced a fine and moving piece of work, deserving of more than the 400 copies capably printed by James Ladd Delkin, Stanford University."[15]

Peggy would look back years later and view the title poem as arrogant, questioning her right to make such a strident statement to the world, but that world had erected hurdles of fear and concern for everyone in the late 1930s and 1940s when she wrote the poems in *Ultimatum for Man*. As a mother of sons, a woman of intelligence, and a lover of peace, she had every right. As her cousin Florence Converse put it in a review of the work, "her heart and mind are filled with visions of the young men who run, 'lovely and smooth-limbed, with their hands full of lightning against the sun.'"[16] Peggy had honestly voiced her insights and her hopes for the future, but it was a volume of work that would haunt her for years to come.

One of Peggy's biggest obstacles was the irony that Los Alamos, a place she knew for its beauty and serenity, should have given birth to the world's most destructive weapon, but she wrote to a friend, "We've met and talked to some of the scientists and their families who've lived up there, and they seem to love the country as much as we did! So from that point, A. J. would, I think, have been proud, and my father, too, to have had their 'paradise' become a spot loved by people of many nations." Such upbeat moments countered other times when the pain still lured her into thoughts of all she had lost.

Endless green buildings and wire fences. The barns and horse stables gone. In their place a large, white wooden building called Theatre 1 dominated the area. In every direction Peggy saw unfamiliar and unattractive buildings seemingly afloat in a sea of mud left by spring rains. At least Fuller Lodge still stood, proud and dignified. And behind it was the Big House, where Ferm had courted her by playing classical records in his room, where she had warmed herself in front of the fireplace on winter evenings, and where Hitch had read H. Rider Haggard novels to the boys after dinner. It was a Saturday afternoon in May 1946, and Peggy, Ferm, and Hugh were visiting Los Alamos for the first time since the war.

Peggy was interviewed in Fuller Lodge and recalled pleasant memories in those surroundings, but at the same time she referred to herself as a displaced person. She was able to laugh about some aspects of the last days before the school closed, getting ready for the evacuation, but she expressed disappointment at the changes she saw on returning. The town, so hastily erected by the army, had no paved streets, and the buildings were typical barracks-style construction. Many of the Ranch School buildings were gone, as were most of the tall, old ponderosas that had stood along the western side of Ashley Pond.

After the meeting in Fuller Lodge, the Churches were driven around the town that their escorts referred to as "the project," a reference to the military designation Project Y. They spotted the school's trading post, still intact and serving a similar purpose, but the district school Hugh and his brothers attended had been turned into the Tech PX. The little stone building that had been the power plant for the Ranch School was the Housing Office. Their log home and the other masters' cottages were occupied by high-ranking scientists and officials and had been nicknamed Bathtub Row because the cottages were the only family dwellings in Los Alamos with bathtubs. Metallurgist Eric Jette and his family were in the house that Connell had built for his sister, May. The classrooms of the Arts and Crafts cottage were home to the new laboratory director, Norris Bradbury. They could no longer knock on the door and chat with their friend Floyd Womelsduff because physicist Robert Bacher was living in his cottage. A world that had once been so personal was filled with strangers.

After the visit, the local newspaper reported that, while considering the loss of her former home, Peggy Church had said, "We felt as the people in the ruins must have felt when some force drove them away many years ago."[17]

Peggy talked to Edith at times about her perceptions of the scientists, gained from the many nights they ate dinner in her home during the war years. Edith had come to know some of the men and women who stayed in Los Alamos after the war and liked them as individuals, recognizing that they, too, had hopes for a peaceful world, but the nature of the work at Los Alamos and its outcome remained a grave concern. While watching the Indians dancing at San Ildefonso Pueblo early one morning, Peggy began to draw some positive and helpful insights from their beliefs and steadfast traditions. "I thought when you come right down to it, the power of life and growth those Indians were invoking was something much greater than the destructive power in the atom, and I wondered if they knew it." For Peggy, the journey was changing, becoming more than ever an inner one.

Chapter 9

New Horizons

"We found life is not what we dream but something that dreams us."

Thank you for the "appreciative things you've said about my poetry," Peggy wrote to William Carson in 1946. Carson was the father of two Los Alamos Ranch School summer campers from St. Louis, and he had taken the time to send kind words after reading *Ultimatum for Man*. In the same letter he expressed his condolences over the closing of the school in Taos.

Peggy responded wistfully. "We hope that we'll be able to keep in touch with all those to whom Los Alamos is not a synonym for atomic destruction, and with everyone for whom, like ourselves, the days on the mesa were 'among the happiest of their lives.'"

Even after three years, Peggy and Ferm were still finding it difficult to leave those days behind. "We know that there is still much beautiful country up there," Peggy wrote in her response, but she described, too, a recent drive through the Jemez to the Valle Grande and the ominous warning signs they encountered along the road—Danger! Peligro! Muerto! Trying to avoid being too negative, she mentioned that "the great basin at the head of Frijoles was as full of golden aspen and crimson woodbine as it always was in October. We've camped beside Tshirege ruin and, except for the hum of distant machinery, found the canyon as timeless as ever." She shared with Carson the spiritual beauty of the recent deer dance at San Ildefonso, when in the predawn she "saw the sacred animals come down from the hills just before sunrise, the women waiting to touch them, the men waiting to scatter sacred meal before them, the drums calling them." Then the pendulum swung, and she couldn't keep from mentioning a disturbing incident involving two army buses that drove through the plaza, honking and causing disruption at one of the crucial times in the ritual. The buses were there to transport workers from the pueblo to Los Alamos, but the drivers could have shown at least courtesy if not reverence. The chorus had performed without a break and the drums had continued, but for Peggy it was upsetting. She reversed her thoughts again to report proudly that son Ted was serving on the USS *Marvin H. McIntyre* in the Philippines, Allen was in pre-veterinary studies at Colorado A&M, and fourteen-year-old Hugh was "a rebel" in eighth grade. On an even stronger note, she ended, "As long as we stay in New Mexico I hope we can be headquarters for any Los Alamos people passing through."[1]

By the winter of 1946 when she wrote to William Carson, Peggy was caught between two ways of thinking about the new Los Alamos. The development of the bombs was something she couldn't accept, but, at the same time, she had met people involved with the Laboratory at Los Alamos and found that she admired them as individuals. Even more, she saw that they were not walking away from the aftermath and the controversy surrounding the potential uses of nuclear energy. There was responsibility to assume, and the scientists understood the challenges they had created for the world with their research. In late August of 1945, twenty-one days after the bombing of Nagasaki, the men and women who had worked on the development of the bombs formed the Association of Los Alamos Scientists (ALAS). Peggy was impressed by the statement of what they hoped to accomplish in the postwar world.

The goal of the ALAS was "to promote the attainment and use of scientific technological advances in the best interests of humanity." The members recognized that because of their special knowledge and position they had "political and social responsibilities beyond their obligations as individual citizens." A newsletter was published to publicly express their views and to encourage international control of peaceful uses of atomic energy. They developed a program of public education on the nature and control of atomic energy, providing lectures, films, and exhibits. Most importantly, the group kept in contact with high-level government officials as well as the press in an effort to influence public policy.[2]

Peggy agreed strongly with the efforts of the scientists and believed in their sincerity, so she pursued the only route she could to help them. She turned over the profits from the sale of *Ultimatum for Man* to the ALAS.

Association of Los Alamos Scientists
P.O. Box 1663
Santa Fe, New Mexico

January 17, 1947

Peggy Pond Church
Box 63

Ranchos de Taos
New Mexico

Dear Mrs. Church:

> *Your kindness in turning over the "harvests" from*
> *the sale of Ultimatum for Man is appreciated far more*
> *than has been indicated to you in the past. Please*
> *accept our heart felt thanks . . .[3]*

Peggy looked at the words again, having read the letter once already. She marveled at such a strange association, though she knew her reasons for supporting this group were valid. She was turning more and more to pacifism, and if the world were ever to attain peace, the control of atomic energy was a necessity. She revisited her decision to dedicate the book to Edith and Tilano and the cryptic words that followed their names —

> *To Edith and Tilano who live by the bridge*
> *and who have seen all that crosses over.*

She turned to the book's concluding poem —

> *And so without words I knew that man is mortal*
> *and doomed both to live and to die,*
> *but what he worships lives on forever.[4]*

Was the choice for the dedication more meaningful than she had thought, in view of the postwar hopes and fears and the "unequivocal ultimatum" that now took on more urgency than when she had first conceived the book's title poem?[5]

The irony struck her that she could be so graciously thanked by one of the scientists of whom she had spoken so harshly in "The Nuclear Physicists," another poem in the book. Her pen had lashed out, "These are the men who / working secretly at night and against great odds / and in what peril they knew not of their own souls / invoked for man's sake the most ancient archetype of evil . . ." She had called their research the blackest of magic and referred to "men who / now with aching voices and with eyes that have seen too far into the world's fate, / tell us what they have done and what we must do." But then the ending of the poem rang true. There had to be "those who listen / and will the world's good."[6] She continued reading the letter.

153

*You have correctly surmised that one of our
more crying needs is for money with which to carry
on our work, and that any amount whatever added
to our slender resources is a help. Coming as it did
during a rather low ebb in our fortunes, your check
. . . has made us particularly grateful. Quite aside
from the money involved, the spirit in which your
poems were written is in itself a contribution, which
we accept with thanks. I think we all realize that
our current problems contain little that is new, that
their only distinction is that they must be solved in a
frighteningly short space of time.*

*We have been especially appreciative of your choice
of stationery.[7] It has perhaps been fully as painful for
those of us who have been here since those first months
in 1943 to know what the name of Los Alamos has
come to symbolize as you say it has been for you. It
has been even more painful for us to realize the extent
of our implication in the madness of these days. If
anything can be considered vital to the continuance
of our civilization, surely the successful control of this
particular weapon must be looked upon as a necessary
thing. All of us recognize that this is only a fragment of
a far more complex problem, but at the same time we
cannot help but understand that unless this fragment
is dealt with successfully there can be little thought of
finally coming to grips with broader issues.*

Thank you again.

Sincerely,

*Robert R. Davis
for the Executive Committee*

From the cold Taos winter, life moved on through spring and into summer. Ferm had taken a position as director at the Harwood Library, and Peggy was serving as treasurer on the Kit Carson Electric Cooperative board.[8] Ted had returned home from the navy, having sailed from the Philippines through the Panama Canal to Norfolk, where his ship was decommissioned. He had returned to MIT, finished his degree in electrical engineering, and was engaged to Elizabeth (Liz) Comfort, a young woman he met in Taos. The two were married in July, and with the assistance of family friend Dorothy McKibbin, Ted was offered a job at the Los Alamos Scientific Laboratory's Z Division on Sandia Base in Albuquerque. Dorothy had been hired by the Manhattan Project in early 1943 to run the Santa Fe office, which cleared all incoming supplies, equipment, personnel, and family members for the trip to Los Alamos. She became known as the Gatekeeper to Los Alamos and rose to a highly respected position. Therefore, Ted was soon working in applied physics for the Laboratory that had caused the family to be exiled from Los Alamos in 1943, but it was a good job and not much was said about the choice.

In Taos Peggy was again in the midst of a writers' and artists' colony but one with a different character. While the Santa Fe colony was progressive in ideals and lifestyles, Taos bordered on the outrageous, attracting as it did some of the world's most talented free thinkers. Peggy was acquainted with many of them but found it difficult to get close or identify with most of them as individuals, particularly with Mabel Dodge Luhan, Frieda Lawrence, and Dorothy Brett. Peggy summed up the triumvirate as "the Mabel-Frieda-Brett ambience—a group into which I did not fit, to which I was not particularly attracted. Something in me could never be 'bohemian'—though on one side I longed to." In later years, from the safe distance of old age, she sometimes regretted the part of herself that always feared and suppressed another side, the free spirit struggling to escape. "How is it that the most truly creative spirits seem to break free of that bondage?" she wondered. She certainly had the opportunity to study that question in the Taos years, for one of those free spirits was a neighbor in Ranchos de Taos. Despite the lack of attraction to the core group of the colony, Peggy found a close friend in artist Andrew Dasburg.

When Peggy met the fifty-seven-year-old Dasburg, he was just coming out of a creative slump that resulted from his years of struggle with Addison's disease. The loss of his energy, even his desire to paint, was in marked contrast to the life he had led up to that point. Born in Paris in 1887, Dasburg had come with his mother as a five-year-old to New York, where he grew up in Hell's Kitchen. He had been fortunate to attend classes at the Art Students

League on scholarship and later studied with Robert Henri at the Chase School. Several summers were spent in Woodstock, New York, in the league's summer program. In the New York City of the early 1900s, his friends and acquaintances were the up-and-coming artists and writers who would dominate the next decades, and some of them he met at the "evenings" hosted by Mabel Dodge in her Fifth Avenue apartment.[9] He fit in from the first time he was invited, and he quickly developed an infatuation for Mabel. Dasburg's free spirit was definitely not afraid to try new things or even, on occasion, dangerous things. Eight months after meeting Mabel, with World War I breaking out in Europe, he sailed to France to join Mabel and her companion, journalist John Reed, who were already in Paris when the fighting began. Disturbed by the sound of artillery shelling and the reports of destruction, Dasburg took a train to a nearby town to see the damage firsthand. On returning to Paris, he shared what he had seen with Reed. The risk-taking journalist was impatient to get closer to the fighting for a better story and talked Dasburg into accompanying him on a similar foray toward the front. They walked from Paris through villages perilously close to the battle lines until a French commandant detained the pair and sent them back.[10]

Dasburg brought a sense of adventure to his friendship with Peggy, but that was not the key ingredient shared by the artist and the poet. The understanding between them centered on an ability that Mabel Dodge Luhan had identified in both of them, something she called the gift of seeing.[11] They looked at everyday things but saw them in extraordinary ways. They shared a sensitivity to life and a love for the land surrounding them. The two neighbors no doubt talked of such things as they sat in the shade of the huge elm tree in front of Dasburg's home, having tea as they often did, sometimes just the two of them and sometimes joined by others who dropped by frequently, as Dasburg was revered by the Taos colony. He was drawn to Taos from his first visit in 1918. The high desert bordered abruptly by forested mountains was seemingly the perfect setting, since one noted art critic referred to him as "the greatest draughtsman of landscape since Van Gogh."[12]

In 1951 Peggy wrote a poem titled "Andrew's Tree in the Moonlight," a poignant work about life and death and the beauty given to us in the years between. It is left to the reader to surmise the reason behind this poem, but it was written at a time when Dasburg was affected by severe depression. Perhaps the beauty of the venerable elm that they both loved inspired her to try reaching him by comparing the tree to "the arch of the rainbow / bending toward the earth," reminding him of "the living, the dying, / balanced in unison like sound, like silence, / of which all song is made."[13]

The poem was printed for mourners at Dasburg's funeral in 1979, revealing its metaphors of life and the friendship that will always remain in its lines.

> Andrew's tree in the moonlight
> is more than a tree; has become for a space a vision
> in which we behold all trees, all times, all seasons,
> all loves, all deaths; our own ascent and returning
> from darkness to darkness, and the light reflected
> in wonder from our eyes.[14]

In Peggy's first years in Taos, there was another important though very different friendship developing, one that would at last fulfill her need to be understood on a deep and insightful level. In a young woman just graduated from college, Peggy found someone who shared her poet's spirit.

Everything is on a track through time—every person, every artifact, every particle of matter in stone or air or water—and each intersection is special. Peggy looked at life that way, seeing each moment as having something unique to offer, perhaps a lesson or a beautiful scene, perhaps silence or the sound of notes blended in music, enhanced by the instruments, the musicians, the quality of the air at a given moment, the temperature, the setting. Each encounter is so intricate that it is beyond our comprehension, and the complexity that we call life is a miracle. It was that kind of insight that Peggy shared with Corina Santistevan. The two women met in Taos in the summer of 1946, and each came to recognize in the other a sensitivity matching her own, a person with whom life's overwhelming moments of awareness could be experienced and their beauty voiced unselfconsciously.

Corina had just returned to Taos after graduating from college in Las Cruces, where she majored in modern languages and education.[15] It was an exciting time for her. In her first summer home, she designed a remedial reading room for the Taos Municipal Schools, and in the fall she began her teaching career. She worked hard to develop her reading classes and spent extra hours helping with the French and Spanish courses at the high school. She met the challenges of a first-year teacher with enthusiasm, but an unexpected change was in store.

Corina had grown up in the small village of Cordillera, just south of Taos. In her teens and early twenties, she had been closely involved with her community, working with adults as well as children. She had organized a community extension club to assist with skills in reading and writing as well as homemaking, farming, and health care. During World War II, she was appointed to the community Victory Council by the U.S. Department of Agriculture War Board in recognition of her work as a volunteer. Now that she had returned as a trained teacher, the people there wanted her to teach their children. She thought long and hard, remembering all of the villagers who had helped her family during hard times, people who held to their traditions and had taught her the sense of community. To those longtime friends she felt gratitude and responsibility, and in the end, her decision was to accept the teaching position in Cordillera's one-room primary school. Corina had come full circle and was back where she started, returning to make her own contributions.

The old Hispanic community had been home to her family for generations. She and her father still lived in the Santistevan adobe that could be dated to 1831 but had existed even before that, so it would have been difficult to say no to a request to teach the local children. Corina had within her the sense of community that is central in Hispanic tradition and the belief that one returns kindness to those who have given it, but her choice was also based on love. She would remain at the one-room school for thirteen years.

Corina was the youngest of five girls, born in 1919 to Don Alfredo and Doña Reymunda Santistevan. When she was two, her mother died suddenly, leaving her father to raise the five little girls with the help of a beloved uncle, until the uncle, too, died in a wagon accident four years later. The four older girls were of school age and attended the one-room school in Cordillera, sometimes taken there through winter snowstorms on a homemade, horse-drawn sled guided by their father. It would have been impossible for Don Alfredo to work with the youngest daughter at home, so, despite the fact that she was too young for school, the teacher allowed Corina to stay with her sisters, providing a cot for her in the back of the room so that she could take naps during the day. Those difficult years were made easier by the supportive neighbors of Cordillera who surrounded her warm and loving family.

Corina graduated, as did her sisters, from Taos High School, but with no means to continue her education, her only option was to work at local jobs and save for her college tuition. There was never any doubt that she would eventually go to college. One of her jobs was a perfect fit—working at the Harwood Library, hired by the National Youth Administration. The librarian was Roberta Robey, who was well known for starting the first bookshop in

Corina Santistevan at her ancestral home in Cordillera, New Mexico, ca. 1940s. Courtesy Corina A. Santistevan.

Santa Fe in the corner of the town's stationery store in 1921. That effort evolved into her Villagra Book Shop in Sena Plaza, a gathering place for Santa Fe book lovers for many years. In the early 1940s, after selling her shop, Robey was sent by the Works Projects Administration to direct the Harwood Library, where she became Corina's cherished mentor. She had Corina begin her day by freshening the hollyhock blossoms floating on a large silver platter. She believed that libraries should be pleasant places! Then in the remaining hours she would teach Corina the skills of a librarian, how to encourage young people to diversify their reading, leading them from, perhaps, Zane Grey to similar books by Harold Bell Wright or Jack London. Corina also helped Robey establish a branch library in Ranchos de Taos. Eventually, through the years of saving, college became possible.[16]

Corina's friendship with Peggy began the summer Corina returned home to Taos, but it developed gradually, "natural and unhurried." At first the two women discussed books or went for a walk or attended a feast day celebration at nearby pueblos. In time, they stole afternoons for picnics or drove to out-of-the-way places to explore. "*Mira!*" Look at this or that, they would exclaim to one another as they glimpsed the magic in a stone or a flower or the moon rising over the mountains. Life's simplest elements became things of wonder when they were together.[17]

Peggy's house in Ranchos was a mile from Corina's home in Cordillera, and on her daily walks, she would sometimes drop in to say hello. Peggy took her walks early in the morning, so her visits often coincided with breakfast, which, from the very first early morning visit, brought about a lesson in Hispanic traditions. She was always welcomed into the Santistevan home, warm and alive with the scent of burning piñon in the fireplace and the aroma of the morning meal cooking or already on the table. In the little village, it was common and quite acceptable for friends and neighbors to just drop in. They couldn't have called ahead because almost no one had a telephone. Peggy was comfortable about visiting, but her upbringing led her to decline Corina's offer to sit down at the table and share breakfast with them, at which point the Santistevan's folded their hands in their laps and allowed their food to get cold while they visited with their guest. During the first such visit, when Peggy noticed that the Santistevans weren't eating, she encouraged them to continue while they talked with her, but that didn't happen as long as she was there. Later Peggy asked Corina why they hadn't continued with their breakfast. Corina answered with dignity, "We're not supposed to!" There were set rules for good manners in the traditional household, and they were not to be forgotten, even after Peggy was accepted and loved by every member of the family. "She had to learn so many of our cultural ways," Corina remembered with a smile long after, recalling the precious memories from the vantage point of her late eighties.[18]

There were many differences between Corina's background and Peggy's upbringing in a family with eastern roots and a boarding school tradition. Taos and the small villages nearby had progressed slowly and still existed more in a bygone time than in the New Mexico that took shape after the war. That difference was one of the things Peggy loved about it.

The atmosphere of Taos was pastoral, with small farms and dirt roads and scattered houses made of adobe. Fewer than half a dozen streets were paved, and the intersection of the state highway with Kit Carson Road had the town's only traffic light. Not long before, the intersection had been the site of the only stop sign in town, a civic necessity so unpopular that writer and poet Spud Johnson paid local children ten cents if they would pull it out of the ground and hide it behind a nearby wall. Peggy's own niece was the recipient of a few of those dimes! In the late 1940s, Taos Plaza was still the gathering place for local residents. Old men sat on benches and talked while children sat nearby and listened to their stories. They learned a great deal of history that way, even if some of it was embellished just a bit. Taos was an isolated place not much affected by the outside world.[19]

Corina taught Peggy about her culture gradually through many shared experiences. Early one morning in the first months of their friendship, Corina was preparing to visit her mother's gravesite. She was almost ready to leave for the cemetery when Peggy stopped by on her morning walk. Corina invited Peggy to come with her. Honoring the dead by remembering and continuing to acknowledge their love is among the important customs in northern New Mexico. Sometime after the visit, Peggy composed one of several poems that she would eventually write as tributes to Corina and the times they spent together. In "Peñas Negras," she wrote of a deeply moving experience.

> We walked in the early morning to the graveyard,
> setting out before the sun had risen,
> the flowers heavy in our arms,
> and the green blanket woven
> by your loving hands to cover the grave of your mother.
> This day, Corina, I came to know tenderness
> that had long been buried in my own heart.[20]

Peggy created a picture of herself walking beside Corina, "like a child, with my arms full of iris." There were meadowlarks and dew that "lay like a mystery on the tall grass." She watched Corina clear the wild grasses from the grave and "spread over it the blanket."

"Oh I might have smiled at you once for this unreasoning gesture of love," Peggy said in the poem, "yet a spirit was incarnate in your face and your pose as you knelt there." Undoubtedly thinking of her relationship with her own mother and how she had so desperately wanted it to be different, Peggy looked deeply into this moment of reverence.

> I saw how the maternal
> is more than the flesh and the bones of the mortal mother.

Through my sudden tears I saw how your mother had taught you
from her place in your heart all that your child's heart needed
to make it a woman's. Then I too knelt
and placed my flowers beside yours, and received this blessing.[21]

Peggy was drawn to Corina's family with its meaningful customs and
loving closeness so unlike her own. Señor Santistevan welcomed her and came
to care for Peggy much as he would have another daughter, and she respected
him in the way of his culture. He was the patriarch of the family and honored as
such. She became friends with all of the sisters—Alicia, Domitila, Cleofista, and
Adela—and treasured special relationships with other members of the family.

Adela's husband, Eli, was a sheepherder and spent summer months in
the mountain pastures with his herd. Peggy often joined Corina and Adela
when they took food and supplies to the intermediate camp halfway up the
mountain. They were met by Eli and other herders, and sometimes they
would continue on to the high camp and spend meaningful hours in that
isolated world of the Rockies, experiencing a way of life that was too rapidly
disappearing. Peggy watched closely as Eli handled his herd dogs, and she sat
in the meadow with him for hours to absorb the astounding beauty of the high
country and the ancient tradition of tending the flock. She came to respect
this gentle and caring man who thrived on the solitude of the mountains, and
despite the fact that Eli never called Peggy anything but "Mrs. Church," they
shared a warm and understanding friendship.[22]

Since childhood Peggy had been able to express her most personal
insights and feelings in poetry, but with Corina she could actually say them.
The two women gradually built the foundation of a lifelong friendship, and
the trust and beauty Peggy knew in that friendship were of great importance
as they became the counterpoint to the unsettled nature of Peggy's life that
marked the Taos years.

The world Peggy had known on the Pajarito Plateau was isolated and slow
paced. Life had been mostly predictable as it followed the seasons and the
regiment of the school year. In Taos she was off balance, as though cut loose
from a mooring and drifting with no course in mind. Even though she and
Ferm were comfortable in the Ranchos house and working at jobs that would
sustain them, she often had the need to escape to something familiar. Peggy
was never as comfortable with the Taos colony as she had been with the
writers in Santa Fe, so despite the added distance, she continued to return

for her needed contact with other writers and poets. On one such outing, a visit to Alice and Haniel Long, Peggy met a woman who would become an anchor for her poetic life, one in whom she immediately recognized a sister in poetry.[23] That woman was New England poet and author May Sarton.

Sarton's first visit to New Mexico came in 1940 at the invitation of Haniel Long. He had loved her first novel, *The Single Hound*, and written to tell her so. Ever the one to sing praises of Santa Fe, he invited her to visit as he so often did when writing to other authors and poets. The letter enticed her to schedule Santa Fe as the first stop of a poetry reading and lecture tour, the first of many such tours she would make from her home in Cambridge.[24]

On that introductory visit to the Southwest, Sarton was immediately captivated by its vastly different landscape. She spent Christmas Day with the Longs and extended her planned stay. She wanted more time on the "tawny earth dotted with these small dark pines" that she called "the leopard land." Haniel introduced her to Santa Fe and to some of the creative people who made it an interesting place, among them Dorothy Stewart, Agnes Sims, Fray Angelico Chavez, and Erna Ferguson, [25] but because Peggy was away for the holidays that year, their important encounter waited for Sarton's return in 1945. On that occasion, the two poets began a friendship that would last for more than four decades, though it was sustained almost entirely by correspondence. The importance of their letters can't be overstated, as there would come a time when Sarton's words and honesty would change the course of Peggy's future and help determine her place in literature.

Peggy and May revealed a vast range of emotions in their letters, but what they truly shared was understanding of "poetry as a truth beyond fact."[26] Long gaps would sometimes occur between letters, but when there was a writer's need to spill out elation or sorrow or day-to-day frustrations, they turned to each other. The heights of joys and deeply felt sorrows filled the pages, and, in turn, sensitivity and support arrived in reply. They exchanged poems and analyzed their work with blunt honesty, and when the muse failed one, the other sent words of encouragement. Grieving the loss of a friend who had lingered for months before dying, Peggy wrote that "now the time is here, poetry seems an underground river I cannot reach," to which Sarton said comfortingly, "I think we all go through this," admitting that she herself had "never been as depressed or as empty as I am this year." Both understood the importance of a poet to express deep emotions in poetic release. She ended with comforting words and insight seemingly for them both, saying, "But I do believe the underground river finds its way out again and also that the dry periods are really growing times, though one does not feel it happening and perhaps in the end without them, we would not be poets at all."[27]

For Peggy, the friendship with May Sarton was the first to provide support from another woman poet. She had found a wonderful mentor in Haniel Long, but their conversations were not the same as talking poetry and writing with a woman who encountered the same emotions. In the exchange of letters with May, Peggy found a comfort that was a new and valuable experience. She needed an understanding and honest friend as she took the next steps in her maturing poetic journey.

Though May was twelve years younger than Peggy, she had seen more of the world and had more publishing experience. May was born in 1912 in Belgium to intellectual and creative parents, one a historian, the other an artist. George and Eleanor Sarton moved with their daughter to the United States four years later to avoid the horrors of World War I. They settled in Cambridge, Massachusetts, where May's father took a part-time teaching position at Harvard to supplement his financial arrangement with the Carnegie Institute to study the history of science. May attended the progressive Shady Hill School, where her first writing efforts resulted in a lifelong love of poetry, just as Peggy's teachers at the progressive Francis Parker School had instilled that love in her. Peggy never finished college, and May never started. She shunned her parents' desire for her to attend Vassar in favor of pursuing an acting career that didn't succeed. An only child, May was indulged by her parents in many ways. They sent her to Belgium on several occasions, the first time at age twelve for the purpose of experiencing European culture and studying at the Institut Belge de Culture Française. Though she had never traveled to Europe, Peggy had been exposed somewhat to European culture through her friendships with Gay Young-Hunter and Aileen Baehrens, but she did not have the associations at an early age that Sarton enjoyed in meeting luminaries such as the actress Eva Le Gallienne, the French poet Jean Dominique, or the English writer Virginia Woolf. Peggy and May were both avid readers who accomplished a high level of self-education through lifelong pursuits. They admired diversity in literature, enjoying a range of interests that spanned from Colette to Paddington Bear. Both women loved New England and New Mexico and spent hours on hands and knees in their gardens, but there were contrasts as well.[28]

May differed from Peggy in one major regard. She was a feminist. Peggy struggled with wanting her independence but honoring her family obligations. May was self-promoting, while Peggy was guarded. May's output of published works far outnumbered Peggy's because May was bold where Peggy was shy about sending out her work. There was also the fact of Peggy's commitment to her marriage and children, an obligation that May explained concisely by saying that in a life of domesticity, "the artist is buried."[29] Peggy countered with harsh honesty in examining May's ultimate dedication to her career when she wrote, "I felt, somehow, how much you had had to live up to, with what devotion you have served the creative spirit—so much so that I could not help wondering if that Genius has not lived at the expense of your human life?"[30] Both recognized the balancing act that occurred between writer and woman.

Of the traits and interests they shared, their love of the northern New Mexico setting was perhaps the strongest. Two poems that resulted from May's first visits to New Mexico reveal her grasp of the soul of the land and its people. She wrote of the horizon "inhabited by mountains" with deep feeling —

> And in the evening without words
> The intense violet light
> Lifted the mountains away into night.
> And I knew I did not have to make a choice
> But only to look at each thing as it came,
> To look as one might listen to a voice
> Unknown, but calling a familiar name.[31]

After meeting Edith and Tilano, her perceptions were keen. In her poem "Letter to an Indian Friend," she asks, "What is the first prayer, Tilano?"

> I have come from far
> To the warm sun and the shelter,
> A long journey to reach here,
> And now it is clear
> That I do not know
> The first step.
>
> . . . .
>
> How many times have you watched the sun rise
> That when I look into your eyes,
> So old, so old and gay, I see there
> That I have never learned the first prayer.[32]

165

The depth of the land and its ancient culture, the things Peggy loved from her first encounters in Pajarito Canyon, seeped into May and lured her to return.

Changes and challenges were in store for the decade after World War II. The laboratory complex that had created the atomic bombs to end the war was expanding on the plateau, and a new road and bridge would soon make travel to Los Alamos easier. The little house at Otowi that had been occupied by Edith and Tilano for almost twenty years was a casualty of the construction. The Indians of San Ildefonso and scientists from "the Hill," as Los Alamos was familiarly known, came together to build a new house for the pair. A small adobe was erected on the south side of the road, nearer to Edith's garden and bordered by cottonwoods that would provide golden autumns.

By the time the Manhattan Project took over the Pajarito Plateau, the future had become uncertain for Edith. The Chili Line was discontinued in 1941, and the tracks were removed. She no longer had an income from the Ranch School, and profits from the tearoom were meager with fewer tourists traveling because of the war. At times she wondered if she might have to leave Otowi to find a job, but the influx of new people at Los Alamos cancelled that concern. The director of the project was a physicist named J. Robert Oppenheimer, and by coincidence he had known Edith before the war. He owned a ranch north of Pecos on the east side of the Sangre de Cristos, and on pack trips years earlier, he had stopped at Edith's place and enjoyed her hospitality. Remembering that visit, he had brought his wife, Kitty, to meet Edith. The couple came to dinner one evening in 1943, and an idea presented itself. Might Edith be willing to serve dinner to some of the scientists and their wives occasionally, giving them time away from the stressful life on the Hill? Edith was willing, and reservations began coming in. The evenings at Edith's house became so popular that reservations had to be made weeks in advance, and there were one or two groups almost every night. The profits from the $2 meals alleviated Edith's financial difficulties, and in addition she developed friendships with world-famous scientists she would never have expected to meet. Hans Bethe, Niels Bohr, Norris Bradbury, Enrico Fermi, Phillip Morrison, Deak Parsons, and Edward Teller, to name a few, sat around Edith's candlelit table and were served by Tilano, who seemed to enjoy the encounters as much as the guests. Edith was generous with extra vegetables from her garden, giving the surplus to the wives who came through her door. So, when the need arose for a new house for Edith and Tilano, the scientists

People from two communities—Los Alamos and San Ildefonso Pueblo—came together to build the new adobe house for Edith and Tilano near Otowi Bridge. Courtsey Los Alamos Historical Museum Archives.

and their families stepped in to help, returning Edith's kindness. They joined neighbors from the pueblo in laying the foundation, mixing adobes, and mudding the walls.

In Taos that summer, another event brought good news. After having three daughters—Joan, Karen, and Gretchen—Peggy's brother, Ashley, and his wife, Lucille, finally had a son to carry on the family name. Ashley D. Pond was born in August 1947, destined to become the second Dr. Pond to practice in Taos—three decades down the road! Rather than using the numeral IV after the name, the family chose the fourth letter of the alphabet as the middle name, designating the fourth Ashley and beginning a new tradition.[33]

Peggy moved forward with the analysis she had begun in California, and she was gaining new insights from the talented artists and writers around her as well as from new friends. In the midst of it all, and in view of her exchanges with scientists from Los Alamos, she found herself turning toward pacifism. On one of her visits to Santa Fe, she attended a Friends' Meeting with Alice Howland, an acquaintance who had once been the headmistress of Shipley Girls

167

School, a Quaker preparatory school in Bryn Mawr, Pennsylvania. Then, in the summer of 1948, Peggy traveled with Corina Santistevan, Wynema Rainer, and Jane Baumann to the Quaker Institute of International Relations at Whittier College in California. While there they heard Amiya Chakravarty speak and were profoundly affected by his comments. His pacifist message was shaped by his years of worldwide travel with the poet Rabindranath Tagore, by serving as the poet's literary secretary, and by his close association with Mahatma Gandhi and their attendance at the World Pacifist Congress at Gandhi's ashram. He had been with Gandhi on the Salt March for the nonviolent protest in 1930, the first in a series of events that eventually led to India's independence from Britain. A poet himself, Chakravarty had much in common with Peggy, and she later sent him some of her poetry in an exchange of letters. Along with her own extensive reading and deep thinking, Chakravarty's reflections on Eastern philosophy, religion, and humanism led her to write in her journal on November 28, 1948, "I became a Quaker." Since Taos had not formed a Quaker Meeting, Peggy traveled to Santa Fe to join the closest one.

The calendar turned yet another year, and family life progressed. Ferm had changed jobs, working for a while as office manager for Kit Carson Electric Cooperative and then signing on with the Philmont Scout Ranch near Cimarron, eventually to become camp director. Hugh worked there as a wrangler in the summers. Older brother Allen, having given up on getting into vet school, provided some excitement for the family when he moved to Hollywood to try acting. He landed small roles in two movies—*The Boy from Indiana* and *Two Flags West*, which created quite a stir because it was filmed on location at San Ildefonso Pueblo and starred Joseph Cotten and Linda Darnell.

For several months, Peggy enjoyed a period of relative calm, but as the new decade approached, that changed abruptly. On a Thursday in the late days of autumn 1949, Hugh stayed home from school with flu-like symptoms. Sore throats and colds had plagued him throughout adolescence, so missing a day of school wasn't out of the ordinary. The next day he felt a little better and went back to his classes. Saturday morning he drove his mother to Raton to pick up a friend at the bus station, a round trip of ninety miles. Though tired from the long drive and the three days of feeling ill, he went to a party with friends that evening. While there he began to feel worse, and even the slightest turn of his head caused severe pain. A friend drove him home, and by the next morning a high fever had set in. Peggy called her brother, who was doctor in Taos. Ashley suggested that Hugh be taken to Holy Cross Hospital, the local medical center.

"All this fuss for just a cold," Hugh complained, but he must have questioned his self-diagnosis when the doctor ordered x-rays and a spinal tap for Monday. Lying in the hospital, he stewed over missed ski practices. An anticipated chance to race at Sun Valley slipped away while he lay in bed, getting weaker each day. He was one of the two top skiers in his class, but that ranking would be gone if he didn't recover soon.

After a week in the hospital, the verdict came. The phone rang at noon, and Peggy answered. "It's polio," said the voice on the other end. Hugh was sent home pending consultations with doctors in Albuquerque to confirm the diagnosis and devise a plan of treatment. In the meantime, the pain settled in Hugh's lower extremities. "Much aspirin and an occasional shot of bourbon helped, administered by parents," he added, recalling those frustrating days. As if polio weren't enough, Hugh was soon back in the hospital with another complication—acute appendicitis. An appendectomy delayed the treatment for his polio, but finally on New Year's Day, his Uncle Ash flew Hugh in his Beechcraft Bonanza to the Carrie Tingley Crippled Children's Hospital in Truth or Consequences, New Mexico, where he underwent rehab and physical therapy for six weeks.[34]

As she always did when her emotions crowded too closely, Peggy turned to writing, composing this time in third person to analyze and distance herself from the moment. Hugh would be returning home in a few days, and she had to deal with the pain she felt, a mother unable to help her son. She pounded the typewriter keys with her thoughts and feelings, issuing two single-spaced pages of sorrow, compassion, and anger.

> *At last, as though she could bear it no longer, she opened the door and lit the stove that had been turned off in the room since the boy had gone away. It was as though she had opened a compartment in her heart that she had tried to shut off. The sun shone in the long west window.[35]*

The day she reentered his room she found a marigold blooming on the window ledge. She had removed the other plants from the room after he had gone but left the marigold, "a shabby plant that had not endured its transplanting well and had been, all fall, a mixture of withered buds and half-hearted blossoms, begrudging the care apparently wasted on it.*[36]* With a change of heart, she trimmed the dead leaves and watered the tenacious plant with a renewed respect. Then she slowly surveyed the room.

> The day the boy left for his convalescence in the Crippled Children's Hospital she had turned off the oil heater and closed the door into his room. Perhaps she had hoped to close off the aching memory of those weeks when he had lain in bed, thin as a horse at the end of a long winter, the ruddy glow of his cheeks paled to a thin flush upon the angular cheek-bones, his eyes huge and weary under the fine dark arch of his brows, his long legs stretched out helplessly under the blanket . . .
>
> As the room grew warmer, the paper pinwheel he had hung last summer from the ceiling above the stove began to spin; idle toy that it was, it smote her heart with recollection of his playfulness, the child so active still in the almost grown boy . . .
>
> Every small, familiar object seemed a witness to the anguish that had faced them . . . How could she exorcise the memory of those weeks? His ridiculous straw hat and the battered Stetson side by side on the bookshelf. The blue jeans and plaid shirt in the drawer; the folded socks and T-shirts—the Philmont pictures tacked up on the wall.*[37]*

Peggy was left with a painful understanding. Her son would return, but the boy would be gone forever.

Hugh lost weeks of school but managed to complete graduation requirements by attending classes half time from March to May. He graduated with his class in the spring of 1950. Polio, however, was not finished with Taos or, for that matter, the Church and Pond families. That summer, Peggy's thirteen-year-old niece, Joan, was diagnosed with a milder case. Perhaps because her

Hugh Church holding the family cat, Mr. Hyde, in Rancho de Taos. Courtesy Peggy Pond Church Estate.

father had just dealt with Hugh's illness, Joan was diagnosed immediately and treatment was successful. Three other young people in Taos came down with the disease before vaccine was widely distributed in the mid-1950s.

By early September, Peggy found herself suffering from empty-nest syndrome, a condition she admitted to Virginia Wirth in a letter. "If you were still my neighbor, I'd have run over this afternoon, I think, and shed a few tears . . ."

"Hugh (né 'Tinker') departed for college yesterday, driving Ferm's Ford truck and hauling, along with himself, two pals and their baggage. I spent the morning cleaning up his room and feeling so damned sentimental and emotional." Two pages of reminiscence later she confided, "Today I feel a little the way one does when Jr. has untied the first apron string and stalked off to kindergarten. Only this is the *last* apron string, and one finds there is a void."[38]

Having recovered to the point of using only a cane and a brace on one leg, Hugh double-clutched his father's four-speed pickup all the way to Albuquerque to begin his freshman year at the University of New Mexico, carrying his two friends along with him.

After the trying months of Hugh's illness, a family trip to the West Coast seemed a good idea for the summer, complete with restful visions of gentle waves along the beach, until the itinerary was filled to overflowing with interesting places they couldn't miss and people they had to see along the way. Ferm, Peggy, and Hugh spent a day in Hollywood with Allen before driving on to Berkeley, where they met up with Jane Baumann for "a wonderful four days" at the Pacific Yearly Meeting of Friends. They continued up the coast to Carmel to camp in Gay Young-Hunter Kuster's backyard and then drove another 200 miles for a stay at Dottie's ranch in Chico. The route home was "via Yosemite, Death Valley, Zion, and the North Rim of the Grand Canyon," as Peggy summed it up, "all in Ferm's two-week vacation!"

Back in Taos, life continued with the day-to-day things that pass the time and distract from worries. As of early summer, there was another war on. This time it was Korea, and Peggy had another son the right age to be in harm's way, though he hadn't been called up yet. Thankfully, there were chickens to feed and the garden to tend and meals to fix. There were also the occasional trips to Santa Fe and visits with old friends. Upon returning from one of those day trips in late October, Peggy found that sorrow had once again visited the house in Ranchos de Taos.

"Our kitty is no more," Peggy wrote to Ted and Liz. "He got some kind of mouth infection." Mr. Hyde had disappeared for two days before being found on Saturday evening by the man who chopped their wood. "He wouldn't touch food or water," she continued. "We fixed him a bed and applied hot compresses." She and Ferm were supposed to be in Santa Fe for a Quaker meeting on Sunday, but Ferm stayed with Hyde while Peggy went on with friends. When she returned that evening, Ferm was taking down bedding from the line. "We've lost or said goodbye to lots of pet animals in our day, but none ever seemed so much a 'person' or so much 'part of the family' as Hyde, I suppose because he's shared so many adventures with us, and changes. Ferm burst into tears when he told me."[39]

By late autumn, the frightening world events infringed on the unwilling residents in Ranchos de Taos. Allen was about to be inducted into the army, which meant that he would almost certainly see action in Korea. Peggy took him to Otowi Bridge to visit Edith Warner. Edith had watched many of the San Ildefonso boys leave the pueblo to fight in World War II and always sent them off with words of wisdom. She offered her gentle thoughts to yet another young man about to go to war. That afternoon, as yet unknown, Edith herself was about to face a battle of a different kind. She mentioned a stomach upset as she visited with Peggy and Allen, but in her usual way made light of the problem.

As 1950 drew to a close, Peggy assessed the events of the past months, some sobering and some rewarding, but among the tally there was one very bright spot, the birth of her first grandchild, Malcolm Spencer Church, born in January to oldest son Ted and his wife, Liz.

Chapter 10

And New Directions
"Write a little something about Edith."

Edith was truly ill. Word traveled through the valley, from the pueblo to Los Alamos, to Santa Fe, and eventually to Taos, where Peggy heard the news. Edith was in the hospital in Chicago, where she had gone for an operation, but the doctors could do nothing for her and were sending her home.

"The place where the river makes a noise"¹ That phrase had always been a comforting one, but this morning it brought other thoughts. Peggy walked briskly in the cold air, but people along the Talpa Road who were used to seeing her every day, just after dawn, would have said her step seemed a little slow. Her mind was on something other than returning from her walk, not even giving much regard to the uneven, frozen ruts in the dirt road. She could hardly remember a time when Edith wasn't at Otowi. It seemed like always. She relished her daily walks in the crisp air, seeing the sun's first rays lighten one side of the dark evergreens and pass through the branches of winter's leafless trees, but today the scene was dreary. It mirrored her thoughts. She regretted living so far away from Edith. Distance would limit what she could do, though she knew friends from Los Alamos and the pueblo would be there for her. They would see it as a chance to return a little of what Edith had done for them. Edith's door had been open to anyone who needed her. The old house beside the bridge had symbolized peace and renewal. The new house, too, was a place of serenity, held in the strong arm of Totavi, the ancient mesa that guarded the house and the stands of cottonwood along the arroyo. Countless people had found healing at Otowi, soothed by the timeless sounds of the flowing river. Edith believed that "there are certain places in the earth where the great powers that move between earth and sky are much closer and more available than others, and this region . . . was such a place."² Having stopped by Edith's house for renewal herself, Peggy understood.

Thinking of the first time she met Edith at Anchor Ranch, she visualized the small, thin wisp of a woman who came to New Mexico to find strength and in turn gave it to so many others. Edith came into her own after moving into the house at the bridge, but it was a challenge to make it livable. Before Edith took over the station, Peggy had passed it as a young girl when she visited her father's school. It was called Haynie in those days, and the two-room wooden house was occupied by a former lumberjack named Macario "Shorty" Pelaez. He rented the house from Julian and Maria Martinez of San Ildefonso and was paid to keep watch over the freight in the boxcar. He acquired a gas pump and turned his living room into a store. Edith expanded on Shorty's idea by opening a tearoom to earn extra money, a wiser venture than her predecessor had tried. Shorty left his position as stationmaster abruptly one day because he was "suspected" of selling bootleg liquor! [3]

The house Shorty Pelaez left behind wasn't much, but it sat on New Mexico soil and that was all Edith cared about. It gave her a chance to stay where she wanted to be and not have to return to Pennsylvania. She was determined to make the situation work. And work it did. Within six years, with Tilano's help, Edith had added a garage, chicken coop, turkey yard, corral, and two-room guesthouse that faced the river. Despite the isolation of the place, friends and guests began to arrive at her door. Visitors on the way to Bandelier National Monument stopped for chocolate cake and cold drinks. Ranch School boys and masters rode their horses to her house, and people from the pueblo were like family and visited often. Edith had thought of the little house as isolated when she moved in, but in time, people from all over the world traveled the road that passed by her door.

Peggy's reverie ended at her mailbox. She turned from the road to walk through snow to her house. Tall grass and chamisa were stiff with frost and glistened in the brilliance of the increasing sunlight. She knocked the snow from her boots and stepped inside to remove them. In the welcome warmth, she shed coat and gloves and walked across the room to her desk. Peggy was a saver of letters, and she had been thinking of one from Edith that was special to her. She opened a drawer of folders and took one out. All of Edith's Christmas letters were there, but this letter was a personal one from years before the Christmas messages had begun. The insight still astounded Peggy as she read it.

Christmas, 1936

Dear Peggy,

Surely you must be home from the Christmas trip, but I haven't seen you pass, nor Virginia, and here sit the Christmas cookies and jam! I didn't want to

175

> *send them up with you not there and hoped you'd*
> *be stopping. Please do when you have a minute.*
> *I spent New Year's Eve re-reading Familiar Journey.*
> *I feel very much an interested onlooker, with even more*
> *than an onlooker's concern. You see, your going back*
> *and forth with all that implies has been part of my life*
> *here. I've hoped that when you needed what was here*
> *you'd come—even though there are times when I've let*
> *mere work overwhelm me. For that I am regretful. I've*
> *felt that through these last years you've been finding*
> *yourself. Now I know it, so for me there was more than*
> *beauty of word and of thought in these poems. There*
> *was seeking and finding. Tears were back of my eyes,*
> *but it was joy, really. I am so glad you gave me the copy.*
>
> *Many wishes and love—Edith*[4]

Always the quiet observer, thought Peggy. Of things outward and of things within.

Within days, Peggy had more news. Edith had returned and almost immediately had taken a turn for the worse. She went by ambulance to the hospital in Los Alamos, where doctors operated on her for four hours, finding most of the cancer. It had spread some, but they were of the opinion that it could be arrested by the use of gold isotopes, a product of atomic research. Peggy wrote to her daughter-in-law to tell her that Edith, though still in the hospital, was feeling comfortable and doing well. She added, "Perhaps we'll have a little miracle and end up having to bless the atom bomb (in a way)!"[5]

But it was not to be. The hopeful treatments failed to stop the advancing cancer. Six weeks later, Ethel Froman, Edith's neighbor and wife of physicist Darol Froman, wrote to Peggy about Edith's condition. "I have some very difficult letters to write," she began. "Edith is at home and has decided to try nothing more." Ethel reported that Velma Ludlow, Edith's sister, had arrived from Pennsyvania, and the doctors had been there. She ended by saying, "I'll try to drop a note every few days." There was also a special plea. "Do write to her. She has told me of how words as you can use them mean so much to her—I wish I had some of your ability this morning." A network of letters and calls among Edith's friends was keeping everyone informed.[6]

Not long after, word came that Edith would like to see Peggy. "I dropped everything and drove down there," she reported to Virginia Wirth after the visit. She found Edith lying in Tilano's bed so that she could look out across the river all the way to the Sangre de Cristos. "She is heartbreakingly thin . . . a weather-beaten rock, her eyes seem enormously large in such a face, but clear and tranquil, and her voice as calm and normal as everyday." Peggy mentioned that people from the pueblo had been to see Edith one by one. Maria and her sister Desideria had said their goodbyes and in their usual concise words gave Edith a wonderful gift by way of a simple compliment. "Other people have tried to interfere," Maria said, "but you have never done that." The comment explained why she had always been accepted by the pueblo. Peggy added that Edith "says farewells as though she were going on the most ordinary journey" and repeated the words of Sarah McComb, who remarked, "she showed us how to live, and now she is showing us how to die."[7]

Peggy wrote on, observing that Edith's thoughts were still of everyone else and of arrangements for Tilano. "She asked about my boys. She asked me to tell you how things were, and said you had written that you and the boys might come by this way in June—and she is sorry she won't be here." Relaying the news that Tilano would be staying on in the house and that Rafael and Juanita Estevan would live there with him, Peggy ended by saying, "So the house will be there. We can still go there, at least for a few more years, and sit and be quiet and remember."

Edith's goddaughter, Henrietta Miller or "Peter," as she was known to all, was expected later that day, so Peggy stayed for less than half an hour, until Edith closed her eyes and said, "I'm afraid I'm tired." They embraced, and Peggy went out, got in her car, and "wept all the way to Santa Clara—because time must have an end and because people can be so wonderful."[8]

Edith died on May 4, 1951. Peggy heard the news while visiting her friend Aileen O'Bryan in Santa Fe.[9] On the way back to Taos, she stopped to visit Ethel Froman, whose house was near Black Mesa on the road to Española. Ethel told her "the end came peacefully." Lois Bradbury had been in the room with her. Lois and Ethel had been taking turns relieving Edith's nurse for weeks. In a letter sent a few days later to May Sarton, informing her of Edith's death, Peggy commented, "I believe Lois has been closer to Edith than anyone these last few years. Edith just closed her eyes and went to sleep and stopped breathing. She was buried that same night, according to the Indian custom, somewhere near the house." Peggy revealed her grief, saying, "Everything seems to change so fast. Edith was sort of a last link with the Pajarito Plateau that was woven so deeply—still is—in my own life."[10]

Many people were touched by Edith's death, and each recalled her in a different context. In regard to Edith's spiritual being, Aileen related to Peggy the story of the abbot of the Trappist monastery near Pecos visiting Edith before she died. He had met Edith and been impressed by her and "thought such a wonderful soul should be Catholic." About five weeks before she died, he went to see her—but came back himself converted. He said that "Edith had something that was worth anything Catholicism could have given her!"[11] Philip and Emily Morrison, a Manhattan Project scientist and his wife, remembered "especially one evening after the war, probably in the summer of 1946, just before some of us left for the east. There was a clear starry sky, and Miss Warner joined us outside after dinner—something she rarely did. We all stood and talked of the Hill, the Valley, the world—various deep and simple things. We do not remember any details, but only a great feeling of calm and peacefulness."[12] Edith's effect on people would be long remembered.

As Peggy knew, life goes on and new life begins. In November, Peggy and Ferm had a small gentleman as a guest. Malcolm was visiting his grandparents while Liz gave birth to Robyn, their second grandchild. The writer in Peggy couldn't pass up the chance to enter little Malcolm's world and pen a note from him to his mother.

> Dear Mommy:
>
> I am having fun at Grandmommy Peggy's and Grandaddy Ferm's house. I play with the kitty. I let the chickens out every day. Sometimes we go visiting. There is a grandfather clock in Granny's house. There is a big swing on the porch at Cousin Ashley's house. When I went out to Arroyo Seco I had a ride on a great big dog.
>
> Yesterday Grandmommy and Grandaddy went to Meeting in Santa Fe. I went with them. I played on the swings. I climbed on the slide. I colored pictures.

We had sandwiches for lunch. Then I took my nap
in the car outside. Then we came home again.

I hope I will see my baby sister soon.

A big hug from Malcolm.[13]

"There's a World Conference of Quakers at Oxford, to which I can't go,
being the last and least of the alternates from Pacific Yearly Meeting," Peggy
explained to May Sarton in an autumn letter full of excitement, "but there
are supposed to be other gatherings of Friends, and our meeting, bless them,
wants a poet to go and listen and try to say something about it when I come
home." She was thrilled at the prospect of a summer trip to England but
daunted by her lack of experience at international travel. "The difficulty is, I
don't know a soul in the whole British Isles, nor anything about where to go or
where to stay. Quakers in general seem great travelers and leap off for Europe
or Asia as casually as I would to Santa Fe, but this is all new to me."[14]

Peggy spent a few days in New York before beginning her grand
adventure, and New York held fascinations of its own. She visited museums
and parks, but the city itself captivated her poet's senses. "Kaleidoscope or
mosaic? The city streets like ballet scenery, and the people coming and going
like dancers. The modern choreographers have made the dance resemble life
so much that life now resembles the dance. Incredible, the people's faces and
the many masks." She sailed for England June 13th, and by the next day she
was writing of the sea. "It is a magic and a mystery, a spellbinder, our ancient
mother, speaking to our blood without words. The sea has been, since we
started, as calm as though it were timeless, rising and falling ever so gently, so
softly, incessantly undulating, hypnotizing, like an incantation."[15]

With the first view of land from the English Channel, Peggy became
uncharacteristically sentimental. "All the ghosts of history and literature I
thought had been forgotten from my school days suddenly came to life, and
at last I went down to my cabin—which was luckily a single one—and wept
for half an hour with utterly unexpected emotion."[16]

The fact that Peggy didn't know anyone in the British Isles turned out not to
matter in the least, as friends gave her names to contact, and she easily made
new friends on her own. In London, she stayed with two of May Sarton's

friends. "I hope I wasn't too awful a headache to them with all my comings and goings," she wrote to May, "and the twice I forgot my keys!" She fell in love with London. There were afternoons in St. James's Park and Hyde Park, where she watched children play. She took a boat up the Thames to Hampton Court Palace and came back on the train to an evening with the English poet Ruth Pitter, an evening that she described as "delightful," all of the time "pinching myself at intervals to see if I'd wake up from a dream."[17]

The World Conference of Friends was held in Oxford, coinciding with the Quaker Tercentenary and drawing an unusually large number of people. Within the crowd, Peggy met two women who would become lifelong friends—Jill Gyngell of London and Margaret Gibbons, "a Scots lass who became a dear friend." They formed a threesome with Peggy one afternoon to walk Pendle Hill, the place where George Fox, founder of the Quakers, experienced in 1652 his vision of gathering people to a new religion. There were visits to other historic sights and lectures from which Peggy took notes to share at Quaker gatherings back home. Groups sat under trees in gardens for discussions amid the scent of roses, expanding on such thoughts as "There is that of God in us which can speak to us" or "God is a circle whose centre is everywhere." Both phrases were written in her notes for further thought, but there were lighter moments, as well. After a lecture on universal love and human kindness, Peggy was sitting on a tour bus that afternoon with the presenter. She asked him with a smile, "We don't really feel we *have* to love everyone, do we? We can have our little jokes about the Texans, and not take it too seriously." After considering such an exception for a moment, he looked at her with an understanding smile and said, "Yes, the Christian discipline is a hard one, isn't it?"

After the days in Oxford, Peggy traveled north to Scotland to attend the Edinburgh Festival. She was excited about the classical music, opera, and theatre available throughout the next two weeks in Edinburgh, but in particular she was looking forward to hearing Kathleen Ferrier perform live, having heard the world-famous singer only on the radio and recordings. She planned also to take in ballet performances and art exhibitions, including a showing of Degas paintings and sculptures, but, upon arriving in Edinburgh, she found that there was a mix up in her hotel reservation. She had no where to stay in a city that was packed with out-of-town visitors. Had it not been for Margaret Gibbons, the two weeks might have been a colossal disappointment. Instead, Margaret put Peggy up for the entire time, and they attended the festival together. It was a memorable fortnight. Peggy heard Kathleen Ferrier perform Brahms's *Liebeslieder-Walzer*, and Margaret planned to visit Peggy in New Mexico the next summer.[18]

The trip to England and Scotland was a resounding success. New friends, wonderful experiences, mental challenges, beautiful scenery, music, and two poems inspired along the way—"Kew Gardens" and "St. Paul's, London."[19] Yet there was one day that Peggy encountered what all New Mexico travelers sooner or later experience, a day when something is just not right. The terrain is too flat or too green or the climate too humid, the people unfamiliar. She was on a side trip to Cornwall when a case of nostalgia set in. Around her the people were "not exactly unfriendly" but "just not friendly, not outgoing to strangers, content within their own special circle . . ." Strangely, she felt "insecure in the most placid and beautiful surroundings. Everywhere scenes of pastoral loveliness. Yet something lacking. The great dramatic tensions of mountain and desert, of sky and earth, of sun and rainstorm." She felt out of place, but the feeling passed. The trip was a wonderful experience, and she sailed from Southampton for home on September 12th.[20]

When Hugh left for college, Peggy lamented to Virginia, "Forty more years to go if I take after the majority of my female ancestors, and what does one *do with all that time*?"[21] It took only a few months for an answer to arrive. It came from Velma Ludlow in the form of another question. Would Peggy write "a little something about Edith?" Peggy wasn't sure about an answer. She didn't consider herself a writer of prose, having produced only books of poetry and a few children's stories to that point. Despite her doubts, she agreed to try. She began to put thoughts of Edith in her daily journal and to exchange letters with Vel and with Peter Miller, Edith's goddaughter, who lived in Pennsylvania. The project was under way, though not at any great speed, and life was crowding in from all sides as usual.

In December, middle son Allen married Carolyn Clarke in Tulsa, Oklahoma, three days before Christmas, and from there Peggy and Ferm went on to Arkansas to spend the holiday with friends. Suddenly it was a new year, and Peggy was working at the Taos Book Shop for the first time, filling in for the "book ladies," Genevieve Janssen and Claire Morrill, so that they might have a vacation. Ferm became a field engineer for Tynes & Loftin, a job that required traveling and long periods away from home. Somewhere in their hectic schedules they found time to visit Tilano just before spring. He had aged in the past year and was lonely. "He seems now for the first time to be as old as he truly is," Peggy observed. He died not long after the visit, and

Peggy was inspired to write the poem "For Tilano of San Ildefonso."

> How shall we learn your language,
> a Bible written in rocks, in the rhythm of the seasons,
> the miracle in the seed, in the branch of the fir tree,
> the voice in a shell, in a bone, in a prayer plume
> planted where invisible beings move?
> How shall we see God in the stone …[22]

A way of life was slipping away and, with it, the ties that Peggy had with the Pajarito Plateau. It was something too important to lose, something she couldn't lose. She began to realize that in Edith's memorial, she had a way to preserve that place in time. She stepped up the pace of her writing, but there was another diversion waiting around the corner, albeit a pleasant one.

Margaret Gibbons arrived for a summer visit with a planned itinerary of speaking engagements at several Quaker Meetings throughout the western United States and British Columbia, and Peggy decided to travel along with her. She drove Margaret to all the meetings, from New Mexico into Canada, on a far-less-than-straight route that eventually covered six thousand miles. They reveled in good times, meeting people, and traveling through breathtaking scenery, but the really memorable thing about the trip was the number of helpful coincidences that occurred along the way. There were so many of these happenings that Peggy and Margaret decided that someone was looking after them. They were traveling with their own patron saint. Finally, they gave her a name. She was St. Co, short for Wholly Coincidence! Or was it Holy Coincidence? Whether on their own or with a little divine help, the pair made it safely back to New Mexico after another grand adventure together.

"That summer was a complete loss as far as any real writing was concerned," Peggy admitted. The calendar turned to 1954, and she managed to start again. "Winter was always my most productive time, perhaps because, in Ranchos de Taos, I was corralled indoors by deep snow and cold," she explained years later in a magazine article about the writing of Edith's memoir.[23] In February she wrote to Peter, "I'm at it again since the beginning of the year . . . first thinking, meditating, then struggling to put things on paper—then throwing pages away, then walking out in the sunlight—then back to it again." Two weeks later, on a more positive note, she wrote to Peter once more: "Working on this book is becoming a wonderful experience—as though a spirit were beginning to be with me, helping."[24] And, as biographers do, she found herself talking to her subject. Her journal entry of April 6, 1954, noted: "As I write about you, Edith, I keep learning things about myself."

Then, Peggy's hard-earned focus on the book was disrupted again. She turned to a different form of writing to send a letter to the editor of the *Santa Fe New Mexican* denouncing the Atomic Energy Commission's decision to revoke Robert Oppenheimer's security clearance. Despite her pacifist views on the atomic bomb and its development at Los Alamos, she admired Oppenheimer for his intelligence, humanism, and sensitive nature. Though never having met him personally, she felt as though she knew him through Edith and her friend Dorothy McKibbin. She admired his philosophical perspective and particularly his world view. "The peoples of this world must unite, or they will perish," he had said in a speech just after the war ended. "This war, that has ravaged so much of the earth, has written these words . . . By our works we are committed to a world united, before this common peril, in law, and in humanity."[25] His words were delivered in front of Fuller Lodge, and his sentiment closely matched Peggy's message in her poem "Ultimatum for Man," written only a few steps from there before the United States entered the war. Her lines held her poet's expression, but the idea was the same: "Love is no longer a theme for eloquence, or a way of life for a few to choose whose hearts can decide it. / It is the sternest necessity; the unequivocal ultimatum."[26]

Understanding that Dorothy would be deeply upset by the Atomic Energy Commission's decision, Peggy wrote to her to say that the letter had been submitted. She included a copy, not knowing if the paper would actually publish it, but it did.

> AEC Acted According to Standards,
> But Men Not Made Loyal by Rules
>
> Editor, The New Mexican:
>
> The decision of the AEC against Dr. Robert Oppenheimer leaves me deeply disturbed. I agree that in accordance with the standards of national security they cannot have acted other than they did. But I have a sad suspicion that when a nation sets military security above every other standard of value it is already doomed from within. If we put more trust in our knowledge of

atomic "secrets" than we do in the qualities of mind and heart which Dr. Oppenheimer so exceptionally combines, we will soon end up by having nothing of human value to defend. Men are not made loyal by security regulations. Loyalty is a fruit of love, and love is a response to value which cannot be coerced.

It does not seem particularly important whether or not Dr. Oppenheimer has access to classified material, but it does seem that we have declared ourselves unable to trust a man of his sensitive human feeling and perception. Whom then are we to trust? Those who have given their discernment between right and wrong entirely into the keeping of the anonymous and frightening entity, the State? If that is so, then we are well on the way to following in the footsteps of those whom we protest to be the enemy of all we have long held civilized and dear.[27]

Peggy Church
Ranchos de Taos

Another divergence from the writing of Edith's memoir occurred when the Quaker magazine *Inward Light* decided to publish some of Peggy's poems. Sonnets had long attracted Peggy to their special and difficult form, and since 1943 she had worked on a series titled Indian Summer, completing the last two only the year before. The sonnets spoke of her marriage to Ferm—the difficult years, the adjustments, the gradual coming together over the long road to understanding. In reality they were poetic pictures of all marriages, and readers saw a reflection of their own relationships in the words. Because of the universal content of the poems, *Inward Light* chose to publish fifteen of the sonnets in the autumn issue of 1954, but the series name was changed to The Ripened Fields, taken from the lines of the first sonnet.

The winds and weathers of our years have blown
all our defences down and set us free.
Let us walk forth now on our ripened fields
and pluck what fruits of love the season yields.[28]

The lines of this sonnet revealed the common ground that Peggy and Ferm had reached in their marriage despite the struggle over differences that marked their early years.

Ironically, Ferm mirrored Peggy's words with his own in a letter to his son Ted, written in the same time period. Giving fatherly advice to Ted as he contemplated marriage, Ferm explained that it was a good thing to have both a job and a future "that looked up" before considering marriage. He told of his sadness at losing two girlfriends in his youth because neither wanted to wait for the security that he felt so necessary. "I should still do it that way," he stated but then added, "Of course, I do not regret, today, the course I followed, because your mother and I are very much in love with each other. As you probably know, we have not always been so and it has taken us many years to learn how to live with each other."[29]

The Ripened Fields sonnets were not only an exercise in writing precise poetic form but also Peggy's way of working through the last analysis of the rough years of her marriage to reach the years of contentment together. The sonnets were well received by the readers of *Inward Light* and also by many non-Quakers who saw the issue. One such reader was Haniel Long, who praised the poems "for all who think about their marriages." As to the writing and structure, he felt a "reverence for what is beautiful and perfect in itself." Sonnets being a more traditional and sometimes flowery form of poetry, he noted a difference in these in "the sincerity of the language, its freedom from the slightest touch of rhetoric, the diction, drawn not from books but from the world that people know today . . . all in an absolute sureness of feeling."[30]

Peggy managed to return to Edith's tribute in the summer, eventually sending a partial manuscript to Peter and Vel for their opinions. Peter liked it, but Vel thought she had used too many quotes from Edith's own writing. Peggy explained that they were needed to put Edith's personality and thoughts into the book. Eventually Vel was persuaded, but then progress stopped again. "Like so many other times," Peggy admitted, "I laid the book aside." It was too easy to let other commitments or temptations like an out-of-town trip take precedence.

At Thanksgiving Peggy and Ferm traveled to Phoenix. Hugh had been dating a young woman named Kathleen Decker for a number of months, and she had invited his parents for Thanksgiving dinner to meet her family. There was also an element of serendipity involved. While visiting the Deckers in Arizona, Peggy received word that her mother, Hazel Pond, had died. In a thank you letter to Kathleen, she explained what a blessing it was for her to be with Ferm when the news came. "If I had been home, he would have

Peggy Pond Church and Peter Miller near Otowi, ca. 1960. Edith and Tilano became godparents to Peter and her husband, Earle, at the time of their marriage, an arrangement taken seriously in the Pueblo culture. Thereafter, Peter always referred to Edith as godmother and to Tilano as godfather. Courtesy Los Alamos Historical Museum Archives.

been far away, and it's good to be with people you love in times of trouble. I loved meeting your father and mother. I was sure from knowing you they'd be grand people and they are."[31]

Three months later, Peggy sent another letter to Kathleen. "I just walked up the hill in a nice wet snowstorm, toting among other things a letter from Hugh which says, 'Kathleen is now officially your third future daughter,' and that made me feel so happy I sat down and cried." She set about accumulating "a few feathers" for their nest and wrote to tell Kathleen that she had put away for her "six sheets, six pillow cases, some new dish towels (among Granny's things), even (don't let this discourage you!) a beautiful dusting cloth!"[32]

The memories of her own shaky start in marriage no doubt prompted her to offer words of wisdom and advice to Kathleen from time to time, much as Ferm had written to Ted. "I think it is a good thing when we learn to trust ourselves to growth and not think that we can somehow make ourselves into whatever we want to be in a hurry." Peggy had learned that the hard way. "Do you know how diamonds are formed, by the way?" She answered her own question, telling of the soft, black carbon being altered by high temperatures deep in the earth. "It takes a long time and a lot of effort to make something so beautiful as diamonds out of that ugly stuff—and then lots of polishing and shaping of the rough stone to make it a jewel. Maybe that's one reason they are used for engagement rings—maybe to help us think how long it takes to make a finished human being—and a finished relationship between two human beings . . ." Then she added, from firsthand experience, "You'll have your moments of tension and fear—but it's what you make out of them that counts. I suppose you'll have lots of times when you haven't anything important to say to each other, but if you can start talking in the end, that's what counts—if you aren't afraid to get angry and sometimes even to hurt each other, and then learn understanding and love out of times of hurt—you'll go a long way to making the promise of the diamond come true."[33]

After the many months of not working on Edith's book, Peggy met with some of the scientists and wives at Los Alamos who had helped the San Ildefonso people build Edith's new house. "Their enthusiastic and humorous recollections brought Edith and Tilano alive for me once more," she said. "I managed to settle down and keep myself working at the book for the next three months." She completed the book on March 17, nearly four years after Edith's death and titled it *Finished in Beauty*.

May Sarton was visiting in Santa Fe when Peggy finished the manuscript, so she sent a copy to May and asked for her opinion. The reply she received was unexpected. May was frank in her evaluation. The book wasn't good enough. She told Peggy that she had talked too much about Edith rather than showing her. She should have presented Edith through her activities.[34]

"To correct the faults would mean not to revise this one but to write the whole thing over again, surely another year's work," she wrote in her journal. "The urge for the Edith book has left me . . . I know my fault and it seems impossible to overcome. When I think of trying to eradicate it . . . I am struck dumb." She put the book aside, and it would be two years before she returned to it.[35]

Peggy found solace in Allen's graduation from Stanford in electrical engineering that spring and also in the birth of his and Carolyn's first daughter, and her third grandchild, just weeks later. Nancy Church was born on July 13. Then, in an emotional turnaround, Peggy received word on July 18 that Florence Pond, her beloved Tante, had died in New York. She had last seen her aunt

Nancy Church enjoys the attention of grandparents Peggy and Ferm on the occasion of her first Christmas, Albuquerque, 1951. Courtesy Allen Church.

three years before, during the week she toured New York City before sailing for England. Tante had been frail even then, yet showing her usual strong, determined will. Peggy, along with sister, Dottie, and her husband; brother Ashley and his wife; and son Hugh, along with other family members, gathered in New York to handle the arrangements and settle an estate that included a luxurious apartment full of beautiful things to be divided among the heirs. Tante had been a kind and generous soul, but Peggy viewed her life as sad and lonely. Her fine, expensive possessions had served an upbringing that was "dominated by rules of taste and etiquette," but they had not brought her happiness. "The underprivilege of wealth," Peggy called it. "How much 'wealth' of feeling was locked within her that she was never able to express?"

> Miss Florence Louise Pond, member of an old
> American family and daughter of the late Ashley Pond,
> prominent Detroit lawyer, died here on Monday at her
> residence, 1220 Park Avenue. She was 88 years old.

What the *New York Times* obituary didn't say was that she "died friendless, her funeral attended only by her heirs and a few servants."

Peggy went back to Taos drained of emotion and energy, but she regrouped to make plans for a visitor in the fall. Her friend Jill was coming from England, and Peggy mapped out a typical Church family outing.

Jill Gyngell came just in time for San Geronimo Day. A Connecticut Yankee in King Arthur's Court couldn't have been more juxtaposed than a Londoner in the midst of Taos Pueblo on its annual feast day! Jill was about to experience the total immersion method for visiting New Mexico, but Peggy was certain she would love the color and pageantry set against the oldest and most beautiful pueblo in the Southwest, surrounded by the scenery of autumn! It couldn't have been better. Jill watched the traditional race of barefoot runners, the dances, and the entrance of the Koshares.[36] She felt the excitement building and was fascinated as it culminated in the climbing of the ceremonial pole. In particular, though, she was interested in the San Geronimo Church and listened closely as Peggy explained that it was built in 1850 to replace a previous church that had been destroyed in the Taos Rebellion. To an English woman, the date 1850 didn't seem so very old, but the structure of the church was the thing of interest, the adobe and design so very different from the stone cathedrals of Great Britain. The hand-smoothed lines of the walls, the carved wooden doors, the contrast of whitewashed adobe with the earth tones. The simplicity. The church was a lesson in beauty as well as in cultural differences.

After that auspicious beginning, Ferm joined them for a camping trip. They were off to Mesa Verde via Chama, Pagosa Springs, and Durango. In the afternoon they went to Cliff Palace and completed the circle drive to see pithouses and kivas and the spectacular Sun Temple. That night they pitched a borrowed tent at the park's campground. The moon was shining, so they all decided to sleep outside the tent under the star-filled sky, a rare option for someone from rainy England. In the middle of the night, the weather changed. Clouds moved in, and rain began to fall. They hustled to get the bedding into the tent and settled down again just as the rain stopped.

The next day they enjoyed lunch in Cortez before heading west to Hovenweep, a national monument "out in the middle of nowhere," as Peggy described it, but of interest because of the stone towers built along the edge of a canyon. They camped there for the second night under a clear sky and a nearly full moon. Another serene evening. In the night, the wind came up, blowing camp gear in various directions and sending cooking pots rolling toward the canyon rim! Peggy leaped out of her sleeping bag to chase them down in the moonlight.

From Hovenweep they headed for Monument Valley, planning to camp somewhere between Kayenta and Dennehotzo, but there was no firewood to be had. Ferm was set on a campfire, so they drove on. And on. The road was the worst that Peggy had ever traveled in a car. Finally, around midnight they found themselves in Shiprock, in a motel, with no firewood.

The three adventurers survived their trip, and Jill passed her course in Southwest 101 with flying colors to return home with a collection of memorable stories!

There was an amazing story in Taos that summer, too. "The latest excitement is that Taos had a bank robbery," Peggy told Hugh's fiancée, Kathleen, "and Ferm was in the bank at the time!" He'd gone into the small vault to open his safety deposit box when he turned and noticed the teller with his hands up. "The teller said out of the corner of his mouth, 'It's a holdup! Better put your hands up!'" Peggy explained. "So Ferm did. The robber collected the cash in a paper bag; then he locked Ferm and the teller in the little vault, and all the other people he sent into the big one but didn't lock it because they told him they'd suffocate if he did. Then he went out and crossed the plaza and jumped in a taxi and ordered the man to drive him out of town. The taxi driver ran out of gas on the hill above Pot Creek, and the robber ran away."[37] With an amusing camping trip followed by a bank robbery, life was picking up the pace in Taos.

Hugh finished his master's degree in meteorology at the University of California, Los Angeles, and he and Kathleen set a wedding date for February 25 in Phoenix. Peggy was already planning a trip to San Francisco for March to pursue her Jungian analysis, so she arranged to continue on to the Bay Area from the wedding. She thought she would stay in San Francisco for two months, but, as it turned out, she and Ferm made an unexpected decision. It suddenly seemed time for a change. They had been to the Bay Area on several visits and again when Ferm did a summer session at Stanford. They felt comfortable there. Within weeks, they had bought a house in Berkeley, and their Taos years came to an end. Berkeley offered a new setting, a change of routine, and the opportunity for Peggy to continue her analysis.

Chapter 11

Berkeley

"What poet could ever create if he were satisfied with the status quo?"

"I feel like something of a traitor," Peggy wrote to Corina as she looked out across Berkeley and the bay to the Golden Gate Bridge, "finding it all so beautiful." The weather was perfect, plum trees were in blossom, and she described spring as a "magical time of year" in California.[1] She had found a radio station that played only classical music and joined reading groups that were studying *The Tempest* and a Greek play. "It looks as though life might get awfully intellectual if I'm not careful!" she added playfully. Life was going well for Peggy in her first weeks in California.

After receiving that letter, Corina finally expressed her thoughts about Peggy's leaving. "I minded so much your going away," she said. "Now I think I understand. You have had what Taos can give you . . ." She knew that the small-town atmosphere had been binding. "You must ever be free to soar."[2]

The move to Berkeley was mentioned again in another letter from Corina a few months later when she admitted her "selfish interests" in writing. "I miss you more than I can say," she said. "I do not know if you were right in going, I only know nothing seems so wrong to me right now as to be in a rut." She understood that the restless spirit in Peggy, her poet side, needed change. "What poet could ever create if he were satisfied with the status quo?" All of Corina's observations spoke to the rightness of Peggy's decision to move to California.[3]

Peggy and Ferm both loved the Bay Area and the therapeutic nature of their new surroundings, but that didn't cancel out the bond they still had with New Mexico. "I was thinking of the feast of St. Francis and how beautiful the valley is at this time," Peggy revealed to Corina later in the autumn, "and how the days are so fast passing when people lived close to the earth." She missed seeing farmers working their land almost daily, the traditions in the little villages, and leaves turning color. Of her hillside home she said, "It is a beautiful and comfortable house—but my heart is still, somehow, in the one in Ranchos!"[4]

Her Christmas poem of 1956 began with excitement, but references to home crept into the phrases. "We've moved to a new house!" Peggy wrote, "halfway up a hillside, forty-seven steps from the mailbox," but it was clear that an adjustment was still being made, even after nine months, when Berkeley was still being compared with New Mexico and the Southwest.

> We look over dark trees and bright ones, like on the side of a canyon.
> It's funny how this reminds me of Mesa Verde.
> When I go down the steps each morning to pick up the paper
> I think of the cliff cities perched under ledges of sandstone
> the way we perch on the Berkeley hills . . .[5]

It would have been impossible not to reflect on home at times, but there were wonderful compensations. Peggy loved her view of Tamalpais, the Golden Gate looming out of the fog, and the bay at night looking like "a jeweled darkness." She attended lectures and concerts and took advantage of many of the opportunities a world-class city like San Francisco could provide. To her surprise, there was even a nearby neighbor from home. Lina Brown, Erna Fergusson's sister, lived a quarter of a mile away. She had bought Robert Oppenheimer's house at 1 Eagle Hill. They sometimes spoke of happenings in New Mexico, but in October of 1956, there was news that they both would rather not have heard. Alice and Haniel Long had died within three days of each other. Their deaths shook Santa Fe, and the shock reverberated all the way to Berkeley. For Peggy, the loss was deep.

Peggy wrote in her journal that night as though she were talking to Haniel. He had brought her back from a breakdown, saved her marriage, and brought out the poet in her. At least by her way of thinking he had done all of those things. "You who came most near to liberating the poet in me—the poet I stifled—how far I was from understanding. You rescued me once in your life; rescue me again in your death. As you found a half of yourself in me (for a time), I found my poet half in you." She lay awake, feeling "as though a thread were being pulled out of a pattern in my life."

Thoughts of Haniel continued in the days to come. They had shared so much through the years. He was a friend, a mentor, and a guiding force in her poetic life. One of his strong beliefs was that along with talent came obligation. "I simply could not accept the burden of that great golden harp you tried to make me carry," she said to him again in her journal. The illusion to the harp came from the book *Taliessin through Logres* by British poet Charles Williams, a collection of poetic tales of Taliessin, the legendary bard of King Arthur's court who carried a golden harp on his back. The music he played was so beautiful that it deeply affected all who heard it. The harp symbolized a gift, in the case of Peggy and Haniel, the gift of words. Haniel tried to explain to Peggy that with the gift came not only opportunity but also obligation to use the talent—to inspire, to invoke thought, and to further the appreciation of beauty. She had trouble seeing herself in that role as she did him. "You not only wrote poetry," she countered. "You *were* a poet. You not only were a poet, you were husband to your wife and love to many women."

He had responded to all of this in a letter once after they had been discussing the Taliessin poems.

> When you and I encountered each other in the
> rose garden, where every thorn brings tears, we ran
> into difficulties because we were identical in our
> poetic nature . . . and if we saved ourselves at all
> it was by the simple human desire to comfort and
> be comforted. That's why I don't particularly like
> it when people are so adolescent as to sneer at any
> form of this comfort the sexes give one another, or
> feel that the virginity of the soul is hurt in any way
> by what one does in the love that is admiration and
> compassion. The horn of the unicorn is neither here
> nor there, just something from fables and tapestries,
> but the weight of the great golden harps we have to
> carry through life is very real.[6]

As though he were truly there, in the house on a hill in Berkeley, she wrote, "It is a hard thing you are asking me to do. To change myself. To stop being the busy Quaker, to take up the harp again—to be *responsible* to the poet in myself."[7]

Apparently her rescue came, for within days Peggy found her poet within and wrote a three-part poetic tribute to Haniel and Alice that was printed in the Southwest Review and selected for the Best Poetry of 1957 by Borestone Mountain Poetry Awards.[8] Titled "Elegy in Three Movements," the poem expressed the beauty of their entwined lives, the aura of Haniel's greatness and mystery, and the mutual love between Alice and Haniel that had inspired and comforted so many of their friends. However, the highest praise for the poem, directed at the second movement, came from the people who knew Haniel best. "You have really caught the elusive being in Haniel," wrote May Sarton, and Ruth Swaine commented that Peggy had "handled a most difficult subject with delicacy and true understanding."[9]

The second movement of the poetic elegy made reference to a unicorn. The image was from "Taliessin's Song of the Unicorn," in which the mythical beast, likened to the poet, inspires humans to love.[10] Peggy used this image to her best advantage in explaining who Haniel truly was.

> I think he kept a unicorn
> in his garden, or even himself was
> partly a unicorn and reverted to the form at certain
> seasons, or under the influence of the moon . . .
>
> It was a difficult affliction
> to bear with the unicorn being
> something unclassifiable, mythological,
> not zoological in an age when
> almost no one believes in mythology.
> If Leda were to confess the swan rape or
> Danae blame her condition on a
> god in a ray of gold, you know what they'd be called now!
> So he was always careful to
> hide the flaw in this heredity from the literal-minded
> who were often a bit puzzled
> by the sharp rim of a hoofprint among the roses in the garden . . .[11]

Peggy walked down the forty-seven steps to her mailbox without much enthusiasm, but finding a letter from Dorothy McKibbin, she climbed back up with anticipation. She walked through the house and into her garden to read in the sunlight. She knew Dorothy would be writing to tell her of Santa Fe's reaction to the loss of Haniel and Alice. She sat down and opened the envelope.

> *November 2, 1956*
> *Dearest Peggy,*
>
> *When you return to Santa Fe you will find them*
> *here. You will know Haniel's smile and will see his*

*eyes crinkle up. And hear that laugh which was a
shout. And his voice with its sort of lovely monotony
. . . And Alice with her cup of tea and her smile.
And the visit with them, which was a resuscitation
of the spirit. So that when you leave the house you
don't actually walk. And you sing inside and are
warm. And you feel that if you had a large spear
you could joust.*

We shall never have less of them in us.

*Peggy looked up from the letter to a rose blooming near the house. Haniel
had loved roses. He had loved gardening. Behind his tall adobe wall was an
oasis, a realm of beautifully pruned trees and shrubs. A tiny orchard with apples,
pears, apricots, peaches, cherries in the company of white and blue hyacinths and
crocuses in the spring. Yellow jasmine and peonies prolonged color into summer.
She could see him there, adding a certain magic . . .*

Peggy looked back at the letter.

*Alice's illness was long. Hardening of the arteries
which went so long that she had to go to the hospital
because Haniel was not able to take care of her, to
help her. And the doctor thought he might black
out any moment. A pitiful situation. So she went to
the hospital on what he thought would be a long,
long run. That she would be ill for a long time. And
therefore he should have his operation so that he
could come back and take care of her.*

*I understand that when he left, she said she might
never see him again. His reply, "Then perhaps you
will come and join me."*

*[Their son] Tony, as you know, was with Alice when
she died, and then flew to Rochester and was with
Haniel.*

*Some time when we are together, old friend, I will
tell you of the service . . . It was an occasion which
could have happened only in Santa Fe. And how
Haniel would have loved it . . .*

*Love,
Dorothy[12]*

*She returned the letter to its envelope. She sat for a long time, wondering
what Haniel would think of this very different garden. Baskets of flowers hung
from the wooden latticework that sheltered the small patio. Verdant foliage filled
the yard. The arbor was covered with fuchsia in bloom, and hydrangeas and lilies
bordered the house. She had planted hyacinths recently in the raised bed along the
stone wall that separated her small yard from her neighbors. One of the things she
liked about California was the ease of growing flowers and the profusion of color.
Finally, she walked toward the house, unconsciously looking for the sharp rim of a
hoofprint beneath the roses, half believing that someday she would see one.*

The last lines of Movement I of the elegy summed up what everyone felt
about the deaths so close together.

> How shall we say it was not a happy ending
> for the two whose lives were joined into one music?
> The last chord sounds:
> the musician's hands fall slowly,
> and every discord now resolves in silence.

Peggy felt the loss for many years to come. In a letter to her friend May
Sarton almost three decades later, she still spoke of Haniel. "Strange how the past
continues an existence of its own. Parts of our past we never quite outgrow."[13]

To pursue her search for self with the Jungian analysts in the Bay Area was
one of Peggy's reasons for moving to Berkeley. She still needed to get past
poor parental relationships, to continue strengthening her marriage, and to
feel better about herself. She knew that the keys to unlocking her frustrations

would be found in her childhood experiences. She had always remembered a day when she and her sister had hidden treasured bits of pottery and glass and little toys at the base of a tree in Pajarito Canyon. "I said I could never go back to find them," she wrote in her journal. "Perhaps I was wrong. Perhaps I *can* go back—to retrieve fragments of my own personality, denied or left behind."

From the time she was very young, Peggy internalized everything and was hurt too easily by comments or actions that she should have brushed off. As an adult, she knew this about herself, but in her childhood she couldn't have recognized the fact. Therefore, a series of words and incidents had shaped who she was and how she reacted to others. It was time to revisit all the hurtful things and decide what the effects were on her personality and what she could do about them. Her analyst put it in clear, concise words: "When you have changed your childhood, come back to me."

> Was there no one at all but herself, no one at all
> Aware of the terrible beauty of her world?
> Was she the only one who heard it call —
> That voice behind the stars, that song of the wind?[14]

In the poem "Thirteen Years Old," written from the perspective of an adult, Peggy had given words to her childhood feelings of separation from family and friends who didn't have the same sensitivities to their surroundings or the need to find the words to describe them. "To find yourself liking and writing poetry at thirteen or fourteen," Peggy decided, "is to find yourself suddenly set apart from the companionship of your peers. Was it the loneliness that started the poetry or the poetry that started the loneliness?" As a child, being labeled as different was devastating, but as an adult the problem had lessened. Her differences as a poet and an intuitive person were respected, and other poets had come into her life as friends and colleagues. There was only one place where the separation was still keenly felt, and that was in her relationship with Ferm. They had always viewed the world in different terms. Where he saw essential forms, she saw metaphors. He lacked imagination, something that was almost constant in her. He wasn't able to change any more than she was, so what would be the solution? In what situations did they come closest to seeing things alike? When put like that, the answer was easy. They shared an equal passion for the western landscape—the lonely places, the shorelines with their crashing waves, the forest with only birds breaking the silence. "When we were together on picnics or journeys, how happy we were," Peggy realized, and "when I was beside him and we both were enjoying a beautiful sound or beautiful music, we were very close." Those times had to be her focus for the marriage. She would eventually write in her journal that "after the Berkeley analysis, we had many happy times together."

Peggy thought deeply about her days in Pajarito Canyon, when she and Dottie both "revolted against dolls and against hair ribbons and excessively feminine dresses" and would have liked to have been boys. They both loved nature and the freedom of the outdoors, the kind of life they saw their father living. They also saw the resentment held by their mother at her captivity imposed by three children and the customary role expected of women. Peggy and her sister were ahead of their time in wanting both roles at once, wanting to achieve a blend of female gentleness and masculine assertiveness. The world they saw was not to their liking, and that was another thing that made Peggy feel at odds with the people around her. In Pajarito Canyon, both she and Dottie escaped into fantasy. Peggy remembered being "immersed in fairy tales" as an escape to another world, one that she could control. Her early poetry was full of fairies and wood nymphs. "Even at Smith College I hadn't shaken the dryads off!" she admitted. She thought, too, of the "lifelong rift" between herself and her sister, "each of us projecting onto the other our own frustrations, each of us envying the other for success or superiority in ways in which we were weak." They competed for parental love, even though there wasn't much of it to win. By their teenage years, they both felt rejected. Who were these parents that she needed to understand from the distance of decades?

"My mother, too, had been once a free young spirit, playful, a young Artemis, perhaps filled with drama, reading poetry," Peggy wrote in her journal in regard to her mother's situation. "And how she loved Zane Grey and the Tarzan stories!" She thought of a photograph that showed her mother when she was perhaps twelve, sitting in a hay wagon, holding a rifle. Another picture showed a carefree teenager striking funny poses with friends at the beach. How different that young girl was from the person who slapped her children's hands when they touched the polished furniture! When did she turn so cold? Her mother's personality changed when she married too young, Peggy realized, becoming both the executive of the family and the domestic without "having ever a life of her own." She remembered a terrible statement that her mother had made once. Tending to Peggy while she was visiting and taken ill, her mother confessed, "I have never done anything because I loved to, but only because of duty."

Focusing on her father, Peggy listed the issues surrounding the "tempestuous, passionate man, whom I both loved and feared." In certain situations, Ashley could show tenderness but only when "someone or something was suffering." Under such circumstances, "his heart was easily touched." Peggy knew that "men in his day were victims of a stereotype," expected to be manly. They were not allowed to develop the womanly side of themselves that might show tender emotion or feelings. And yet, she remembered that two of her father's favorite books to read to his children were *Mopsa, the Fairy* and *The Prince and the Pauper* and that he occasionally composed rhymes and read poetry to them. He was not only a victim of stereotyping but also of a stern and cold father who was a poor role model in how to be a parent.

In regard to her parents, it was time for at least understanding if not forgiveness. With her parents both gone, the pain of the past could not be worked through entirely, but she could still make amends with Dottie. It was long past time, and the opportunity was finally at hand with her sister living only three hours away.

Dottie was living on a ranch outside Chico, California, with her second husband, Courtney Benedict. Each had endured an unpleasant first marriage and waited long enough to be certain of the second. They adored each other and shared a simple life based on their love of the outdoors. Dottie's attraction to horses that began in Pajarito Canyon as a young girl continued throughout her life. She raised and showed Arabians and was "an amazing rider." Her love for her horses even extended to "retrieving ones she had sold if she felt they were not being cared for properly!"[15] A number of other critters roamed the ranch. Dogs, cats, chickens, ducks, geese, strays, and rescues of every two and four-legged kind were ever present, and they all had names. Peggy began to visit the ranch and became reacquainted with her bohemian, free-spirited sister. She liked what she saw, in both Dottie and herself.

Dottie and Courtney never seemed to slow down during the day, but in the evenings "they relaxed with homemade applejack (deadly strong) and sit-down meals with conversation." They were avid readers of almost everything and were always willing to advocate for a cause in which they believed. They were also "politically active, socialist in an idealistic way," and, in retrospect, observed one niece, "rather childlike and innocent."[16]

Peggy remembered when Dottie "seemed so locked in herself as a little girl. One could feel her seething with furies inside her to which she never gave voice as I did in my fits of tempestuous rage." It was good to see her finally at peace and living a life she loved. The reconciliation between the sisters

Peggy, Ashley, and Dottie in a rare reunion at Dottie's ranch in Chico, California, ca. 1958. Courtesy of Ashley D. Pond and Family.

lasted, and their visits continued even after Peggy returned to New Mexico and Dottie and Courtney moved to a ranch at Grants Pass, Oregon.

The importance of the reunion with her sister and the regret for their lost years can be seen in "Perhaps in Our Old Age," a poem Peggy wrote for Dottie.

> Perhaps in our old age,
> we can return again to being children,
> return to our playful places,
> to the magic world we were once part of
>
> . . . .
>
> Let us unearth our childhood
> like a bone hidden and long forgotten

by an old dog, and gnaw the marrow of it
and bring the taste back again
of those times when our imaginations ran free
and every straight stick became a pony
and our real ponies steeds of fire.[17]

*By the second Christmas in Berkeley, the new environment was more familiar,
but the holiday still seemed incomplete without New Mexico traditions. Then,
unexpectedly, two boxes arrived. Peggy untied the ribbon from the first one, a box
sent from a local floral company. Inside she found beautiful red roses with a card
from Corina, and tucked in with them was tree holly added by the florist. After
removing brown paper and string from the second package, she discovered that Lou
had collected twigs and sprigs of juniper and mistletoe and sagebrush. Decorations
from Taos! Before Peggy knew it the house was filled with reminders of home. She
put the roses in a tall, green pitcher and placed them on one side of the fireplace.
At the other end of the room she put a white pottery Madonna and Child in the
center of a black plate that Tony Reyna, a friend from Taos Pueblo, had given her.
Around the plate, she made a wreath of Lou's evergreens and the holly. Instead of
a Christmas tree, there was a large poinsettia in a pot wrapped in crimson foil. It
sat on a chest in front of the picture window that looked out over the bay, radiant
in the afternoon sun. Red holly berries and red candles completed the picture and
looked rich against the dark, polished wood that dominated the room. She had her
traditional Christmas after all, but "No Snow," Peggy lamented in a thank you
note to Corina. "Everyone is rushing off to the mountains to ski—but it takes four
hours to get there, and when I go to the mountains I don't want to go in crowds,
but alone, or with you." Peggy shared a memory from a time they had gone to U.S.
Hill near Taos. "It's a place in my inner country," she told Corina, realizing that
she could always go back, just as she could always have a New Mexico Christmas
in the Berkeley Hills.[18]*

The first years in Berkeley were a period of inner change. While Peggy continued
analysis off and on for several more years, she had begun to struggle free of

the past and add new dimensions to her life. She and Ferm began to enjoy a new compatibility and the sharing of many good times—concerts, opera, Shakespeare at Ashland, visits to Dottie, and meals at The Nut Tree along the way.[19] They took memorable drives up the Mendocino coast and to the Olympic Rain Forest. And as they did with music, they approached their travel experiences with a "silent sharing," creating their own kind of communication. They were elated, too, to have a fourth grandchild in the family. Janet Church was born in 1958, a second daughter for Allen and Carolyn.

Eventually, many loose ends came together, with one of the most important being the unfinished manuscript that "wasn't good enough." Peggy finally returned to her work on Edith Warner's memoir. She accepted May Sarton's challenge and began rewriting the book. In so doing, she took another large step toward healing. While working on the first draft in Taos, Peggy had noted in her journal, "As I write about you, Edith, I keep learning things about myself." In the end, *The House at Otowi Bridge* was a reexamining of self as much as a biographic glimpse of Edith Warner, and what emerged was a beautiful story destined to become a classic.

Chapter 12

The Making of a Classic
"The Bridge Is Out!"

As it turned out, reworking the manuscript about Edith wasn't the struggle that Peggy had expected. When she moved to Berkeley, she put the work off for more than two years. She would take the manuscript out occasionally and try to work on it but end up putting it back on the shelf. In the beginning, Berkeley was "an exciting new environment that took a lot of exploring and enjoying." Then one day, in October of 1957, a friend asked her about the book she was writing. "The book I don't seem able to write," Peggy countered, "and that I can't rest happy till I do." Nevertheless, she told the friend a bit about the book. Thinking afterward about the exchange led Peggy to return to writing about Edith in her journal. She began to see a new approach for the book. She needed to emphasize the importance of the two ways of life between which Edith had lived—the Indians with their culture and spirituality rooted in the belief that we must live in harmony with nature and the atomic scientists who used the power of man's mind to control nature. "Yet they too—the physicists—loved the land," she thought, "the landscape, and the feeling that Edith and Tilano gave them of rootedness."[1]

In her journal, she contrasted these concepts, describing first Edith and her environment. Some of the words from the journal pages became part of the book. "She walks in her brown moccasins, the soft buckskin lapped over at the ankle with a silver button," Peggy wrote. "She is thin and straight. She moves gracefully and precisely with the economy of movement of a feeding deer. She is self-effacing, too, like a wild animal that instinctively melts itself into a pattern of a leaf-shadow." Then she considered what parts of Edith's world and her activities she should show to make her come alive within the context of that spiritual world that existed with nature. She jotted down ideas. "She lives her daily life with her feet on the ground, her hands among the fruits. The river is a singing river; the mesas are rooted earth-powers; the wild geese are the sign of measure and returning cycles—the mariposa lily—the gathering of pine knots . . ."

Peggy's comments on the control of nature in the form of nuclear energy were harsh. Her upbringing and her Quaker beliefs made it clear which philosophy she favored. The journal read, "We've lived with it for nearly twelve years: the mushroom cloud of the atom bomb; the evil, flattened head of a venomous snake, an eruption like a disembodied volcano, a gushing up out of nothing, a gush of light, fountain of naked fire, as though a thundercloud were to flash into solid lighting . . ."

In the spring of 1958, she removed the manuscript from the shelf and took a long look at it. She concluded that the book needed only to be reorganized and touched up. Within weeks she had made the changes she felt were necessary, and what resulted was a dual memoir. Peggy had observed early in her writing that she "could not be truly objective. I kept connecting Edith with me," she admitted, but rather than detracting from the story, that helped place Edith in the setting of people as well as the land. In the end, the book came together beautifully.

On a trip to Albuquerque that summer to visit her sons and their families, Peggy showed the manuscript to Erna Fergusson, long-time friend and respected New Mexico author. Erna immediately showed it to her friend Roland Dickey, director of the University of New Mexico Press. He accepted it "almost at once" for publication in the *New Mexico Quarterly*, the university's literary magazine.[2]

As Peggy put it, "Mr. Dickey didn't give me much chance to linger complacently on cloud nine." When she went back to Berkeley, she had a list of changes and additions that he wanted completed in six weeks! The first thing on the list was a new title. The manuscript had been presented with the working title *Finished in Beauty*. That changed before she ever left New Mexico. Sitting on the platform of the Belen train station, waiting to leave for Berkeley, Peggy decided to call the book *The House at Otowi Bridge*.[3]

Exchanges between Peggy and her editor continued through the next five months. Dickey worked on the manuscript at his home on Lobo Place in the evenings, so as to avoid interruptions and have the quietness he felt to be a "necessity for this piece." In a letter to Peggy, he wrote, "I have rarely seen anything which was so of one piece and one mood, and therefore editing calls for almost complete recall of details and structure. This is *good* . . . so few things have this marvelous quality, and I find myself disappearing completely into the world of Edith Warner . . ."[4]

Dickey was a skilled editor. He took the time to teach and point out subtleties of word usage in addition to the usual errors of spelling, punctuation, and repetitive words. In view of too many adjectives in the manuscript, no doubt a natural mistake for a poet, he compared the overuse and the loss of effectiveness to a baroque church in which "it is difficult to focus upon a single ornament, and the excess is a little cloying." He showed how "a bit of judicious trimming will increase the total impact" and how "substituting strong verbs" can decrease the need for qualifying adjectives. He grasped the fact that Edith "drew her strength from the land itself" and made sure everything in the manuscript supported that premise. "The whole thing borders on what might be called religious experience," he commented, and edited with care "to cleave to the essentials of the experience" and remove phrasing that bordered on "preaching." Peggy realized her good fortune in having Roland Dickey as her editor, and when the book was published, she wrote an article for *New America* magazine in which she credited him as being a fine example of a gifted editor and stated "how much Roland Dickey contributed to the building of a sturdy Bridge."[5]

Dickey was complimentary as well. "I was constantly plunged deep beneath the surface of the manuscript," he remarked, "lost completely in that San Ildefonso world, which makes for rather poor perspective on the part of the editor, but reveals the power of the author. It is a very, very fine book, and I think I have been changed by working with it . . ."[6]

The House at Otowi Bridge was first released in two installments in the *New Mexico Quarterly*, complete with the illustrations by Connie Fox Boyd. It was the first book-length work published in the *Quarterly*, and the first installment went on sale in the 1958 winter issue. Readers had to wait until the next issue in the spring of 1959 to finish the story, at which time Peggy began to receive letters of praise for what she had written.

"I knew it would be beautiful," said an admirer after reading *The House at Otowi Bridge*, "and I looked forward to getting acquainted with Edith Warner because I had only heard of her and never met her, but I had not known that it would be a song of New Mexico and of the Indians, and the story of your soul and mine and of all people who love New Mexico."[7]

The release of the installments in the *Quarterly* initiated a flood of letters in praise of the piece, some being short memoirs in themselves, from people who had known Edith or Peggy or both. Many of the accolades came from her fellow writers in both Taos and Santa Fe. If there had been any doubt in Peggy's mind that the book was anything but a success, these letters would have convinced her otherwise.

April 15, 1959

Dear Peggy—

The enclosed clipping by way of telling you how much I enjoyed the first few chapters of The House

at Otowi Bridge—and that I'm looking forward to
the next installment.

> Affectionately,
> Spud [Johnson]

Dearest Peggy—

A quote from Fray Angelico Chavez—

"The Peggy Pond Church piece on Edith Warner is
superb. More on it when I return your copy of the
Quarterly."

I'll send on his additional comment when I get it.

> With love,
> Erna [Fergusson]

> June 1, 1959

Dear Peggy—

. . . I, too, had been in that house, had known that
I was face to face with a great soul . . . Only a poet
could have written The House at Otowi Bridge.

> Dorothy Pillsbury

> June 26, 1959

Dear Peggy—

Your second quarterly is out, and people are loving
it . . . The first is out of print . . . Everyone is
talking and looking forward to the book, and your
story of Edith is in the air, where it should be,
with the clouds, the moving rain, and the sun . . .
everything is alive and loved, and Edith is
there, and you.

> [The Oppenheimers] both said that you re-created
> the spirit of the country and of Edith poignantly.
>
> Dorothy [McKibbin][8]

Shortly after the second installment was released, copies were given to the university's publications committee so that *The House at Otowi Bridge* could be considered for printing in book form. Roland Dickey made the final decision for the content of the *Quarterly* but not for the selection of books for the press. However, he admitted years later that he had done everything possible to tip the scales in favor of *Otowi Bridge*. He knew that if he proved the book could be a moneymaker for the press, it had a better chance, so he over-printed the two issues of the *Quarterly* in the belief that it would sell. That enabled him to report high sales figures for those issues. In addition, he designed the pages of *Otowi Bridge* as though they were a separate book but in such a way that they would blend well with the usual format for the *Quarterly*. As a result, no extra cost would be incurred for setting the type should the press choose to publish the book. Needless to say, the financial picture convinced the committee. *The House at Otowi Bridge* would become a University of New Mexico Press book.[9]

With a second chance to make changes, Peggy spoke to Dickey about the line drawings used with her installments in the *Quarterly*. She hadn't particularly liked them. "Having lived so long in Edith's world, I had my own way of seeing it, and Connie simply hadn't seen it the way I did," Peggy admitted. Ferm "objected strenuously" to the illustrations, and other friends had voiced negative opinions. Vel Ludlow didn't think there should be any drawings at all and offered to send some photographs instead. Peggy wrote to Dickey on Vel's behalf and suggested photographs. He replied, "I felt the drawings had just the right amount of strength and simplicity, and reflected my own feeling for the country, since Mrs. Boyd did the drawings on the spot." He didn't want to make a final decision just yet but added that photographs should absolutely not be used.[10]

His reasoning against photographs was valid. "A photograph is of one place and one time . . ." he pointed out. "With some exceptions . . . Weston and Ansel Adams, perhaps . . . most photographs tie down the imagination rather than free it." He felt strongly, too, that the book should not be illustrated (as opposed to decorated), adamantly saying that the book "stands on its own."

Many readers have "their own recollections of the Otowi country," and the line drawings are simply reminiscent of those memories rather than attempts at reproductions.[11] After sending the issue back and forth for several months and postponing decisions, Peggy finally bowed to Dickey's expertise, and the drawings stayed.

With that disruption resolved, another one followed close behind, but it had nothing to do with publishing the book. In late September 1959, Ferm's job recalled him to New Mexico. Peggy decided to come along for what would be a two- to three-month stay, but after being back for that long, they both realized that they wanted to stay permanently. At first it seemed the move would come at a bad time, with the book projected to have a pre-Christmas release, but the press date was delayed. And delayed. As the next September approached and the book was still not out, Peggy began to lose patience. She knew that the press was understaffed and had experienced unexpected problems, but the wait was wearing thin.

Finally the project began to move forward again. Proofs arrived and, with them, a question. It was a relief to have the final phase under way, but the question collided with one of Peggy's pet peeves.

"Would you fill out the enclosed biographical sheet . . . ?" Dickey asked innocently. There was no response for three weeks. Finally, Peggy returned the page proofs and enclosed the form.

> Here, too, is the biographical memo—which I think is just plain silly! Who cares about all these banal details anyway? . . . What a holy cow we make of our formal education when most of what we end up knowing we haven't learned at school at all. The books I have read since I left school, the people I have met, the insight gained in analysis, the joy of traveling in the United States, up and down the backbone of the Rocky Mountains and the Pacific Coast, are much more a part of me than those long-ago left-behind school days. I think Shakespeare and Bach and the Bible (read as literature) have been my most persistent teachers. And not touring Europe but entertaining European and Asiatic friends at my own breakfast table! What a lack of degrees and military experience and prizes

and honors, but quite a lot of experience in just being a human being. I studied astronomy when I was at Smith and learned to call quite a lot of stars by their Greek names, along with the Greek alphabet which I have since forgotten! But what I still know about the stars are the names of the constellations my mother pointed out to me and the Greek legends that went with them. And think of all one learns from living in the Indian world, from sleeping on the ground at Hovenweep and shivering at the Shalako! No, it seems to me these biographical facts have nothing at all to do with the price of beans! But for whatever they are worth, here they are. Good luck.[12]

If nothing else, Peggy's response demonstrated the rapport she and Roland Dickey had developed in almost two years of working together and exchanging letters.

"Thank you for your always good letter," Dickey calmly said, "and for your reaction to standard biographies." He very tactfully left out all references on the cover to formal education and made mention of Shakespeare, Bach, the Bible, and Indians!

On November 18, 1960, Peggy's journal entry read: "THE BRIDGE IS OUT."

The accolades began again. The first was actually presented to the original publication in the *Quarterly. The House at Otowi Bridge* had won a 1959 Longview Literary Award, one of thirty-three such awards given each year for literature published in small magazines and collections.

Roland Dickey followed that with high praise for his author in a note to Claire Morrill of the Taos Book Shop when he thanked her for an invitation to a book signing. "We feel that *The House at Otowi Bridge* is one of the most remarkable books that we have had the privilege of publishing, and we feel that it will gain not only regional but national recognition," he wrote. "Certainly it is a sensitive work, beautifully written."[13]

Peggy added an addendum to Dickey's comments in her *New America* article. "Since Roland didn't go on to say sensitively edited and beautifully designed and produced by Roland Dickey of the University of New Mexico Press, I will take the liberty of saying it for him at long last. It does take two, at least, to build a bridge!" And in the acknowledgements in the front of the book, she credited someone else who had played a large role in making *The House at Otowi Bridge* a better book. She wrote, "I owe more than I can say to May Sarton for her severe and loving criticism of the first draft." With that statement, Peggy closed the circle on one of her most important life experiences.

A wider audience had access to *The House at Otowi Bridge* in book form, and more letters began arriving.

May 11, 1961

I like the way you have wound your own story into the pages with the other story. You and Edith each make the other's part in the narrative more vitally inherent.

Yours ever, Hal [Bynner]

1967

Dear Mrs. Church:

Thank you for making it possible for me to take my remembering heart "back home" for a little yesterday.

Yes, Miss Warner was a remarkable woman. But it seems to me the fine book evidences that another of grace has made a pretty enriching, gratifying pilgrimage in life.

Your father had a magnificent dream. I am glad to have been one of its beneficiaries . . . and there is none, I vow, who has drawn more life-long value from the experience.

It has been a long trail since my first trip up the Mesa in June of 1925. It has led many places to many wonderful environs, but none has been "heart's home" to the same extent or degree. No other place has ever matched . . .

James M. Gilchrist, Jr.
December 1, 1960

Dearest Peggy,

I don't believe there will be another Christmas present like yours that came day before yesterday—the beautiful enriching book, how much it brings me, of you, of Edith and Tilano, and of the place where I have felt closest to earth and sky, and most blessed . . .

Happy Christmas, dearest Peggy.

Love always, May [Sarton]

January 25, 1961

No one except a sensitive poet like yourself could have written this book and woven into it such deep understanding. You have written a beautiful and moving interpretation for all of us who love New Mexico.

Ruth Laughlin[14]

The people who had known Edith and Los Alamos before the war had gone through a painful time of change, and the loss of Edith was, for many, the culmination of their pain. Their world would never be the same again, but the finest parts of that former world would live on within the pages of the book. The people of wartime Los Alamos and those who stayed afterward mourned Edith, too. *The House at Otowi Bridge* represented a closure for them all.

Chapter 13

The Santa Fe Years
"The landscape has a being of its own."

It seemed natural to be back in New Mexico. At the same time, Peggy observed, in a letter to May Sarton, "I find it so strange to be living again in Santa Fe, where I've been only a visitor since 1924 when I married." To others, the length of time didn't matter. People still recognized her and remembered her family's presence in Santa Fe, even though her father had been dead for almost three decades and her mother had moved to Taos many years before. "Out for a walk one day, I was stopped by the mailman," she told May. He said, "Mrs. Church, do you remember me?" Peggy didn't, though she had learned his name at Christmas so that she could give him a small gift. He was Arthur Ortiz, and he continued, "Your father used to take me fishing with him a lot." He spoke of Ashley and how he had founded the fire department. He asked about her sister and brother, and then he said, "You still look very much like your mother." Within days, it happened again. While having dinner in a restaurant, Peggy put on her glasses and bent down to look at a book. "Oh, how much you look like your mother when you do that," the hostess said. Peggy had never been keen on looking like her mother, but she was, indeed, home again.[1]

Within weeks of moving back to Santa Fe, Peggy was invited to an evening with the Baumanns to read poetry with old friends, including Witter Bynner and Winfield Scott and his wife, Ellie. As usual, there was much talk of old times in the conversation.

"Why don't we get together and write a petition against paving the upper end of the Acequia Madre?"

"Why do they have to pave all the streets?"

"Why don't they leave us some bare ground to walk on?"

"Because there are so many people now," Peggy said, "and they all drive cars fast and spread the dust around." She quoted the evening paper. "By 1980 they estimate the population of Santa Fe will be 67,000! It's 34,000 now, almost five times as many as when I came to live in Santa Fe as a little girl of thirteen and used to ride my horse up and down Palace Avenue and play jacks in front of the bank on the plaza."

Ellie Scott commented that if worse came to worst they could always move on.

Everyone looked at her, and someone asked, "Where to?"

Peggy knew the answer. She had just lived somewhere else for five years, a place where she had been happy in a beautiful setting, but there was no place like Santa Fe.

Peggy settled easily into her new routine, and Ferm returned to familiar terrain in his work as a field engineer, designing and staking power lines and substations for rural electric cooperatives throughout the Southwest. He traveled in the first months to Twining, No Agua, Nambé, Gobernador, and Jemez Pueblo in New Mexico and to areas around Creede in Colorado. For him, the best part of the job was being outdoors much of the time in beautiful surroundings and solitude. "I can't count the miles I have hiked over mountains, mesas, and deserts," he once remarked. Many times he returned to special places he had worked and took Peggy with him.

They bought a home on Victoria Street in an older section of Santa Fe that still had the old, familiar atmosphere of unpaved roads and adobe houses, and Peggy rented a small stone hut on the back of neighbor Ed Pigeon's property to use as a new poem cabin. With the tendency for nicknames in the Church family, the hut was soon referred to as the Pigeon Coop. Peggy was eager to return to poetry after her venture into prose.

After moving into the new house and getting it organized, Peggy's thoughts turned to something else she wanted. "I was paying my habitual visit to the animal shelter, driven by some instinct, feeling the lack in the human being for an animal," she explained in her journal, when in one of the outdoor pens among the tangle of puppies she saw "two furry Teddy bears, one tan, one white." Even better, the attendant told her they were Samoyeds. She had wanted one for years. "At least the pup was partly Samoyed," Peggy said, setting the record straight. "We named her Poli-kota, White Butterfly in Hopi, because at eight weeks, and only perhaps eight inches long, she bounced about so lightly she hardly seemed to touch the ground." Ferm was on the road for days at a time, and a dog would keep her company and go along on hikes. Poli, as she came to be called, was the companion Peggy had hoped for. On good days, Peggy would pack a sandwich and her usual baby food jar filled with sherry, and off they would go to some favorite trail. Carrying a pocket-size spiral notebook, she would stop occasionally to record thoughts or lines for a poem, while Poli delighted in examining everything in the range of her nose. They made a good team, and eventually, as with so many of Peggy's friends, Poli got her own poem, "White Dog with Mushrooms."[2]

The first years back in Santa Fe were also a time of travel and catching up with friends and family. Peggy and Ferm returned to the Bay Area more than once and went to Boston for an overdue visit with Ferm's brother Vallette and his family as well as a reunion with Lawrence Hitchcock and his wife. In addition, there were two longer trips for Peggy that greatly expanded her horizons. In 1961 she had the opportunity to attend another Quaker meeting overseas. She flew east, stopping first to see Peter Miller on her farm in Pennsylvania, and continued on to London, where she met Margaret Gibbons at the Britain Yearly Meeting. From there, it was on to Paris for a few days and then south to the Dordogne region of France to meet up with small groups of Friends, including Jill Gyngell, who would be staying in villages and on farms with host Quaker families.

～

As the Britain Yearly Meeting of 1961 came to a close, Margaret Gibbons handed Peggy a list of names and contact information for Friends in various parts of France. "These might be useful," she said. The second part of Peggy's summer trip was about to take her across the English Channel to Paris and on to stay with a Quaker family in the Dordogne. From London, where she had stayed with her friend Jill Gyngell, she was eager to brave new ground, but upon landing in Paris, her confidence quickly downgraded to panic. Everyone was jabbering away in French, and the confusion in the airport was overwhelming. She took a deep breath, removed her pocket dictionary from her purse, and forged on. After a few attempts to communicate, her pronunciation and her confidence improved. She checked into her hotel, a little tired but determined to beat the cold she had acquired as a souvenir of England. However, as days passed, she felt worse and worse. Coming in from an afternoon of exploring museums, she stopped at the hotel desk and mentioned that she wasn't well. A kind woman appeared at her door to check on her. "Ah, la grippe!" she said. So that's how they say "flu" in French, Peggy thought, and wondered what they called a sinus infection. The woman left and returned with soup and a pitcher of water and continued to reappear from time to time, taking care of Peggy's needs. Despite the kindness, Peggy continued to feel weaker and was sure she had a fever, so finally she sent a note to a woman whose name Margaret had given her.

Marguerite Czarnecki owned the Quaker Center in Paris, and she came right away. She got Peggy into the American Hospital at Neuilly-sur-Seine, where she was treated with antibiotics and stayed for two days. Peggy carried with her the trusty pocket dictionary and, as she would explain to friends later, "managed to cope pretty well, even with the French doctor who laid his ear on my chest instead of using a stethoscope!"

When Peggy had recovered, Marguerite put her in a taxi, accompanied her to the station, and saw her settled on the train to her next destination, even showing her how to get a ticket for the first serving in the dining car. Reflecting on the care and concern of Marguerite and the hotel staff, people she hadn't even met before, Peggy thought, "Aren't people wonderful!"

Six and a half hours later, she found herself in the Dordogne looking out the window at a rich and rolling countryside passing by. Fields were beautifully tended, and families were working together in the midst of a wheat harvest. There were even large, wooden wagons drawn by oxen. The scene was an Impressionist painting come to life! A few tractors and combines were in use, but most of the harvesting was being done in the old way. On the farm where she stayed with other Quakers, she was in a typical, old stone farmhouse, with living quarters on the second floor above sheds and storerooms. A living room and kitchen were combined in a central room, with a bedroom on each end. The rooms were furnished with immense, heavy furniture—roperos and trasteros and miscellaneous chests. Her favorite of all the furnishings was a large, cello-shaped grandfather clock that insisted on striking twice about three minutes apart, whatever the hour! She awoke in the mornings to the sound of the eccentric clock and to French roosters crowing.

The Quakers from Britain, including Jill, were staying in other farmhouses and nearby villages. Peggy met up with them most days to browse outdoor markets for milk, long loaves of bread, country fresh butter, vegetables, peaches, and anything that struck their fancy for a good lunch. Together they would eat in fields or on the banks of a river at midday, and in the evenings, they dined in small wayside restaurants with outdoor tables, sitting under a tree or sometimes a grape arbor, always with a good local wine. In the afternoons there were quaint villages and centuries-old churches to explore.

Peggy was having a "lovely, lovely summer" when she found a moment to write to Corina from Magnol, prés Puybrun, but she admitted, "I'm finding myself eager to get home now. One can spend just so long drifting and visiting and rootless and then longs for the familiar routine of one's own life and to tend the flowers in one's own garden." New Mexico was calling.³

Four years later Peggy crossed the Atlantic again, traveling with Dorothy McKibbin. They had a wonderful time touring Spain and Egypt. "I recall the daybreak in Luxor when I woke to the call of the muezzin, the crowing of a cock, the onslaught of hot consuming day breaking over the cool edge of night," Peggy recorded in her journal. "I am glad I had that experience of another ancient land, another climate, so remote in tradition from my own . . . to feel my way back into the past along the fertile and irrigating Nile." But once again, she was more than ready to return home. To May Sarton she wrote, "When I was in Cairo I longed to get back to New Mexico and go into a canyon away from people and lie under a pine tree."[4]

Staying at home was satisfying for Peggy, and there was never a shortage of friends arriving on her own doorstep, among them Gay Young-Hunter Kuster, who returned to New Mexico often, and Margaret Gibbons, who came a second and third time from Scotland. During their first decade back in Santa Fe, youngest son, Hugh, and his wife, Kathleen, presented Peggy and Ferm with three more grandchildren—Julia, born in 1963, Eric in 1964, and Leigh in 1968. Spending time with their growing family was another advantage to being back in New Mexico. With the family's population increase and their enjoyment of entertaining visitors, Peggy and Ferm moved to a larger house, a adobe on Camino Rancheros surrounded by enough land for Poli to run and Peggy to have a garden and trees. It was also a one-story house, an advantage they knew would be a good idea as they got older. They called the new home Quinientos, a name derived from the street address. Life was smooth sailing, which, in retrospect, should have made them suspicious.

In 1966 Taos author Frank Waters released a book titled *The Woman at Otowi Crossing*, and a storm of disagreement that would last for decades settled over northern New Mexico. For many people who had known and loved Edith Warner, the book defamed her character, but since the book was written as fiction, not much could be done about it. Peter Miller, Edith's goddaughter, was irate, and Vel Ludlow, in her distress, met with Roland Dickey at the University of New Mexico Press for advice, but he suggested that the best thing to do was "nothing." Anything more could "blow it all up by making a 'cause célèbre.'" Frustration set in.[5]

It was clear whom the main character in the book represented, but Waters had given Edith a different name. He had also given her a child from a fictitious marriage, a lover, and an altered personality. Other characters had been renamed and changed as well. Edith's spirituality was referred to as psychic ability, which holds a different connotation, and that psychic power was the focus of the novel.

Peggy had been aware that Waters was planning to write a book about Edith, so when Vel Ludlow asked her to write the "authorized version," Peggy tried to discuss the subject with Frank. Janey Waters, Frank's wife, was a good friend of Peggy, so, over lunch with them one day, Peggy spoke up. "I told Frank what I had been asked to do, and suggested that perhaps we should compare notes in order not to tread on each other's territory." In a letter Peggy wrote later to Harry James, a friend of Edith, she recounted what happened. "Frank was kind of sulky, but said he was 'planning to give her a love affair, and a child by a previous marriage.'" Peggy was shocked but suggested courteously "that since she had sisters and close friends living, wouldn't it be better to stick closer to her character?" Frank didn't reply and never spoke to Peggy again. After Frank's book came out and she had read it, Peggy sent him a note, trying to smooth things over. In her letter to James, she explained what she had said to Frank, writing, "The first time I had read *The Woman at Otowi Crossing* it made me mad; the second time it made me sick; the third time I had read it I was slightly laid up with a virus and did it the justice of reading every word." She graciously added that she had found "things about the book that I liked." Continuing, she related her further words to Frank. "I regretted the hurt to living people and hoped that if we met we could meet as friends . . . for the sake of the things we had in common." The overture was ignored.[6]

If Peggy was willing to be generous with her opinion, others were not. In the Santa Fe Gadfly, a column in the *New Mexican*, Spud Johnson admitted to being "confused in such a cross-fire between fact and fiction," referring to real people turned into fictitious characters who journey to a real Santa Fe and Los Alamos but to a fictitious Taos and Alcalde. To those who resented the book "as a false picture (even though sympathetic) of a real and much-loved person," he offered the consolation that "Mrs. Church's biography . . . has already solidly established the real Edith Warner in a beautiful and enduring book."[7]

Many decades later, despite the fact that *The Woman at Otowi Crossing* has remained in publication on the stature of Frank Waters's name, the true story of Edith Warner still has strong champions. In the 2006 book *Larger Than Life: New Mexico in the Twentieth Century*, the respected historian Ferenc M. Szasz referred to *The Woman at Otowi Crossing* and boldly commented, "Taos novelist Frank Waters fictionalized this story . . . but Warner found her Boswell in Peggy Pond Church's *The House at Otowi Bridge* (1959), a southwestern classic that has never gone out of print."[8]

When the furor died down, Peggy and Ferm set about enjoying Quinientos, their active grandchildren, and their many interests. Ferm finally retired and joined Peggy in her Quaker involvement. Sadly, they lost a good friend in artist Olive Rush, but in a kind gesture she had left her home on Canyon Road for the Friends' Meeting House, giving them a permanent site for the first time. Peggy had her writing and a new piano, and she and Ferm looked forward to the Santa Fe Opera seasons and miles of hiking trails to explore. For most people that would have been enough, but as the decade neared its end, they both found themselves with new projects to add to their already full lives.

Though he described himself as not being a "joiner," Ferm became a founding member of the New Mexico Citizens for Clean Air and Water and a very active one. He served as the group's newsletter editor, fundraiser, and treasurer. With his geology background and his engineering degree, he could contribute through this organization to a goal in which he believed deeply—a sound ecological philosophy for a sustainable future. As he said in his biography prepared for his fiftieth anniversary report to Harvard in 1971, "I believe it is vital for everyone to develop the ecological approach—what Aldo Leopold called the 'Ethic of the Land'—otherwise I see no future for man and his surroundings." He was concerned when pulp mills and power plants began to threaten New Mexico's blue skies and clear streams. Ferm was not one to sit back and talk about a cause; he became a determined advocate.[9]

Peggy's new undertaking began in 1967 when Crowell Publishing Company was looking for an author to write a biography of Mary Austin for a young people's series. The challenge of such a project had a certain appeal. She had long been fascinated by Austin, and writing a biography would be an opportunity to look deeper into the life of a unique woman, learn who she really was and what motivated her writing. Peggy took *The Land of Little Rain* from the shelf and reread it. It was the first and best of Austin's books, considered an American classic by many critics, and it had inspired nature lovers since its first publication in 1903. After some serious consideration—and lured by the love of the land that she shared with Austin—Peggy contacted Crowell and agreed to try it.[10]

For several months, Peggy studied as many of Mary Austin's published works as she could find. Almost all of her titles were out of print and difficult to find, but in that regard, Peggy was lucky. As she reported to her publisher, "My neighbor Jack Schaefer, author of the book from which the movie *Shane* was made . . . happens to be a Mary Austin fan and owns 'everything she ever wrote' and lends his collection most generously. He happened to have two copies of the little book of verse, *Children Sing in the Far West*, and made me a gift of the spare one!"[11] Austin was known as a novelist, nature writer, folklorist, poet, feminist, and crusader for community causes. Her body of work covered a wide range of genres, and within that range Peggy observed changes between the young woman who wrote an American classic in the California desert and the egocentric, confused woman she had known in Santa Fe in the 1920s and 1930s. She had the first glimpse of an intriguing research journey.

After immersing herself in the reading, Peggy planned a road trip through Mary Austin country in California, and Ferm went along. Years later, in looking back at their adventure, Peggy would say that the trip west, on the trail of Mary Austin, was "the best of our journeys." Their first destinations were Lone Pine and Independence in the Owens Valley, where Austin had written *The Land of Little Rain* in the shadow of the Sierra Nevadas. "I wished to see the fierce land through her eyes," Peggy said. It was a land that hadn't changed appreciably in the sixty years or so since Austin had lived there, but the economic character of the valley had changed dramatically from the homesteading era of Austin's day, when small ranches, farms, and dairies, with a few fruit orchards, had dotted the region surrounding the two small towns. The change had been well under way by 1913 when the first Los Angeles Aqueduct began to drain the Owens Valley of its water and channel it 250 miles for the needs of the growing city. When Peggy and Ferm visited in the late 1960s, they found a small-town economy bolstered only by the Los Angeles Department of Water and Power and the National Park Service, which managed recreational sites in the nearby mountains. Mary Austin and others had tenaciously fought the construction of the aqueduct, knowing what the project would do to the valley, but they were small voices against bureaucracy. The ultimate loss was a disillusionment that Austin never got over.

"East away from the Sierras, south from Panamint and Amargosa, east and south many an uncounted mile, is the Country of Lost Borders," Mary Austin wrote in the opening of *The Land of Little Rain*. Peggy and Ferm walked the "high level-looking plains full of intolerable sun glare," and visited the "hills, rounded, blunt, burned, squeezed up out of chaos, chrome and vermilion painted, aspiring to the snowline."[12] When asked once to explain her ability to interpret the desert, Austin replied, "I looked. By and by I got to know where looking was most worthwhile. Then I got so full of looking that I had to write to get rid of it and make room for more."[13] So Peggy and Ferm looked, too, and Austin's words came alive as they explored mile after mile of the parched Owens Valley, remembering that, "Void of life it never is, however dry the air and villainous the soil."[14] Standing in front of a brown, nondescript house in Independence, bordered by a picket fence and looking west, Peggy saw what Austin saw every day from her home—the majesty of 12,598-foot Kearsarge Peak, a mountain not even the highest in the range, for Mt. Whitney topped 14,000 feet a few miles to the south. Desert country it might be, but it was dramatic. It was important for Peggy to trace Austin's footsteps, a way of connecting, a kind of communication not easily explained but deeply felt.

Peggy's days in the Owens Valley were invaluable. She increased her comprehension of Austin's life on the edge of the Mojave Desert and talked with long-time residents who shared recollections and stories. She imagined the solitude of the day-to-day life of a young woman living in that small, isolated town in the 1890s and surmised how stifling the place could have been for someone of Austin's intellect. Was that what led to the intimate relationship she developed with the desert and the minute and sensitive observations she made of the wild country and its natural inhabitants?

Understanding that the serious writer that Mary was becoming in the desert and the self-centered old woman she had become in Santa Fe were joined somewhere in childhood experiences, Peggy began to assemble the history of Mary Austin's early life in order to make the connections.

Austin was born in Carlinville in 1868 to George and Susannah Hunter. Her father was an educated man who had been a lawyer before serving as an officer in the Civil War. In addition to his law books, he had a small library of classics and poetry by noted authors, many of them first editions. Young Mary took after him and at an early age declared her intentions of becoming a writer, but when she was ten years old, her father died. She lost the only member of the family to whom she could relate. After that, there was no one who understood her intellect or bookishness. Her mother couldn't comprehend why her daughter wanted to read anything other than the Bible, much less the literary titles that Mary consumed. She felt like a misfit, alone and unloved. She spent time wandering in the woods near her home, but those solitary hours laid the foundation for her observations of nature.[15] Peggy identified with those hours alone and with the mother who could not understand.

Austin was already interested in natural science when she arrived in California in 1888, a twenty-year-old graduate of Blackburn College in Carlinville, Illinois. Despite being an avid lover of books, she had chosen science over an English major in college, saying that she could teach herself literature but needed a teacher and a laboratory to learn science. Mary's family had been lured to California by cousins who were homesteading near Bakersfield, but not enamored of farming, she took a teaching position nearby. She soon met a young graduate of the University of California at Berkeley named Stafford Wallace Austin. At the time, he owned a vineyard but had no apparent skills to ensure its success. Though Mary had little experience with young men and almost no concept of what lay ahead, she married Wallace in the summer of 1891. Predictably, the vineyard failed, and the couple moved to Lone Pine, where he obtained a teaching job. The following year, Mary gave birth to a daughter they named Ruth, but within months, it was obvious that the child was mentally disabled, a problem that added stress to a marriage already showing signs of insecurity. That same year, Mary had her first story, "The Mother of Felipe," published in the *Overland Monthly*. Encouraged by this bit of success and feeling stifled and unhappy in her marriage, Mary made a drastic decision. She took the baby and moved forty miles north to teach at an academy in Bishop for several months. While she was gone, Wallace gave up his teaching position to file on a homestead near Independence, so Mary returned to help. The homestead failed, and Wallace became the registrar at the land office in Independence. Consequently, Mary took another out-of-town job at the Los Angeles Normal School. There she met Charles Lummis, editor of *Out West* magazine, who published some of her stories and introduced her to local writers such as Sharlot Hall and Frederick Webb Hodge. Inspired by these contacts, she made more time to write and had a story published in the *Atlantic Monthly*, then other pieces in *Cosmopolitan* and *St. Nicholas*.[16]

After a year away, Austin returned again to Independence, where Wallace was building a house for the family. This was the house that Peggy had stood beside in Independence, seeing the open desert so close and knowing firsthand the temptation to leave domesticity behind and seek the solitude and the inspirations for written words. She had answered the same call in her early married days when she rode the trails of the Pajarito Plateau. It was from this house that Austin had wandered the arroyos and hillsides, gathering her thoughts for the essays that filled *The Land of Little Rain*. The book was a success, which gave Austin the possibility of enhancing her husband's income to give them a more comfortable living, but Wallace couldn't accept that. Her family, too, wanted her to stop wasting her time writing stories and settle into her role as wife and mother. No one offered the slightest consideration for her need to write. She had high aspirations that weren't understood or even acceptable for women by the standards of her day. She had reached a crossroads. Mary decided to leave her husband and strike out on her own. As a single mother, she came to the conclusion that she could no longer care for Ruth, so she placed the child in an institution in Santa Clara, California. With that decision, she could have a life of her own, one in which her potential would not be wasted.[17]

By the time Peggy left the Owens Valley, she had a better picture of what Mary's life had been like in the desert and the motives for her decisions. She understood Austin's inner drive for expression and the conflict between the domestic life and the creative one. Peggy had known the frustration of living with a husband who saw life in a different reality, but writing of that in a letter after the trip, she revealed her hard-learned lesson on that subject by acknowledging "what a hard time said husband really has of it!"[18] She had been fortunate to have Ferm who, despite his different viewpoint, encouraged her writing and was not threatened by her success, who even took pride in her accomplishments. And there he was by her side, driving long miles to help with her research. As they continued on, they talked over Austin's reactions to her desert life and her marriage. There was one thing that troubled them both: the decision to put her child into an institution. Was the child better off there, or was it Mary Austin who was better off because the child was there? That question, which couldn't be answered with certainty, was the first hint of the emotional rollercoaster Peggy would encounter as she continued her research.

From the Mojave Desert, she and Ferm drove to the San Joaquin Valley and eventually on to Carmel, where in 1906 Austin had joined a group of young and somewhat radical writers and artists that included names destined for fame or at least notoriety—Jack London, George Sterling, Sinclair Lewis, Ambrose Bierce, Robinson Jeffers, Upton Sinclair, and Lincoln Steffens, to name a few. In looking into this phase of Austin's life, Peggy began to see a different person, one pursuing not only expression but also ultimate freedom to try new things. Austin rented a small house and then proceeded to build a wickiup like the ones she had seen the Indians build in the Owens Valley, only she put hers high in the branches of an oak tree to use it as a writing retreat.[19] Having escaped those who would tell her what she should and shouldn't do, she transitioned to exercising that prerogative herself by bossing others and offering her opinion where it wasn't always wanted. The other writers and artists in the Carmel colony began referring to her as "God's mother-in-law" because of her overbearing personality.[20] Even with such behind-the-back jibes, her reviews were mixed within the colony, as they would continue to be throughout her life. Jack London "had a great respect for Austin's mind, and for her achievements," but like his fellow writers "could not refrain sometimes from poking fun at her."[21] Another member of the colony, Arnold Genthe, saw beyond her façade in the Carmel days, saying, "Her little idiosyncrasies did not prevent her from being a real person and a true genius. She had about her a kind of majesty, and when one got beyond her forbidding surface, there was warmth, loyalty, and genuine humor."[22] Another opposite opinion, years later, would be that she had "no glint of humor." Which was the real Mary Austin? Peggy's research wasn't making that question any easier to answer.

Peggy and Ferm took advantage of a house exchange in Carmel. Their friend Terry Allen was residing at Quinientos in Santa Fe while they stayed in her home in Carmel. Terry had been the creative writing teacher at the Institute for American Indian Affairs, and the previous year Peggy had substituted for her for five months while Terry was on sick leave. With the convenience of a house, Peggy could take her time on the Carmel research. She learned that in 1910 Austin was instrumental in establishing the Forest Theater, the first outdoor theater west of the Rockies. She gave poetry readings there and produced at least two of her own plays. The theater was still thriving in the 1960s, a lasting legacy of which Mary Austin would no doubt have been proud. Peggy needed to determine Austin's place in the bohemian colony that had been populated by varied personalities and diverse talents. She concluded that Carmel had been a starting point, a place for Austin to examine who she was and who she could become. Peggy knew that after Carmel an even more ambitious Austin had spent time in New York, London, and Italy, continuing to write and establish herself in the literary world of the early twentieth century. Wrapping up the Carmel research, Peggy felt that she had established a good foundation of understanding for Austin's California years and how they related to her earlier life and the years that followed.

Peggy and Ferm returned home in time to see *Madame Butterfly* open at the new Santa Fe Opera pavilion before greeting their summer visitors, beginning with Lawrence Hitchcock and his wife. In August, Dottie and Courtney—and Dottie's horse, Oma—stopped in Taos and Santa Fe on their way to the National Arabian Horse Show in Albuquerque.

To be in physical contact with the warm earth, savoring silence, was Peggy's idea of a perfect moment. "One afternoon / she lay there / among the slanting rays of winter, / caught in the golden vase of autumn," she wrote in 1974. "Perhaps I will take root here like the pines" (from "She Will Want Nothing But Stones"). Courtesy Peggy Pond Church Estate.

Surgery in the autumn forced Peggy to put aside her research for a time, and it was difficult to settle into it again. As she always admitted, "Applying the seat of the pants to the seat of a chair is an acrobatic exercise I have never entirely mastered." Life simply got in the way. There was the traditional Thanksgiving picnic, a trip to the Monastery of Christ in the Desert that she didn't want to miss, a drive to the Valle Grande in the Jemez with granddaughter Robyn and Margaret Gibbons, a party for the Warings, and Christmas Eve dinner at the Pink Adobe. There were wild geese to watch and camping trips to Santa Clara Canyon. She and Ferm followed the skiing progress of granddaughters Nancy and Janet as they raced to first place in their respective classes. And another dog, Baba the Turk, joined the family. In the summer of 1970, to celebrate Ferm's seventieth birthday, they traveled to Banded Peak Ranch in Colorado, spending wonderful days where Ferm had tutored the Hughes twins in the mid-1920s. The boys' father, Lafayette Hughes, had played a significant role in the financial stability of the Ranch School, and Ferm had stayed in touch with the family for years.

The trip to Colorado and the memories brought back by the visit to the Banded Peak Ranch made them realize how fortunate they were, still healthy and vital and growing together into old age, a time of savoring their shared joys and their appreciation of the landscapes around them. "Too many riches to chose from within arm's reach" was how Peggy described it. On a picnic near Cochiti Lake some months later, she recalled, "I told Ferm, laughingly, I had married him so that I might live among scenes like this, and that I had certainly got my money's worth. Our marriage was really founded on a rock," she added, sitting in the presence of so many beautiful stones. Then she heard Ferm mutter something about the rock being "a volcanic one!" But, at last, they were in a place of comfortable companionship enjoying their picnics and outings.

Since the release of The House at Otowi Bridge in 1960, Peggy had been giving the royalties from the book to San Ildefonso Pueblo's church fund in memory of Edith. She sent a check each year to the governor of the pueblo, different men as the years passed. She wasn't sure if the governors understood why the money was sent, as the checks were cashed but never acknowledged. Finally, Vel Ludlow mentioned something about it to Santana Martinez, the daughter in law of potter Maria Martinez.

On a Sunday afternoon in February 1973, Peggy and Ferm, along with Vel and her housemate Betty Morgan, were invited to the pueblo for "tea." They arrived at Tewa Center, where the gathering was to be, but found only two women beginning to set tables as if for a banquet. It seemed they were too early, so Vel suggested that they visit with Maria Martinez for a few minutes. They walked across the north plaza to where Maria was living with her sister Desideria. Another sister, Clara, was there, too, and also Juanita, who had cared for Tilano after Edith died, so they all had a fine time reminiscing. Finally, they returned to the hall to a "tea" that more closely resembled a feast. The women had prepared a buffet meal with posole, frijoles, sopapillas, and chili, followed by two colors of jello salad with bananas in a kind of frosting and a rose-pink cake. It was a large, family affair with husbands, children, young women with babies, and grandparents, but the hosts were the ladies of the Sewing Circle Group of Pueblo de San Ildefonso. As it turned out, the ladies hadn't known about the book royalties, but they knew that Peggy made donations each year to the pueblo and wanted to thank her. She explained the best she could about the royalties.

"I've sent the money because the book was about Edith and because Edith loved the pueblo," she told them, adding, "I have, too, as long as I have known it, which has been ever since I was a little girl of ten or eleven. Because I knew Edith would want to do something to make the pueblo happy, I have turned over the money for the church, and I hoped it would be something to make the pueblo people happy." The room filled with many friendly smiles. The women had made her a gift as well, "all wrapped up in three layers of colored paper, which, after much unwrapping, turned out to be a very handsome apron with stripes of all colors and a pair of marvelous pockets." Peggy was wearing a turquoise and black wool skirt that day, and she tried on the apron so the women could see that she liked it. The colors were perfect together. "I hardly see how I can wear the skirt without it after this!" she told them. She was also presented with a copy of Maria: The Potter of San Ildefonso *by Alice Marriott, even more of a treasure because it was autographed by Maria and the seven ladies of the sewing circle. Most of the pueblo had gone to Cochiti that day for a buffalo dance, but this group had stayed behind to honor Peggy.*

She was moved by the beauty of it all, writing later to Virginia in praise of the pueblo women, "so low-voiced and gentle." She ended her reveries of the afternoon by saying, "When they laugh they are as musical as birds. I wish they were all my sisters." [23]

Eventually Peggy did resume her Mary Austin research, seeking the help of two people who could clarify the Carlinville years and Mary's relationship with her family. She began to correspond with Harriet Stoddard, a professor of English at Blackburn College and an Austin scholar who was an expert on Mary's Illinois background. She also met Austin's niece, Mary Hunter, who knew her aunt better than any other surviving relative, having lived with her off and on during Austin's Santa Fe years. With the depth these two women added to Peggy's understanding, she finished the first section of the manuscript which contained the early years of Austin's life preceding her family's move to the San Joaquin Valley. Peggy titled it *Wind's Trail*, taken from an Indian poem that Austin had liked—"Wind's trail I am seeking." Then, she couldn't go on. When she tried to gather her thoughts to write the California years, something was holding her back. Had she learned too much with the research? The young Mary Austin offered an enjoyable study of a developing adolescent girl, but the later Mary Austin lost that innocence, swallowed by her driving ego. Had Peggy's opinion changed concerning the woman she once knew in Santa Fe?

Peggy remembered the audience she'd had with Austin as a young poet, too young even to really appreciate the encounter. "She was so kind as to read my poems and invited me to her house to discuss them," Peggy recalled in a letter to her publisher. When Peggy arrived, Austin was in her kitchen making pepper pot soup, a specialty of hers. The memory was still keen. "I was amused that even at that occupation her hair was piled regally on her head and held in place with a tortoise-shell Spanish comb. Irreverently I found myself wondering how she kept the comb from falling into the soup as she stirred the kettle."[24] That was early in Austin's Santa Fe decade, before she lost the respect of most friends and acquaintances.

As early as 1918, Austin began visiting New Mexico, spending time in Taos and Santa Fe and giving lectures and poetry readings. In the process she became concerned with the preservation and revival of Hispanic and Indian arts and culture, and ultimately decided to settle in Santa Fe, building her house on Camino del Monte Sol and calling it Casa Querida, the Beloved House.

Austin acquired the backing to found the Spanish Colonial Arts Society in 1925, joined by many of the influential citizens of Santa Fe, among them Ruth Laughlin Alexander, George Bloom, Ina and Gerald Cassidy, Kenneth Chapman, Leonora Curtin, Bronson Cutting, Andrew Dasburg, Margretta Dietrich, Alice Corbin Henderson, Cyrus McCormick, John Gaw Meem, Frank Mera, Sheldon Parsons, Cady Wells, and Mary Wheelwright. Austin had the ability to assemble powerful people for worthy causes, but she managed also to eventually alienate most of them.[25]

For Peggy, writing the biography was becoming a juggling act between Austin's abrasiveness and her endeavors to do good, between her genius and her ego. Even as early as the Carmel days, Austin was "too consciously concerned about posterity and her place in it."[26] Something was driving Austin to be a literary celebrity, to be important, but in Santa Fe, in the end, "she was remembered for the most part only with ridicule."[27] With Peggy's background in Jungian analysis, she looked for answers in Austin's earlier years and concluded that "all her life she was seeking a tempting and evasive spirit, like the wind, and losing her grip on the solid reality of earth."

Peggy began to see Austin's life as a tragedy, an example of the destructive side of genius. She believed that Austin had "sacrificed her husband and child to the demand of the creative spirit for self expression." In addition, some of

Peggy's analysis of Austin's problems hit too close to home. In letters to Harriet Stoddard, Peggy described Mary Austin in words she had used to describe herself in her own soul searching. She wrote of "the longing for her father's approval," "the unfeeling mother," and "the feeling that her spontaneous imaginative self was not acceptable." She even referred to how much the young Mary looked like her mother! Peggy had dealt with her own analysis. She didn't think she could go through it again with Mary Austin. "I am neither psychologist nor artist enough to deal with the depth of her tragedy," she wrote to her friend Lawrence Clark Powell early in 1973.[28] She mentioned that she was seriously considering abandoning the Austin biography.

Later that year, Peggy sent the *Wind's Trail* manuscript to Powell, perhaps at Powell's request, for he knew how much effort she had put into the project already. After reading the manuscript, he responded, "You have dug deep into her life and soul. I don't see how you could not continue. Let the momentum of these first chapters carry you, or have you lost it?" He recognized the quality of her presentation of the early years in Carlinville and urged her on. "You have made a deep initial dive. Don't stay under. Come up and take another deep one!" Powell advised her to go to the Huntington Library and "get fired up by what is there."[29] Peggy knew she should return to California to explore the papers and letters in the Mary Austin collection at the Huntington before making her decision. Perhaps it would make a difference, she thought, but the coming months were busy ones and the trip would have to wait for a more convenient time.

Unforeseen sadness mingled with the busy schedule when Poli, the beautiful white dog, died and left a void in Peggy's life. She loved her other dog, Baba, also a Samoyed cross, but Poli had been the favorite. However, a new affection between Peggy and Baba resulted from the loss. The younger dog had always misbehaved to get attention, but a new, gentle personality emerged when there was no longer competition. Baba became a consoling companion for both Peggy and Ferm. The Thanksgiving picnic for 1973 was on U.S. Hill near Taos, continuing an outdoor tradition for that holiday that started in the California years, and once the new year began, thoughts turned to their fiftieth wedding anniversary. The family was, of course, planning a celebration. Forty-two relatives descended on Santa Fe for a picnic—or the tribal rites, as Peggy called it. The attendants at their wedding had been Margaret Kelly and Ashley III, and in a quieter celebration of the milestone, Peggy and Ferm took Margaret and Ashley to dinner at Bishop's Lodge. Both occasions were memorable and appreciated.

Fermor and Peggy Church, on the right, celebrated their fiftieth wedding anniversary in 1974. On the left are Peggy's brother, Dr. Ashley Pond, and his wife, Lucille. Courtesy Joan F. Pond.

A few weeks after the anniversary, Peggy and Ferm took a trip to Lake Powell, enjoying some of their favorite landscapes along the way. While there, they took a day's trip by tourist boat to Rainbow Bridge. Peggy thought that it was sacrilege to go by boat, along with a lot of tourists snapping photos and disturbing the quiet beauty, but she knew it was the only way she and Ferm could still see it at their ages. She fell in love with Navajo Mountain, and they drove past Shonto Trading Post and the ruin of Betatakin. As they passed by Shiprock and the Four Corners, they were both disturbed by the mobile homes and television antennas that had replaced the traditional hogans they remembered. Ferm was "strangely silent and uncommunicative all the way," but she thought it was just a reaction to the changes and to the strip mining and power plant plumes ruining the views. Then a week or so after returning home, he began hallucinating. He was hospitalized and diagnosed with a brain tumor.

Fortunately, the tumor was in a place where it destroyed the pain centers, so he experienced no discomfort, though he did lose some ability to interpret reality and to react emotionally. The doctors wanted to do a biopsy, but Peggy said no. She and Ferm had talked about just such an eventuality and agreed that "death was a phase of living" at their stage of life and should not be interfered with. She shared the diagnosis with Ferm in a direct manner. He looked out the hospital window at the golden cottonwood trees and said, "That's the way Santa Fe looked when I came in 1921." He was saddened that it was time to leave. She knew he had fallen instantly in love with the land, and "that was the great bond between us," she thought. A poem that she had associated with Ferm almost from the beginning of their marriage ran through her mind.[30]

The grandchildren and great nieces and nephews of Peggy and Fermor Church. First row: twins Briget and Kersti Tyson, Dawn Boulware behind Jono Tyson, and Adrienne Pond. Second row: Eric Church, Leigh Church, Julia Church, Teresa Trujillo, and Ashley E. Pond (V). Behind them are Fermor Church, Elizabeth Boulware, Peggy Church, Patty Boulware, Nancy Church, and Robyn Church. Courtesy Joan F. Pond.

> Who loves the rain,
> And loves his home,
> And looks on life with quiet eyes,
> Him will I follow through the storm;
> And at his hearth-fire keep me warm;
> Nor hell nor heaven shall that soul surprise
> Who loves the rain and loves his home
> And looks on life with quiet eyes.
>
> — Frances Howard Shaw[31]

The doctor agreed with Peggy's decision. He gave Ferm medication to control seizures and sent him home. In some ways, Ferm seemed himself. Friends visited, and he and Peggy managed two or three autumn picnics, but he was gradually fading. With the help of visiting nurses, Peggy was able to keep him at home for almost three months. Eventually he began to drift into a coma and went back to the hospital. He was in and out of consciousness. Peggy visited three times daily to help feed him. Then, she came down with the flu and had to stay away. Before she could return, Ferm died.

Peggy's neighbor, Ruth MacPherson, came to tell her. She had just gotten up the morning of February 2 and was having early morning tea when Ruth came in. "It's all over," she said gently. Peggy didn't realize what she meant, so she said it again. "It's all over. The hospital just called me."

On a warm day a few months later, the family assembled to scatter Ferm's ashes in Garcia Canyon. They chose a site "on the slope of a cliff under some fine caves" and above the pines. "It seemed the very right place for it," Peggy said, "on the Pajarito Plateau in country similar to Los Alamos . . . looking both toward the Jemez and the Sangre de Cristos." Afterward they all had a picnic amid the scenery that Ferm had loved so much.

Peggy had so admired Virginia Wirth after Cecil died, developing into an independent woman out of the safe family pattern, earning a living with her teaching skills and raising her two sons. So many women she knew had lost their husbands and had to make their own way, "sturdily creating their own wholeness or being created by that potential within themselves." But could she do it?

Adjusting to life alone wasn't easy. "Ferm had always taken the hard responsibilities for me," Peggy admitted. "As independent as I had come to think I was, I was not so after all." She thought of the lesson from *I Heard the Owl Call My Name*, when the old woman advises, "Do not look back,"[32] but that wasn't entirely possible. However, she did understand that "whatever life is ahead must be new."

She made repeated efforts to be strong, to be realistic, but they were followed by repeated regressions. Everywhere she looked, there was a memory of Ferm. Something as simple as picking up a smooth stone in the garden was a reminder of how much she had delighted in his knowledge of geology, the many questions she had asked and his patient answers. Hearing Tosca on the radio brought tears because it was his favorite opera. The sound of rain, clouds building to the west, wind in the pines—almost everything had an association with Ferm.

She talked to Dottie often and even flew to Oregon for a visit. The closeness that had grown between the two sisters was a blessing in coping with Ferm's loss. And the closeness went both ways. "Dottie phoned to tell me how disappointed she was that I hadn't looked back from the ramp to wave when the plane left Medford," Peggy wrote in her journal. "How warm she sounded."

She needed time with friends as well. Frances McAllister, a Quaker friend, came from Flagstaff, and together they went to three operas and a chamber music concert as well spending a day in Bandelier National Monument. Vel Ludlow, and eventually two more of Edith's sisters, moved to Santa Fe, and Peggy was glad to have them close. Staying busy was a key to recovery, as was something else she had missed in recent years.

It had been three decades since Peggy had published a book of poetry. In 1976 Ahsahta Press at Boise State University, a relatively new publisher dedicated to western poets, brought out *New & Selected Poems*, which included several of Peggy's previously published favorites but also eleven new poems, among them "Lament," which she wrote for Ferm. Tom Trusky, one of the founders of Ahsahta Press, was interested in doing a book of women poets of the West. He called one evening to talk over the idea with Peggy. "Why are women poets of the West so neglected?" he asked. "Why have you been so neglected?" Peggy answered, "Because I have neglected myself," she told him and then wondered all evening why she had betrayed the poet within herself until it was too late. She hadn't promoted her work as she should have. But maybe it wasn't too late. There was still more inside her to share.

A year later she dusted off the sonnets that had been printed in *Inward Light* in 1954 and added a new one. "Sonnet XV: For F.S.C. 1900–1975" was a tribute to Ferm and perhaps her best effort at mastering the difficult fourteen-line structure and rhyming scheme of sonnets.

I am thinking this morning of the beauty of the earth
as you and I loved it, wondering
how my vision is still half yours—the broken surf
of morning over landforms; slant light; rolling thunder
at the edge of our summer picnics; the high dancing
flight of the sandhill cranes, their cry that echoed
like water rippling over smooth stones, over the far expanse of
bright air. Within and all around us time flowed,
making, unmaking mountains: the crystal essence
still glitters in the sand grains of dry rivers.
Nothing seems lost—light's changes, wind-swept silence,
the arid land reflecting the shape of water.
I gather pebbles feeling your quiet presence
companion me still in all we loved together.[33]

Lightning Tree of Santa Fe published *The Ripened Fields: Fifteen Sonnets of a Marriage* in 1978. In the introduction to the volume, Lawrence Clark Powell praised Peggy as "one of the few poets to grace the Southwest—I mean poets, not versifiers with which the region abounds." In celebration of *The Ripened Fields* and the occasion of Peggy's seventy-fifth birthday, Lightning Tree and Villagra Book Shop hosted a party for Peggy at St. John's College that was a tremendous success.

A new appreciation for her poetry was evident in the readings she was asked to give around Santa Fe, and her knowledge of Pajarito Plateau history was making her a popular speaker in Los Alamos, even with her constant reminders that the entire town, with few exceptions, mispronounced Otowi. "OH-tow-wee," she would say slowly to her audience, with deliberate accents, as she led her lessons in pronunciation, beckoning the audience in Fuller Lodge to repeat the word. "OH-tow-wee." If they weren't fast learners, they had to do it again, with a reminder that "the accent is on the first syllable!" As more and more people met her, she became a revered part of Los Alamos history.[34]

Peggy was lonely without Ferm, but she had managed to put her life together and fill it with meaningful times. She read, enjoyed music, took seminars at St. John's College, and went on outings with friends and family. She learned Spanish in order to read the poetry of Pablo Neruda in its original language, even translating her own version of his epic poem, "Alturas de Macchu Picchu." And, as always, there was time for the outdoors.

Baba pulled on the lead as if to say, "Hurry! I know where we're going!" Peggy locked the car and began her hike up Big Tesuque Trail. The dog excitedly checked the scent of every blade of grass and wildflower along the path, walking hurriedly with her head down and her tail up. The warm sun of early autumn accented the gold of the turning aspens. As she walked over a familiar knoll, she found herself thinking of how one might build a cabin there among the pines. She stopped and sat beneath a tree to give Baba some water. Taking out a pocket-size spiral notebook, her hiking journal, she jotted down memories brought back by her thought of building a cabin.

"I remember the little cabin—the hut I had at LARS, that Ferm and Hitch built for me. I haven't thought of it in such a long time. I used to go there in winter and build a fire in the tiny stove, watch the snow falling, falling in the canyon below me, for the hut was built on the very edge. I would lie on the spool daybed. How I wish I had it now."

She leaned back against the tree, digging her heels into the mass of pine needles surrounding it, and wrote more. "To the south the sky is the color of a bluebird's feather. The slender young aspen lift their singing leaves against it. The wind quickens and the leaves rain down. Wind and color make music together." And then, a different thought. "Will I be able to come here again another year?"

Baba was eager to go on, so she put the journal back in her pocket and continued. She walked for some time, the dog eventually slowing to stay patiently beside her. In another half mile, they reached the place where she usually ate her sandwich and drank her sherry. After eating, she brought out the notebook again.

"Baba, my old dog, lies beside me. Blessed companion of these last years. Her lovely independence mingled with affection—like my own." She was still for a time, just petting the dog, before looking at her comments from the earlier stop. "I am so aware of the body's increasing refusals," she wrote. "My soul still aspires to climb mountains, to wrestle with gravity. The human body does not willingly drop its leaves as the tree does. It is not death but aging that is the problem." Recently, she had been writing a fictional narrative, an autobiography she called Littlebird in which the child growing up called herself Quince. Thinking of that child, she added, "Quince is still so alive within me."

Lying back in the grasses, she closed her eyes and listened, thinking. "Life seems so simple on this mountainside. This moment is the eternal moment. No conflict. I sink into the life of the trees, the grasses, the tiny bird, the leaning rock decorated by a yellow-green lichen, the light stir of the wind. The world exactly as it is. Silence and solitude. I slip free from my ego. I become the mountain on which I sit."

Peggy finally made the return trip to California and spent days at the Huntington Library in San Marino, studying the letters and papers of Mary Austin. As Powell had predicted, it was a productive trip. She was excited when she returned home, sitting down almost at once to tell Virginia Wiebenson about the research and the train trip, which mirrored some of the route she and Ferm and Hugh had taken to California in 1943. She stayed awake coming back to "look at the full moon on the desert" but was disappointed to find so many houses and lights between San Bernardino and Needles. "Only the country between Flagstaff and Gallup seemed spacious and uninhabited as it used to be." She related the pleasure of seeing flocks of Navajo sheep and a boy on a paint pony being followed by a colt. Then she finished the letter. "Well, it's fifteen minutes past Walter Cronkite, so I suppose I'd better stop rambling. With love, Maggie." It was a name she used only occasionally to sign Virginia's letters, when she was feeling especially sentimental.[35]

Peggy was eager to begin the Austin project anew, as her journal from those days reveals.

> All day yesterday so filled with delight in starting work again on Mary A—the coming again into focus, the effort to be articulate about insight, insight into the workings of the soul, for as I peer into Mary I see at the same time myself. Where does the subjective leave off and the objective begin?

And there it was: the underlying problem from her previous stall, lying in wait. The enthusiasm regenerated by the Huntington visit didn't last long. Ultimately the subjective views collided with the objective and couldn't be separated. Peggy loved the research journey she had taken, and she was still intrigued by Austin and admired her early writing, but she began to see that it wasn't possible to write about a complex woman like Mary Austin and "serve it up for teenagers." There was too much depth of human relationships and inner conflicts. If they were too deep for her, they were far too deep for young people. In the end, she saw Austin's life as a tragedy: the destructive side of genius. As Peggy noted in her journal, "What price 'genius' if the human being is sacrificed?" For Peggy, the real Mary Austin was the young woman who wrote *The Land of Little Rain* and had such promise. That was the woman she wanted to remember rather than the one who had spent her last years in Santa Fe after a lifetime of frustrations and disappointments, ending friendless and in fear. Fear of dying and fear that her legacy would not live on. In the end, a few perceptive people who were aware of "the tortured human being she really was" came to her aid. Ina Sizer Cassidy had the compassion to sit with Austin in her last days as she lay dying. She was "a poor, helpless, friendless old woman," Cassidy said, and she "couldn't leave her to die alone."[36] It was Ina Cassidy who made the arrangement to have Austin's ashes entombed atop Picacho Peak in the Sangre de Cristos.

Peggy spent months in turmoil before deciding that she could not write the Mary Austin biography. She kept the *Wind's Trail* manuscript of Austin's early years and turned the remainder of her research over to Augusta Fink, who wrote *I-Mary: A Biography of Mary Austin*, released in 1983. And finally she acknowledged another reason for giving up the project. It was "because I just want to," she said. "I want to make the most of what active life is left me, and have time to write poetry of my own, if possible, and meditate upon the mystery of the end of life in my own way, not Mary's." It was time to move on.

Chapter 14

Looking Back

"I believe in writing in order to keep things from getting lost."

A young girl, perhaps twelve or thirteen, danced gracefully beside the stream that passes through Frijoles Canyon in Bandelier National Monument. It was the summer of 1980, and Peggy sat nearby at a picnic table with Evelyn Frey, Frances McAllister, and Betty Hoyt, a group of old friends enjoying an afternoon in a place that could also be called a longtime friend. In Peggy's younger days, she had lived not far from this canyon that became a national monument in 1916 during her Pajarito Club days. Evelyn, who was in her mid-eighties, had lived in the canyon most of her life, coming in 1925 with her husband to manage Ten Elders guest ranch and later operating concessions for the National Park Service. The other two women were visiting from Arizona; one of them, Frances, remembered spending glorious days in the canyon as a young wife with her husband in one of the guest cottages. The canyon held a special place in their collective memories.

As the women ate their lunch and talked, Peggy focused on the girl who had wandered away from her family, fascinated by her surroundings. Words formed in Peggy's mind as the scene unfolded before her. The girl stood looking at the stream "as though the murmurous water had enticed her / into some secret world." She stepped onto a fallen tree branch that was partly submerged in the water, wrapping her toes around it for balance. She extended her body "in a ballet dancer's position, / left leg horizontal, / arms reaching forward." She practiced the "delighted balance" over and over, "as though the voice of the stream were teaching / her the grace of its own movement." The young dancer was experiencing oneness with nature as Peggy had as a child. It is possible that in this serious young girl Peggy saw her younger self in her own "secret world" in Pajarito Canyon. Whether or not she made such an association, the picture before her inspired "The Rito: Frijoles Canyon," one of Peggy's longest poems.[1]

Over the next few days, she shaped "The Rito," as the poem is familiarly called, into a poignant look back at a simpler time and as a tribute to the physical beauty of the canyon she and her friends treasured. The poem personifies nature. The stream runs "with her clear eyes." She tears "at her banks and heals them" and is "patient." The kind of relationship that Peggy

Peggy and Evelyn Frey shared a bond in their love for Frijoles Canyon in Bandelier National Monument. They met as young women in 1925 and remained friends for more than sixty years. Courtesy Los Alamos Historical Museum Archives.

and these women had with the canyon was unmistakably one of longstanding love combined with respect for the "millenniums of time" that nature took to form such a wonder. In her words, Peggy laments the changes she sees from her perspective of old age—the loss of silence, the crowds of people, and their children who will never know "what the canyon itself would teach them / growing up in the rhythm of its seasons." She is keenly aware of time flowing and the world she is gradually leaving behind.

> We who spent our young days
> among the mounds and shards of a vanished people
> must count ourselves now among the vanishing.
> What we remember
> cannot live after us.
> We smile at one another
> as though the present were a dream around us.
> Within us the canyon and the still melodious river
> lead a secret life that only we can enter.[2]

"The Rito" wasn't the first poem in which Peggy used such a comparison, as she wrote in "Morning on Tseregé" of greeting the "child who will stand here / upon Tseregé" and "feel under her questioning hand, the living grasses / weaving substance of sunlight and the dust of a fallen city." But that poem offered a vision of optimism, that there would be another child who, despite the encroaching present, would come and appreciate and feel the connections to the past.[3] She once commented in her journal that this was that poem that most focused her feelings about the world she had lived in.

As the decade of the 1980s began, Peggy was taking pleasure in the resurgence of her poetry. In 1981, she joined her friend Jeannie Pear, a Denver illustrator and publisher, to bring out a collection of poetry and drawings. Beginning in 1928, Peggy had written poems to send out to friends each Christmas, and she resurrected eight of those poems, dating as far back as 1934, for *A Rustle of Angels*. Pear's haunting drawings and the meaningful words were a successful combination.[4] Even more important, she was writing new poetry. She produced "Stones on an Arid Hillside" to follow "An Afternoon Among Stones," written on Peter and Earle's ranch two years before, and on a visit to Garcia Canyon, where the family had scattered Ferm's ashes, she wrote "Sandhill Cranes in February." The words were reminiscent of times she and Ferm had watched the flights of cranes moving across the sky. "We looked upward again and again and saw them flying / and as they flew they called to one another." Peggy remembered a conversation they had shared on just such a day. "As the sound ebbed we spoke wistfully of dying, / when our time came, into such ecstacy."[5]

Peggy's New and Selected Poems *had been well received and was collecting good reviews. She wanted to write Tom Trusky at Ahsahta Press and share some of the comments with him. She sat down to type the letter, glancing out the window as she did. It was a beautiful day, sunny, inviting. She picked up a piece of paper and looked again. Beautiful summer clouds were forming over the mountains. The sky was blue. She put the paper in the typewriter and began.*

Dear Tom —

I thought I'd spend the afternoon writing letters. I put this blank sheet of paper in the typewriter and thought, "On such a lovely afternoon, how much better to take Baba and go walk somewhere in the mountains." So, I will leave it in the typewriter where it can't possibly get away till I come back!

The call of the mountains won out. Peggy spent her afternoon walking through ponderosa pines, grassy dells, and patches of bluebells and wild onion. Tom got his letter—just a day later!

Unexpected recognition came to Peggy in the early 1980s from a very different venue—a concert hall. New Mexico composer Michael Mauldin had contacted her in 1976 to ask permission to use phrases from *The House at Otowi Bridge* as narration to accompany music he was composing for *Enchanted Land: Suite for Narrator and Orchestra*. Out of respect, he had asked her first before approaching the University of New Mexico Press, the holder of the copyright. He included the passages he had selected, and she replied.

> I can't say how enchanted I am by the selections you have made from The House at Otowi Bridge. You seem to have selected passages that give what is to me the essence of the book, the land, and Edith Warner's own outlook. Now I can hardly wait to hear the music that goes with it.
>
> That you should have the work start out with the phrase ". . . there are certain places in the earth where the great powers that move between earth and sky are much closer and more available than others . . ." seemed so fortuitous, because I had been thinking so often of those words the last three days. Peter Miller and Earle, her husband, and I

took a picnic Saturday to the petroglyphs south of
Galisteo in the great volcanic dike that runs from
west to east. The glyphs were marvelous, reminding
me of a kind of zodiac. After we'd done our
tramping around we lay for half an hour or so on
the tip of the dike and were so aware of "the powers
that move between earth and sky" that I intended
to go to the book soon and look up the passage—
and there it was at the beginning of your excerpts.

I really must thank you so much, and do let me
know when the suite is to be performed.

Eagerly,
Peggy Church

The first performance of the work was by the Chamber Orchestra
of Albuquerque, under David Oberg, at the University of New Mexico's
Keller Hall in 1981. Peggy was unable to attend, but the performance was
broadcast live on the radio by KHFM, so she was able to hear it. "I'm
still dripping with tears on my way to bed after tonight's *Enchanted Land*,"
Peggy wrote to Mauldin. "The narration was superb and the music blended
perfectly. You made a poem of the book," she concluded.[6] *Enchanted Land*
was released in 2000 and has taken its place in the arts and cultural tradition
of New Mexico.

*In the Pueblo culture, Coyote is the trickster, always pulling pranks and making
mischief. Peggy had a small wooden carving of a coyote that she was fond of
and kept on a bookshelf in a place of prominence. There was a reason for his
presence.*

*One morning, Peggy walked around the house, noticeably agitated. She
opened the drawers in her desk. She looked under newspapers haphazardly piled
on the table, checked the pockets of the robe she'd worn earlier, and looked in the
kitchen. Then she went into the bathroom to look by the sink. She even got down
on hands and knees to search under the bed.*

Finally, she marched to the shelf and reached up to turn Coyote around. "You're going to face the wall until you let me find my glasses!"

In the early 1980s, Peggy felt the pull back to the Friends' Meetings she had found meaningful in previous years. She and Ferm had once been dedicated members of the Quaker community, attending the Quaker Meetings in Santa Fe and traveling to the Pacific Yearly Meeting of Friends, but they eventually questioned their beliefs. As Peggy revealed in a letter to Dody Waring, they stopped attending Meetings because they "felt that too much energy was devoted to trying to 'do good' in all parts of the world, to the neglect of the powers that struggle in each individual." She further explained that "to identify with the good, to be convinced that it is our duty to show 'the truth' to others, to try to use love as a 'power'—however nonviolent—is, we felt, to turn away from our main task of growth in the light of our own truth." Then she made a poignant observation related to Edith Warner. "How are we to live in this world and continue to believe in and to seek the 'silence and peace' which Edith found by living her individual life with such conviction and devotion?" In thinking about Edith's life through the years, Peggy knew that Edith's personal growth and development had been "rooted in her daily life, her acceptance of the struggle of each day and its mixture of beauty and disappointment and quietness and effort."[7]

Peggy had always devoted a significant amount of time to examining her beliefs, which ultimately were a combination of Quaker pacifism, Native American spiritualism, Eastern philosophy, and the Christian faith. She had read voraciously a number of books that helped her clarify her thoughts and ideas. "How much it meant to me when I first read the one-volume edition of *The Golden Bough*!" she mentioned in her journal. She identified the book as one which "liberated her from the dogmatic tradition of the Church" and opened an awareness of an ancient community of which she felt herself to be a part. She noted that she believed in "sin and repentance" and that "purgatory is an inner state and inescapable." In her opinion, "what we are punished for longest are our sins against love, our failure to be kind." And, while discussing religion with Corina, she stated her belief that "heaven and hell are not opposites" and that "death and rebirth are going on all the time within us. Not one after the other, but always simultaneously in our eternal life."[8]

As her life advanced, obviously moving toward its conclusion, she began to give even more serious thought to what she believed and what she had learned on the journey. She liked to refer to the beautiful portrait of Tilano that Laura Gilpin, the photographer, had given her. When she looked at the picture closely, Tilano seemed stern, his mouth tightly set, but from a distance, he was standing tall and gently smiling. "Whatever the secret of his wisdom is, childlike and yet ancient-of-days," Peggy said, "we must find it for ourselves."[9]

Peggy lamented the loss of many friends in the last years of her life, and in many cases she wrote poems in their memory. "For a Mountain Burial" was for Jane Baumann, and "For Gus" was a goodbye to artist Gustave Baumann, both of them beloved friends of a lifetime.[10] In 1982, she bid farewell to John Gaw Meem in "The Agéd Man." In Jungian analysis she had learned to record her dreams and attempt to decipher their meanings. In her journal of October 1, 1982, she recorded,

> I dream I am at the Meem's large house (not exactly
> like the real one) . . . John is in the beautiful sunny
> living room and begins to sing, seated on a sofa
> near the window. Frail as he is, he can still sing—or
> perhaps he has just discovered he can sing. His
> voice seems to grow stronger and stronger as he
> ends the song, rich and full. I am so moved I go to
> him and kneel down and bury my face in his lap
> and weep.

Meem died August 4, 1983, and at his funeral Peggy read a tribute to her family's friend, ending with the poem she had written.

> It has been my good fortune to have known John
> Meem through many different phases of my
> life, beginning at least as far back as 1924 when
> he planned a house for my mother and father
> on Palace Ave. In 1932, fifty-one years ago, he
> designed a stone addition to our log house at the
> Los Alamos Ranch School, where the magnificent
> Fuller Lodge had been constructed a few years

earlier. In spite of some unfortunate additions, the Lodge still stands as one of his most inspired and original masterpieces. In the same year he stood as godfather to our youngest son. The godfather relation was never pursued, due in part to geographical discrepancies, but I have always cherished it in my heart, making me aware always of where John's life was most deeply grounded.

This poem, "The Agéd Man," grew out of a vivid dream I had about John last October. Though, of course, it was "only a dream," still, dreams have their own reality and often teach us things about each other's souls we can learn in no other way. Because this dream reflected for me so much of John's true spirit, because it has become part of my own joyful memories of John, I wanted to share the poem with all of you who also loved him.

The Agéd Man
for John Gaw Meem

The agéd man sang in my dream.
I heard him sing
love of his long years,
love of the bright flame
that blazed up and consumed
his life's last remnant.
I heard the gathered song pour from his wasted frame
and fill the room and echo in the caverns of my heart.
Music became a fire
that fed itself on every mortal part
like flame on knotted wood.
How could an agéd man find strength to sing
approaching his life's end?
In dream I went to him and knelt
and laid my face between his knees and wept
while that music rose within me like a sea.[11]

Many of Peggy's poems held underlying sources and complexities, as with "The Agéd Man." Whether they were conscious or not isn't known, but this poem has associations to the thoughts expressed in William Butler Yeats's "Sailing to Byzantium," which was a poem that Peggy admired and committed to memory.

Within this same time frame, Peggy was writing perhaps her most complex and enigmatic poem, "Old Man by the River." It seems to interpret life and death in its cryptic allusions to her life, events, and people. The content of the poem confirms the fact that Peggy was analyzing her view of life as a series of learning experiences and preparing to take her leave. She worked on this poem off and on in her last years, and it seems that the final version in her workbook for this poem may not yet have been to her satisfaction. "Old Man by the River" was never published. Peggy used the flowing river as representative of life, as she did in several poems. With so many references to rivers and water in her works, the question of unconscious memory arises. What effect might a journey through life-threatening flood waters have had on a ten-month-old child?

> Do not trust yourself to the rising river
> that sweeps onward like time;
> trust yourself only
> to the old man who lives beside it
> with his thin white hair like a child's
> and his eyes as young as starlight.[12]

With so many of her friends passing away, Peggy became concerned about Virginia Wiebenson, who had recently been hospitalized. As she took out writing paper for a letter, Peggy reflected on how many memories she and Virginia shared, particularly the world in which they lived their young married lives. She once commented to Virginia, "With you, I often think how blessed we were to have had what we did." In 1983, she wrote again of those days.

> You and I share so much that no one else knows
> of. Please take care and stick around a while—
> though I myself am not quite sure I want to. Still,
> unexpected joys come our way.
>
> I love you dearly,
> Maggie[13]

Virginia Wiebenson and Peggy became friends when they were the young wives of masters at the Los Alamos Ranch School. "Do you remember those days, Virginia, when we were young and time was innocent?" Peggy asked in her poem "Letter to Virginia." Courtesy Peggy Pond Church Estate.

Ted's birthday, April 26th, fell on a Tuesday in 1983. Peggy looked at the calendar, unbelieving. It was already Tuesday the 26th, and she hadn't sent her son a card! Imagine, she thought, a mother writing a belated greeting. She'd run errands all day on Monday and been in a tizzy over company coming for dinner, and it just happened. She sat down to write the card—late!

Whatever happened to Monday? I wasn't so busy on Saturday, April 25th, 1925—busier on the 26th!

Lots of love,
Ma[14]

In the autumn of 1983, while visiting with Nancy Wirth, her friend Virginia's daughter-in-law, Peggy commented with a tinge of apprehension, "In just a little over three weeks I am going to be an octogenarian." Nancy said, "No such thing. What you are going to be is an octogeranium." Peggy relayed that lovely idea to May Sarton. "You have no idea how that cheered me up," she admitted. Then she told a funny little story about her friend who claimed to be a witch. The woman was in the hospital at the time, recovering from a car accident. "I went to see her," Peggy said, "and asked if she thought she could turn me into a geranium on my birthday." After some consideration, the woman told Peggy that she would have to be quite sure she wanted to be a geranium from then on. "Apparently there is no reversing the process," Peggy wrote, "but wouldn't it be nice?" Peggy penned a poem entitled "Silly Song for My Eightieth Birthday" and turned eighty, perhaps establishing a new word for the dictionary.[15]

Peggy's still keen sense of humor was balanced by sober thoughts of aging, thoughts that were magnified by the loss of her dog, Baba. When it became clear that Baba was too ill to get well, Peggy began to consider having her put down, but the decision was harder than it had ever been before. "I have had to make this decision about other dogs and my cat, Colette," she wrote in her journal, "but the decision about Baba has been tearing me to pieces—my dear companion ever since Ferm died. She is part of me—the nomadic part. The part that loves to wander. My companion on the blissful mountain walks." With great difficulty, Peggy wrote "On Putting to Death an Old Dog," and ended it with a grim outlook, saying, "and I, an old woman, clutching at a dream's end / wordless in the steep shadow / of my own death."[16]

There was no doubt that Peggy realized time was slipping away quickly, but she remained active as much as possible. She still gave poetry readings and an occasional lecture. At one such event she shared a favorite anecdote and a comment about the change she perceived in her life.

> When I told the mother of my great granddaughter
> that I was going to be an octogeranium, she said,
> 'Does that mean you're going to get potted on your
> birthday?' I don't think I'd have had the nerve to
> say such a thing to my grandmother—who never
> thought I was grown up enough to have her recipe

for pickled peaches, worse luck! This is leading up
to that old cliché that times have changed. I started
writing poetry when I lived on the Pajarito Plateau
among the caves and ruins of the prehistoric people
who had vanished 400 years before—yet in some
ways I felt closer to them than I do to my own
grandchildren who are now into a computer world
that baffles me.

Another instance of looking at the time gap occurred between Peggy
and her granddaughter Julia, older daughter of Hugh and Kathleen, but their
exchange of a letter for a poem is among the most beautiful things Peggy left
behind. In January 1984, Peggy sent this poem to Julia.

Lines for a Granddaughter Aged 20

I sit across from you at the morning table;
the birds fly in quick wreaths outside the window
and the snow is limned with the shadow of winter branches.
We are two women who have come here today to share life
across a barrier
that only birds can cross
or thoughts like birds
free to the mutual air.
It is time that holds us
too far apart for touch,
time wide as a continent
or as the space through which light travels
from one star to another.

I look at you as sorrowing Demeter
must have looked at her straying child, Persephone,
as at her own lost youth.
The rift of separation
is wide between us.
I have been part of
a time that is long gone by;
your time has not yet

ripened its memory.
You travel ahead of me,
younger than I and yet much wiser;
the trees of life grow taller
as the generations pass.
How can I show you
what my own spring was like?

Our journeys bring us together at a crossroad
where you must go one way and I another.
The maps I have made will have no meaning for you;
the landmarks are not the same.
You will be traveling in a different season
by a path that must be your own.
My own way now leads downward
like the winter's leaf
toward death and dissolution.
What is there I can leave you
but a moment's glimpse of the rainbow
the setting sun casts at evening
on the last cloud?[17]

In reply, Julia wrote this letter to her grandmother:

January 20, 1984

Dearest Grandmother,

    I have had your poem for a week, but have
been waiting for the "right" time to come along and
with it, the "right" words by which I can tell you
how much the poem meant to me. I don't know
that I'll ever find the words to thank you for those
lines and the meaning they hold. For now, all I can
say is thank you, they are beautiful.

    I, too, feel the "rift of separation" between us
and the barrier across which we share our life and

time. I often wish that I could go back in time to your youth which was so very different than my own. I imagine what it must have been like for you as a young girl growing up, going to school away from home, or living in a poetic dream world in the serenity of the mountains. I wonder what it was like for you to be married to a man you hardly knew and at such a young age. I wonder what I felt as the mother of three sons, one of which was my own father. I wonder what you experienced with the other men in your life. I wonder so many things about who you were before I came along. I wonder if I will look at my own granddaughter in 60 years as my own lost youth.

I suppose that I will never really know what your "spring" was like. I can picture it in the words you say and the words you write, but I know that your landmarks are not the same as mine have been, or will be. I can only hope that when I am in the winter of my life I will have lived a productive life, as you have. The landmarks of your maps are not the same as mine, but the overall map of your life is a great inspiration to mine and at that crossroad where you and I meet, a part of me will stand forever.

Grandmother, I will hold your rainbow in my heart, long after your sun has set.

Best love, Julia[18]

Peggy was a saver of letters, journals, books, lecture notes, photos, and such. Having done research herself, she realized the value of these items to future generations. She began to consider what she wanted to do with her papers and related artifacts. She knew the Ranch School papers should be placed in Los Alamos. The personal journals and letters, as well as the Edith Warner and Mary Austin research and a collection of Austin's books would go to the Center for Southwest Research at the University of New Mexico. A few letters and copies of journal pages were to be included in the Haniel Long Papers at the University of California, Los Angeles. Making those decisions, however, was the least of the task. Everything needed to be evaluated, sorted, and readied for donation, and for that she needed help. She called on Shelley Armitage, a young woman she had met three years before. Armitage had become an English professor at West Texas State University, and she was pleased by Peggy's offer. "It was a profound experience to work with her," Armitage recalled. "She had arranged things in certain ways and wanted only certain things published." She had multiple versions of some poems, so Armitage was amazed to find that she also "recorded the history of poems to see her own odyssey in finalizing them." Armitage would eventually serve as Peggy's literary editor for a time and author *Bones Incandescent: The Pajarito Journals of Peggy Pond Church.*[19]

Organizing and packing up decades of research and writing was difficult, but there was a more daunting task that Peggy had been avoiding. Many of her friends had moved to retirement communities, but she couldn't imagine leaving her house on Camino Rancheros, even though there was a very nice alternative in El Castillo, a popular retirement complex near the Santa Fe Plaza. She would miss her garden, her solitude, and the view from windows that opened onto the past. "I love this room in winter," she said once, standing at the west window, "because I can look through the bare branches of the trees at the familiar outline of the Jemez—Pajarito Mountain, Tsikomo, which I know as well or better than my own heart." A decision was forcing itself ever closer. "The thought of El Castillo as a refuge grows impossible," she said, "but the effort to stay on in this house grows impossible, too."

The care of the house was too much for her to handle alone at her age. Finally practicality won out, and she added her name to the waiting list at El Castillo and put her home up for sale. It sold quickly, which might have been a problem if not for the fact that the person buying the house wasn't in a hurry to occupy it and agreed that Peggy could live there until something opened up at El Castillo. The new owner was Larry Hagman, at that time a star of the popular television series *Dallas*. His daughter had been Peggy's neighbor for some time, always kind to help Peggy and look in on her, knowing that she lived alone. When the house went on the market, she mentioned that her father was thinking of buying a Santa Fe property and that he might be interested. Hagman made an appointment to see the home. He knew that

Peggy was a poet and must have mentioned the fact when they met, at which point, to be polite, she asked, "And what do you do?" When he told her, she apologized, explaining that she didn't watch much television, but he thought it was wonderfully funny, not bothered in the least by the fact that Peggy was one of perhaps a dozen people in the country who didn't know who his character J. R. Ewing was. When Peggy received the Governor's Award for Excellence and Achievement in the Arts a few weeks later, Larry Hagman and his wife, Maj, were among the first to send congratulations by way of a telegram.[20] The award was established in 1974 to celebrate the contributions and lifetime achievements of living artists, craftspeople, and arts supporters in New Mexico. Peggy earned the coveted honor in 1984 in the category of literature.

To her surprise, Peggy liked El Castillo once she got settled. Her apartment opened on a large courtyard. There were trees and beds of beautiful flowers. Some residents even had small gardens, and a man who was no longer using his plot gave it to Peggy. She returned to Camino Rancheros and retrieved some plumbago and cactus. The Plaza was close enough for her to walk there. She enjoyed revisiting old memories as she lingered under the portal of the Palace of Governors, a place "where, during World War I, I used to sell vegetables from my mother's victory garden," she remembered. Other things she observed on her walks weren't so nostalgic. She was not happy with the amount of property being bought up for more "malls and boutiques and galleries beyond number." In her opinion, Santa Fe had commercialized itself into ruin.

Jill Gyngell, Peggy's friend from London, wrote to say that she was considering a similar move. Peggy had trimmed down her possessions when she relocated to El Castillo, and Jill wanted to know how she was getting by with less. Peggy had adjusted, but she was amused by another woman's viewpoint on such things. Jill had sent along a delightful anecdote. She had asked one of the oldest women in the "home" she was considering if she had been able to bring her own furniture to the new apartment. The old woman had smiled and replied, "I haven't had any for forty years, apart from a few books. It all went with the bombing. Losing it gave me such freedom." Peggy liked that other way of looking at possessions.[21]

Peggy remained active, walking in Frijoles Canyon, attending the basket dance at San Ildefonso, and picnicking along the Rio Grande, but she also acknowledged a hearing loss that made outings and communication less enjoyable. She had mentioned the problem months before to May Sarton in regard to poetry readings. "More and more I love to read poetry out loud, especially to occasional visitors and friends," she wrote, emphasizing, "the sound and the taste of words." But she couldn't listen to someone else reading poetry unless the reader was very close and in front of her. "The only poetry readings I can go to any more are the ones where I am the reader! A happy frog in a small puddle," as she put it.[22]

Peggy may have considered herself to be in a small puddle, but she had one more splash to make. In 1985, her *Birds of Daybreak* was published by William Gannon of Santa Fe. The book contained twenty-one poems, of which fourteen were new, written in 1980 or after. Peggy had turned into a productive poet again. The book's dedication read, "To the memory of my husband, Ferm Church, who shared with me fifty years of clouds and stones and desert rivers." The book included not only "Sandhill Cranes in February" but also "In Memoriam: FSC 1900–1975," the third poem she had written for Ferm since his death. Also in the volume were two poems for Dottie, "A Memory of Horses" and "Perhaps in Our Old Age," as well as "The Rito: Frijoles Canyon," "Black Mesa: Dream and Variations," and "A Lament on Tsankawi Mesa," which had been issued as a single poem in a special limited edition in 1980 by Thistle Press of Santa Fe.[23]

Early in November, Peggy went on her last adventurous outing. Some new friends offered to take her out on Cochiti Lake in a canoe, and on a lark, she accepted. Paddling ten miles north, almost as far as Frijoles Canyon, before turning around, they were on the water for seven hours. The sun went down before they returned, and in the darkness the stars were reflected in the water. "There was not another soul on the lake," Peggy recalled when describing the trip. "Such magnificent silence." She was so cold she could hardly stand up when they returned to shore but added, "It was worth it. Quite an adventure for an old lady within a few weeks of her 82nd birthday!"[24]

The year 1985 had held some good memories for Peggy, but it ended in sadness when news came that Dorothy McKibbin had died peacefully in her sleep on December 17. Peggy and Dorothy had been friends for more than fifty years. At Dorothy's memorial service, Peggy read her poem titled "For D." that she had written in the early days of their friendship. "Her love, like the evening star / shines clear for everyone," Peggy had written, knowing from the beginning what a special person Dorothy McKibbin was.[25]

As the new year began, Peggy's time in the outdoors was becoming limited. She had developed chemical sensitivities and was having trouble going

Canoeing with friends, Peggy was on Cochiti Lake for seven hours on a November day in 1985. They paddled almost to Frijoles Canyon. She called it "quite an adventure for an old lady within a few weeks of her 82nd birthday!" Courtesy Peggy Pond Church Estate.

Eric Church, Peggy's grandson, escorts his grandmother down the aisle at his sister Julia's wedding in June 1986. Peggy read two sonnets from *The Ripened Fields* during the ceremony. Courtesy Peggy Pond Church Estate.

anywhere outside her apartment. She was likely to encounter bothersome substances or pollution at the bank, the post office, the grocery, or even in a friend's home. Her eyes were irritated much of the time, and despite cataract surgery a few months before, her eyesight was beginning to fail along with her hearing.

She grudgingly began to give up things she loved to do. Music and the piano were the first to go. She could no longer hear the music clearly. She had trouble reading and canceled subscriptions to *The Guardian* and *The Atlantic Monthly*. She cut out watching most television programs in favor of reading books, but some days she could read only a few minutes at a time. The days were shrinking.

As Peggy had once said, there were still unexpected joys in life. In March 1986, she garnered another honor when she was named a Living Treasure of Santa Fe, joining a select group of revered elders chosen each year. In June Peggy was given an honor of a different kind when she read sonnets XII and XIV from *The Ripened Fields* at her granddaughter Julia's wedding. Such moments were special interludes in months that were becoming more difficult.

Eventually her own apartment began to cause the chemical sensitivity discomforts, and her eyes were inflamed much of the time. Her friend Mary Bryan, living in a retirement home in Pennsylvania, had once spoken of encountering her first severe illness and then commented that "it gave her hope that after all she might not take such a long time dying." Peggy identified with Mary's words.[26]

Life no longer held the quality that allowed Peggy to do the things she loved. Her hearing and eyesight were failing rapidly. Writing, reading, listening to music, hiking—all were beyond her.

Peggy wrote a last letter to her friend May Sarton to express her concern about May's health, but she mentioned, too, an inability to write poetry any longer. "I'm glad to have lived in the New Mexico times when I did but am coming to feel that enough is enough," she said, signing the letter, "With my love, May, a handclasp, Peggy."[27] May's heart was failing, but she wrote a short letter in return. "Maybe poems will come," she said encouragingly. "Hang on." It was signed, "Your old May."[28]

Peggy called Corina and her sisters, a few other friends, and her family, and then, on October 23, 1986, Peggy took her own life.

She left a letter behind.

It has long been my belief that in old age when the body fails we should be permitted to lay it down at a time of our own choosing and allow the spirit to go free. To a poet, death is another phase of life. In this age of vociferous right-to-lifers, I feel that death has rights too and needs to be made a friend of.

I regret that circumstances make it impossible to say farewell to my many and dear friends. Those who know my books will know I have already said all there is to say.[29]

"Oh never fear death for me,
for I have looked at the earth and loved it;
I have been part of earth's beauty
beyond the edge of living."[30]

"Now I, old willow tree from which the birds have fled,
through whose branches the sap no longer rises,
leave my own vacancy on the waiting air."[31]

The words in Peggy's letter revealed the poet, but an excerpt from her journal, written years earlier, revealed the person.

In the hour before dawn, the earth lay covered with a light frost that shone palely, reflected from frosted leaves.

I moved about the dark kitchen, half awake, smelling the sharp odor of the toast I had burned last night, but my room had been full of the rose petal potpourri scent from the little box I'd opened in the night.

And I thought of all the beauty I had felt and experienced in a lifetime of housewifely hours, the beauty I have been aware of, consciousness, to have been an awake and conscious human being. Moments of adoration.

What does it matter whether one has gone here or there or done this or that or satisfied one's own or others' expectations so long as one has had these epiphanies, these moments of awareness? The lifelong accumulation of autumn mornings.

Afterword

Peggy Pond Church ended her life in her chosen way, according to the guidelines of the Hemlock Society, an organization now known as Compassion and Choices, but in many ways her life goes on. Her words, both poetry and prose, continue to touch the lives of all who read them, and her friends and family continue to honor her legacy. In an obituary in *The Taos News*, November 13, 1986, reporter Meg Scherch wrote that "those who attended services at St. John's College, Santa Fe, November 3, say they were struck by the many different types of people who attended." Peggy counted among her friends the young and the old, among them housekeepers, gardeners, archaeologists, teachers, librarians, scholars, poets, authors, artists, architects, ranchers, and many more. They came not only from the United States but also from Japan, Scotland, England, Finland, Canada, France, and India. In short, her impact was far reaching.

The House at Otowi Bridge is still in print after more than fifty years. Three books of poetry are also still in print, including two volumes published since her death: *This Dancing Ground of Sky* (Red Crane Books, 1993) and *Accidental Magic* (Wildflower Press, 2004). In addition, *Wind's Trail: The Early Life of Mary Austin* was edited by Shelley Armitage and published by the Museum of New Mexico Press in Santa Fe in 1990. A children's story, *Shoes for the Santo Niño* (Rio Grande Books, 2010), has become a children's opera that will premiere in December 2011. Another book of short stories for children, with illustrations by Elizabeth Church, is pending with the University of New Mexico Press.

Peggy's life goes on, too, in the day-to-day activities of her descendants, one of the youngest being great-granddaughter Hadley Margaret Sherman. At age ten, Hadley wrote this poem, words that are reminiscent of another young girl almost a century ago who wrote poetry at that age.

Misty Night
by Hadley Sherman

The bitter mist
hovering, above the ground
trees, limp and bare
the ground on fire from red and yellow leaves

all the world seems magical but . . .
    lonely
a swift, cold, silver wind slices my face
the sky, dim, full of mystery and . . .
    wonder.

In the autumn of 2010, members of the Pond and Church families gathered in Los Alamos, New Mexico, for the dedication of a New Mexico Historic Women's Marker honoring Peggy. The marker stands beside Ashley Pond, a small body of water named for her father.

Peggy Pond Church
(1903–1986)

Peggy Pond Church, author of the Southwest classic *The House at Otowi Bridge* and daughter of Los Alamos Ranch School founder Ashley Pond, will forever be "The First Lady of New Mexican Poetry." As she rode the Pajarito Plateau and camped beneath tall pines, she came to understand that "it is the land that wants to be said." She captured it in her sensitive poems.

In a beautiful coda to her grandmother's life, Robyn Church Hatton has said, "One of my favorite memories of Grandmother Peggy is of her voice. When she read us her poems, I could hear the land she loved."

DESCENDANTS
of ASHLEY AND HARRIET POND

Theodore Spencer Church
(1925–2011)

Stanley B. Pond   Allen Bartlit Church
(1869–1873)   (1928–   )

Jared Pond ——— Ashley Pond ——— Ashley Pond Jr. ——— Margaret Hallett Pond ——— Hugh Whitney Church
(1790–1856)   (1827–1910)   (1872–1933)   (1903–1986)   (1932–   )

m. Statira Bartlit   m. Harriet Pearl   m. Hazel Hallett   m. Fermor Spencer Church
(1802–1872)   (1842–1900)   (1885–1954)   (1900–1975)

Florence Pond   Dorothy Pond   Joan Florence Pond
(1867–1955)   (1906–1989   (1937–   )

m. Courtney Benedict   Karen Hazel Pond
(1903–1979)   (1939–2011)

Ashley Pond III ——— Gretchen Ragnhild Pond
(1908–1986)   (1942–   )

m. Lucille Olson   Ashley D. Pond
(1912–2000)   (1947–   )

---

m. Keyes Danforth   DESCENDANTS
(1841–1882)   of OZRO AND MARY HADLEY

Addie Hadley ——— Mary Tetard
(1852–1890)   (1889–   )

m. Louis Tetard
(1888–   )

Ozro A. Hadley ——— Altie Hadley ——— William Hadley Hallett   Theodore Spencer Church
(1826–1915)   (1857–1951)   (1879–1889)   (1925–2011)

m. Mary Kilbourn   m. William Hallett   Homan Danforth Hallett   Allen Bartlit Church
(1832–1903)   (1848–1901)   (1881–1946)   (1928–   )

Hazel Hallett ——— Margaret Hallett Pond ——— Hugh Whitney Church
(1885–1954)   (1903–1986)   (1932–   )

m. Ashley Pond Jr   m. Fermor Spencer Church
(1872–1933)   (1900–1975)

Horace Allis Hallett   Dorothy Pond   Joan Florence Pond
(1889–1893)   (1906–1989)   (1937–   )

m. Courtney Benedict   Karen Hazel Pond
(1903–1979)   (1939–2011)

Ashley Pond (III) ——— Gretchen Ragnhild Pond
(1908–1986)   (1942–   )

m. Lucille Olson   Ashley D. Pond
(1912–2000)   (1947–   )

DESCENDANTS
of AMY CANNON SPENCER

Amy Cannon Spencer
(1859–1942)

#1
m. William A. Cape
(1860–1886)

John J. Cape
(1886–1956)
m. M. A. Gillette

Jackie Cape
(1922–1986)

John J. Cape Jr.
(1918–1942)

William S. Cape
(1884–1945)
m. E. G. Gillette

Evangeline Cape
(1882–1957)
m. Louis T. Wallis
(1882–1959)

Herbert Spencer Wallis
(1913–1977)

Malcolm Wallis
(1917–1981)

#2
m. William Church
(1858–1927)

Vallette Church
(1894–1975)
m. Isabella Ashcroft
(1899–1973

Fermor Spencer Church
(1900–1975)
m. Margaret Hallett Pond
(1903–1986)

Theodore Spencer Church
(1925–2011)

Allen Bartlit Church
(1928–   )

Hugh Whitney Church
(1932–   )

Endnotes

Much of the quoted material in this book comes from the volumes of Peggy Pond Church's personal journal, which she kept for most of her life. In the interest of space and ease for the reader, such quotes will not be included in these endnotes. The reader may assume that unreferenced quotes are taken from the journal. All other quoted material will be noted, and source abbreviations from the following list will be used.

CAS
Correspondence between Corina A. Santistevan and Peggy Pond Church currently resides with Corina Santistevan, Taos, New Mexico. Quotes from these letters are used with permission.

CFP
The Church Family Papers are currently in the possession of Hugh and Kathleen Church unless otherwise noted. Some materials are in the possession of Allen Church. It is the intention of the family that most of these materials, which consist of files, correspondence, legal documents, and photographs, be turned over to the Center for Southwest Research at Zimmerman Library, University of New Mexico, as an addition to the Peggy Pond Church Papers (Mss 231). Use of these materials is with the permission of Kathleen Church, literary executor of the Peggy Pond Church estate.

CSWR
The Center for Southwest Research in Zimmerman Library at the University of New Mexico holds the bulk of the Peggy Pond Church Papers in Manuscript Collection 231. In addition to personal papers and correspondence, the research for *The House at Otowi Bridge* and for *Wind's Trail: The Early Life of Mary Austin* is housed at the center in Zimmerman Library. Use of these materials is with the permission Kathleen Church, copyright holder for the Peggy Pond Church Papers, and by permission of the Center for Southwest Research, University of New Mexico.

LAHMA
The Los Alamos Historical Museum Archives maintains a collection of historical papers concerning the history of the Los Alamos Ranch School, among them the personal papers, photographs, and research of Peggy Pond Church regarding Ashley Pond Jr., the history of the Pajarito Club, her early life on the Pajarito Plateau, and her years as a faculty wife at the Los Alamos Ranch School. Use of these materials is with permission of the archives.

PPC
The journal of Peggy Pond Church consists of handwritten and typed volumes. The volumes from the Los Alamos Ranch School years no longer exist. The surviving notebooks of the journal reside with Hugh and Kathleen Church but will eventually be presented to the Center for Southwest Research at the University of New Mexico as an addition to the Peggy Pond Church Papers (Mss 231). Use of these materials is with permission of the Church family.

UCLA
The Department of Special Collections, Charles E. Young Research Library, University of California, Los Angeles., holds the Haniel Long Papers in Manuscript Collection 672. Within the collection are papers donated by Peggy Pond Church which reference her relationship with Long.

INTRODUCTION

1. Mabel Dodge Luhan, "A Poet of Los Alamos, New Mexico" (a review of *Ultimatum for Man*, 1946), *The Chicago Sun Book Week*, December 1946.
2. Peggy Pond Church, "Morning on Tseregé" (1945), first published in *Ultimatum for Man* (1946), *Birds of Daybreak* (1985), *This Dancing Ground of Sky* (1993), and a special broadside edition (1976).
3. Peggy Pond Church, "Ultimatum for Man," title poem from *Ultimatum for Man* (1946), *Saturday Review* (August 1946), *New and Selected Poems* (1976).
4. Stanley Noyes in *Birds of Daybreak* (1985).

PREFACE

1. Mike Shearer, "Peggy Pond Church: An 'Octogeranium' Speaks," *New Mexico Magazine*, February 1985.

CHAPTER 1

1. Tshirege is the spelling that Peggy Pond Church used in later years for the ruins above Pajarito Canyon, an ancestral site for the people of San Ildefonso Pueblo, but through time, and still today, the spelling has varied: Tsirege, Tseregé, Tzirege. The name was published two different ways in the title of Peggy Pond Church's poem "Morning on Tseregé," carrying that spelling in *Ultimatum for Man* (1946) and *This Dancing Ground of Sky* (1993) but spelled Tshirege in *Birds of Daybreak* (1985) and on a separate broadside issue of the poem.
2. Peggy Pond Church, "Sangre de Cristo" (1921), unpublished poem, CFP.
3. W. David Laird, review of *A Rustle of Angels in Books of the Southwest*, May 1982. Laird said of the book of Christmas poems, "Nothing southwestern here except that these two fine, creative spirits are soaked through and through with the essence of New Mexico. Church, First Lady of New Mexican poetry, should be in all poetry collections." By "spirits," Laird referred also to illustrator Jeannie Pear.
4. Peggy Pond Church, "Trails Over Pajarito," text of a presentation to the Los Alamos Historical Society, 1982, CFP.
5. Ibid. The name *Ramon Vigil Ranch* came from the Spanish land grant days. Though the land changed hands many times, Vigil was the owner of record when the American courts established the Spanish land grant titles as private land, and, thus, his name became attached to the grant. In actuality, Ramon Vigil owned the grant for only eight years.
6. The Los Alamos Ranch School (1917–1942) began as a health school where sickly boys with respiratory illnesses could recuperate in the high mountain air while enjoying the outdoor life, but it soon evolved into a combination of academics and outdoor activities that included camping and riding. Each boy was assigned his own horse for the time he was at the school. A summer camp with pack trips was also offered in many years. In the era when ranch schools were popular with young men, the Los Alamos Ranch School held a respected position among such schools and was nationally known for its academic program.
7. Peggy Pond Church, "Trails Over Pajarito," CFP and LAHMA (1982).
8. Peggy Pond Church, "And in the Late Afternoon" (1935), *Familiar Journey* (1936).
9. Peggy Pond Church to May Sarton, October 1951, CFP.
10. Peggy Pond Church, "East of the Sun and West of the Moon" (1935), *Familiar Journey* (1936) and *This Dancing Ground of Sky* (1993).

CHAPTER 2

1. Peggy Pond Church, "Return to a Landscape" (1983), *Birds of Daybreak* (1985) and *This Dancing Ground of Sky* (1993).
2. In 1982, Peggy Church and her longtime friend Mary MacArthur Bryan traveled to Mora County to visit their past. Mary Bryan was born to a ranching family in Wagon Mound, New Mexico, in 1897. "Return to a Landscape" was a tribute to Bryan as well as a memoir to the common roots they shared. Mary Bryan left behind a short but special memoir—*Mary MacArthur Bryan: Childhood Days in New Mexico, 1897–1911*, as told to Doris Schwartz, Foulkeways, Gwynedd, PA, February 1985, CFP.
3. Personal files of Peggy Pond Church on the history of the Clyde Ranch, CFP.
4. Notes of Peggy Pond Church for "Preface to an Autobiography" (1934), a poem edited by Haniel Long and published in *Space*, September 1934, CFP.
5. Stephen Dorsey was a United States senator from Arkansas. He won his seat in the Senate as a carpetbag politician after the Civil War. Some reports say he bought the necessary votes to be elected. He had been involved with shady deals in stocks and railroad bonds before moving to Arkansas. In New Mexico he bought up large amounts of ranching acreage and acquired the Uña de Gato Grant with a deed later determined to be a forgery. He was also part of the corrupt Star Route mail contracting business, an involvement that cost him dearly in legal fees to avoid a prison term. In an effort to recoup some of his money, Dorsey formulated a plan to buy the Maxwell Land Grant and subdivide it, but the venture failed. The Dorsey Mansion, a Victorian home built at Chico Springs near Springer, New Mexico, and completed in 1886, is today a historical attraction sometimes open to the public. (*Rogue! The Life and High Times of Stephen W. Dorsey* by Thomas J. Caperton, Museum of New Mexico Press, 1978.)
6. Personal files of Peggy Pond Church on the history of the Clyde Ranch, CFP.
7. Susannah North Martin was the ancestor who was hanged as a witch in old Salem. She was executed along with four other women on July 19, 1692, in Salem, Massachusetts. The famous Rev. Cotton Mather remarked that Susannah was "one of the most impudent, scurrilous, wicked creatures of this world," but the author of the *History of Amesbury* defends Martin by saying, "The idea of snatching this hardworking, honest woman from her home to be tried for her life by those who never knew her, and witnesses who were prejudiced against her . . . is almost too much for belief . . . Allowed no counsel, she was her own lawyer, and her answers are remarkable for independence and clearness. She showed herself to be a woman of more than ordinary talent and resolution." Another historian of the period claimed that her real offense was likely that she had more wit than her neighbors. It is just possible that Peggy Church inherited some of that wit from her long ago relative, for her own was always keen. In her papers on family genealogy, she noted that "Susannah's daughter Jane married Samuel Hadley and bore him eleven children. Their next to last son, Joseph, had twelve children, and at that rate the witch's strain must have been pretty much diluted by the time it got down to my mother, Hazel, granddaughter of Ozro A. Hadley, 8th generation down the line from the witty and hapless Susannah."
8. Files on Hadley Family Genealogy, CFP.
9. *Illustrated History of New Mexico*, Chicago: Lewis Publishing Co., 1895.
10. Personal files of Peggy Pond Church on the history of the Clyde Ranch, CFP.
11. Peggy Pond Church, "Return to a Landscape" (1983), *Birds of Daybreak* (1985) and *This Dancing Ground of Sky* (1993).
12. Personal files of Peggy Pond Church on the history of the Clyde Ranch, CFP.
13. Ibid. In this passage, when Church says, "Afternoons, memory said, or my mother," she is referring to ancestral memory or in Carl Jung's terminology, the "collective memory" that

he defined as inherited traits, intuitions, and collective wisdom of the past. She was an avid reader of Jung's psychological theories and pursued Jungian analysis for many years.

14. Peggy Pond Church, "Preface to an Autobiography" (1934), *Space*, September 1934.
15. Ashley Pond Jr.'s boyhood friends Roy Chapin and Henry Joy became chief executives of the Hudson Motor Car Company and the Packard Motor Company, respectively. They were also to become partners with Pond and two other Detroit men in the Pajarito Club, a failed venture to establish an elite hunting resort in northern New Mexico (see Chapter 4).
16. Linda K. Aldrich and John D. Wirth, *Los Alamos, the Ranch School Years*, Albuquerque: University of New Mexico Press, 2003.
17. Biographical notes on Ashley Pond Jr. from the Peggy Pond Church papers, LAHMA.
18. Ibid.
19. Ibid.
20. Peggy Pond Church, "For My Mother Who Claims That I Have Never Written a Poem to Her" (1934), *Accidental Magic* (2004).
21. Florence Pond to a friend (Louise) (c. 1903), LAHMA.
22. Personal files of Peggy Pond Church on The Watrous Years, CFP.
23. Peggy Pond Church, "For My Mother Who Claims That I Have Never Written a Poem to Her" (1934), *Accidental Magic* (2004).
24. The Watrous Years, CFP.
25. Hadley Family Genealogy, CFP.
26. The Watrous Years, CFP. The two-story brick house continues to stand in Shoemaker Canyon despite flooding and years with no occupancy. Renovation has been considered and would save a beautiful and significant piece of New Mexico history.
27. Notes of Peggy Pond Church from a visit with Gertie Tipton Lynch in Craig, Colorado (1977), CFP. After the age of four, Peggy didn't see Gertie again until 1977, when she and Gertie were reunited after seventy years. In the course of her genealogical pursuits, Peggy found Gertie still living in the high mountains of Colorado where she and Albert had homesteaded. The two exchanged letters and enjoyed a visit, and Gertie filled in many details of Peggy's early days in Mora County.
28. Fritz Thompson, "The Flood" in *IMPACT, Albuquerque Journal Magazine*, March 15, 1983.
29. Ibid.
30. Daniel Scotten to his family in Michigan, Autumn 1904, The Watrous Years, CFP. Scotten's letter was also published as part of an article in the *Detroit Free Press*, October 17, 1904.
31. Fritz Thompson, "The Flood" in *IMPACT, Albuquerque Journal Magazine*, March 15, 1983.
32. Scotten letter, The Watrous Years, CFP.
33. Ibid.
34. Ibid. The small black dog described by Daniel Scotten did not survive the disaster, but another dog was a heroine that night. At the time of the flood, Ashley owned a Great Dane named Princess, and that dog may have saved the people on the Pond ranch. She began to bark around 2 a.m., waking Ashley and alerting him to the danger. When he stepped out of bed, the water was already ankle-deep in the downstairs rooms of the house. Princess was too large to carry to safety, but when Ashley and Daniel Scotten returned to the house late the following morning, Princess was found swimming in the parlor!
35. Ibid.
36. Ibid.
37. Fritz Thompson, "The Flood" in *IMPACT, Albuquerque Journal Magazine*, March 15, 1983.
38. *Las Vegas Optic*, October 4, 1904.
39. *Las Vegas Optic*, October 8, 1904.
40. Scotten letter, The Watrous Years, CFP.
41. Ibid.

CHAPTER 3

1. Linda Aldrich and John Wirth, *Los Alamos, the Ranch School Years*, University of New Mexico Press, 2003.
2. Three Mile Lake is now called Lake Angelus, a change that occurred in the 1920s.
3. Obituary of Ashley Pond Sr., *Detroit Free Press*, January 13, 1910.
4. Ashley felt the pressure of an only son because of the death of his brother Stanley in December 1873. As well, he was competing for family laurels with two talented cousins, Allen Bartlit Pond and Irving Kane Pond, highly successful architects in Chicago.
5. Peggy Pond Church, "Handprints in the Sands of Time," unpublished account (ca. 1944), CFP.
6. Peggy Pond Church, "Sister" (1976), *Accidental Magic* (2004).
7. "Handprints in the Sands of Time," CFP.
8. Notes from a visit of Peggy Pond Church with Gertie Tipton Lynch in Craig, Colorado (1977), CFP. Gertie and Albert Horton stayed in Michigan for only a year. Albert wanted to join his brother in Colorado, so he bought three horses from Pond and shipped them west to begin his own ranch. He and Gertie homesteaded near Craig on the Dry Fork of the Little Bear River in 1908. Albert died in 1940, but Gertie remained on the ranch until she moved into Craig in 1958. She died November 12, 1986, at the age of 100. Her story stands high in its own right and can be found in an article called *County Profile: Alice Gertrude Lynch* by Sylvia Becker in the *The Daily Press* (Craig, CO), March 29, 1978.
9. Ibid.
10. Peggy Pond Church, "Gertie" (1977), unpublished poem, CFP.
11. Notes on Gertie Tipton Lynch, CFP.
12. Ibid.
13. Ibid.
14. Ibid.
15. Peggy Pond Church, "Gertie" (1977), unpublished poem, CFP.
16. "Author, Peggy Pond Church," *The Santa Fean*, September 1978, p. 22.
17. Peggy Pond Church, "Handprints in the Sands of Time," CFP. Peggy sometimes hung on to thoughts for decades. In 1964, she wrote a humorous Christmas poem titled "All Granma Wants." It was about a tree toad. That poem is published in *Accidental Magic* (2004).
18. Ibid.
19. Ibid.
20. Ibid.
21. Ibid.
22. Peggy Pond Church, "Five Years Old," (1925), *Children—A Magazine for Parents* (n.d.) and *Foretaste* (1933).
23. Mark Twain was known to be especially fond of children. He and his wife, Olivia, had three girls and a boy. The son died in infancy, and Twain later lost two of his daughters. The youngest girl, Jean, died only a few months before Twain watched young Peggy Pond playing on the Bermuda beach in 1910. He was in poor health when he visited Bermuda, hoping the warm climate would be beneficial, but the climate didn't help. Twain returned home in April and died a week later, April 21, 1910. Peggy used the scenario from the beach in "Old Man by the River" (1982), an unpublished poem about death (CFP), and according to her oldest son, she kept a photograph of Twain on her desk for many years. In the picture, Twain was relaxing in a chaise lounge, location unknown. A significant quote in her journal refers to her encounter: "She learned . . . the ocean . . . when she was six and they spent the winter months in Bermuda, picnicking on the coral islands, whose surfaces rasped her bare feet and where she played hide-and-go-seek around the rock with the white-haired old gentleman whom they called Mark Twain."

24. Peggy Pond Church, "Background," (1926), unpublished poem, CFP. This poem also exists under the title "When She Was Small."

CHAPTER 4

1. Peggy Pond Church to Ted Church, January 21, 1976, CFP.
2. Mary Hadley died June 11, 1903. O. A. Hadley sold the Clyde four years later and moved to California to be near his daughter, Altie, and his grandson Homan. He died in the Lakeview Hotel in Los Angeles on July 18, 1915.
3. "Trails Over Pajarito," CFP.
4. Ibid.
5. "Author, Peggy Pond Church," *The Santa Fean*, September 1978, and notes by Peggy Pond Church for a presentation titled "Early Days at Los Alamos," presented to the Newcomers Club at Los Alamos, July 25, 1973, LAHMA.
6. "Trails Over Pajarito," CFP.
7. "The Days Before Los Alamos, Parts I & II," Los Alamos Historical Society Newsletter, December 1995 & March 1996, LAHMA. Note: The story of Hazel's arrival at the house in Pajarito Canyon is also told in an unpublished fictionalized account by Peggy Pond Church titled "Canyon Summer" (Mss 231, Center for Southwest Research, University of New Mexico).
8. Ibid.
9. Ibid.
10. "Trails Over Pajarito," CFP.
11. Peggy Pond Church to Ted Church, January 21, 1976, CFP.
12. "Early Days at Los Alamos," 1973, LAHMA.
13. Ibid.
14. "Author, Peggy Pond Church," *The Santa Fean*, September 1978.
15. Rosanna Hall, "Words a way of life for Peggy Pond Church," *Santa Fe New Mexican*, Living/Santa Fe, Section D, June 28, 1981.
16. Visitors to the Pajarito Club as well as to local hotels were listed in the *Santa Fe New Mexican*.
17. "Trails Over Pajarito," CFP.
18. "Early Days at Los Alamos," 1973, LAHMA.
19. Peggy Pond Church, "Thirteen Years Old" (1925), published in *Children's Magazine*, August 1927, and *Accidental Magic* (2004).
20. Peggy Pond Church, notes on mythology, CFP.
21. Peggy Pond Church, "Ten Years Old" (1925), unpublished poem, CFP.
22. Lines of Peggy Pond Church's first poem recounted from her personal journal, CFP.
23. Peggy Pond Church, "Ode to a Flower" (1916), *Accidental Magic* (2004).
24. Peggy Pond Church, script for a poetry reading, Santa Fe, College of St. John, December 11, 1983, CFP.
25. "Trails Over Pajarito," CFP.
26. "Trails Over Pajarito," CFP, and "The Whiffenpoof Pool" (ca. 1950), *Accidental Magic* (2004).
27. Ibid.
28. Peggy Pond Church, "Quince" Journal and "Morning at Tserege" (1945), *Ultimatum for Man* (1946), *Birds of Daybreak* (1985), and *This Dancing Ground of Sky* (1993). Peggy kept an autobiographical journal in the form of a first-person narrative for a time. In this journal she called herself Quince. This form of self-representational writing or autobiography as fiction is therapeutic in psychoanalysis. Peggy took this cue from Doris Lessing. Peggy did have her collection of arrowheads from Pajarito Canyon on display at

the Pan-American Exposition in San Diego, and she complained occasionally about the Exposition authorities because they never gave her arrowheads back!

29. "Trails Over Pajarito," CFP.
30. Ibid.
31. Ibid.
32. Edgar L. Hewett, *Pajarito Plateau and its Ancient People*, revised by Bertha P. Dutton, University of New Mexico Press, 1953, p. vi.
33. The words—"When you come to the end of a perfect day"—are from the lyrics of the World War I song, "A Perfect Day," by Carrie Jacobs-Bond, 1910.

CHAPTER 5

1. The Los Alamos Ranch School was slow in getting started. Lancelot Inglesby Pelly, the son of a British consul stationed in Seattle, may have been the first student, but records are uncertain. Wirth and Aldrich record that at least two other boys spent some time as students at the school in its first year. A Boy Scout from Santa Fe named Bill Rose was brought in for companionship for the early boys, and Connell's nephew also spent some time at the ranch. Enrollment may have reached eight or nine by the second year, with Bill Rose and Ashley Pond III on the student roster by then. In an attempt to gain a meaningful endorsement for the school and boost enrollment, Ashley Pond wrote to his commanding officer from his Rough Rider days, who was by then President Theodore Roosevelt. The result was disappointing, though honest.

   Sagamore Hill
   Aug 13th 1916
   Dear Mr. Pond,
   I dislike to say "no" to an old Rough Rider; but, my dear sir, I never endorse a school or anything else unless I know it, and can speak from personal knowledge. Any other course would render my endorsements worthless.

   With regret
   very truly yours
   Theodore Roosevelt

2. "Early Days at Los Alamos," 1973, LAHMA.
3. Arthur Rackham was a popular British illustrator of fairy tales and fables in the early twentieth century. He provided artwork for such stories as Peter Pan, Aesop's Fables, Cinderella, Sleeping Beauty, Mother Goose, and The Wind in the Willows as well as Peer Gynt, A Midsummer Night's Dream, and Gulliver's Travels. He is referenced in Peggy Pond Church's "Children Remember Knowing Aphrodite" (1926), *Accidental Magic* (2004).
4. Aileen O'Bryan, *Seven Gardens* (ca. 1950), an unpublished autobiography in possession of the author.
5. Aileen Baehrens was born Mary Aileen O'Bryan in Las Vegas, New Mexico Territory, in 1889. As a young girl, she moved to Paris with her paternal grandparents, where in 1911 she married Alfred Baehrens, an American expatriate musician. In 1913, they had a son, Deric. Baehrens died three years later, and Aileen returned to New Mexico with her young son. She later married archaeologist Jesse Nusbaum. When that marriage ended in divorce, she went back to her maiden name of O'Bryan.
6. "Children Remember Knowing Aphrodite" (1926). A shorter version of this poem honoring Aileen Baehrens is called "Tribute" (1925). It was published in *Children's* magazine. By the time these poems were written, Aileen was married to archaeologist Jesse Nusbaum.

7. *El Palacio*, No. 19, Vol. V, December 1918; "New Mexico in the Great War, At the Front," *New Mexico Historical Review*, No. 2, January 1920, p. 17. After Pond returned from France, he continued on the Board of Directors for the Ranch School but was never again involved in its day-to-day management.

8. Peggy Pond Church to May Sarton, December 1983, CFP; "Girl Scouting in N.M. To Celebrate 75 Years," *Journal North*, March 11, 1987.

9. Files and camp records of The Aloha Foundation, RR#1, Box 91A, Fairlee, Vermont 05045-9737. Harriet and Edward Gulick were founders of Camp Aloha.

10. Prize Winners of the Atlantic Short Story Contest for Schools and Colleges, The Atlantic Monthly Company, Boston, 1921–1922.

CHAPTER 6

1. Peggy Pond Church, "Betrothal Gift" (1939), unpublished poem, CFP.

2. Peggy Pond Church to her granddaughter, Robyn Church Hatton, August 1, 1979.

3. Audio tape (R-1864a/68.5 F.S. & P.P. Church—Los Alamos Ranch School 7/73), LAHMA.

4. Ibid.

5. The Ranch School secretary that first year in the Pyramid was Walter Fessenden, called "Fezzy." He occupied the other half of the Pyramid, and by agreement, Peggy cleaned his quarters as well as her own.

6. Audio tape (R-1864a/68.5 F.S. & P.P. Church—Los Alamos Ranch School 7/73), LAHMA.

7. Ibid.

8. Peggy Pond Church, "Return to a Landscape" (1983), *Birds of Daybreak* (1885) and *This Dancing Ground of Sky* (1993).

9. Shelley Armitage, "Introduction," *This Dancing Ground of Sky* (1993). Armitage, University of Texas at El Paso, became friends with Peggy Church when she helped Peggy arrange her personal papers for donation to the Center for Southwest Research (CSWR) at the University of New Mexico. In addition to the Introduction for *This Dancing Ground of Sky*, she also wrote an Introduction for and edited *Wind's Trail: The Early Life of Mary Austin* (1990) by Peggy Pond Church. She has given presentations on Church's poetry, published *Bones Incandescent*, a literary analysis of Church's Pajarito Journals, and authored the Boise State University Western Writers' Series volume on Church.

10. Whether by edict or luck of the Irish, no girls were born to Ranch School masters until Tommy and Anita Waring had a girl in the last years of the school's existence.

11. Audio tape (R-1864a/68.5 F.S. & P.P. Church—Los Alamos Ranch School 7/73), LAHMA.

12. To provide water for the Ranch School, a small dam was built in a canyon in the mountains above the school, creating a reservoir that has been improved but is still in use. A gravity-feed pipeline supplied water to a wooden water tower at the school. Overflow from the tower was diverted to a nearby natural pond that was surrounded by tall ponderosa pines and used for canoeing and swimming in the summer and ice skating in the winter. In the first years of the school, it was referred to as the Duck Pond, but eventually the too-common name fell victim to the sense of humor of William Mills, an early faculty member, and the small lake was thereafter called Ashley Pond. During the Ranch School years, ice was cut from the pond, which sometimes yielded as much as a two-year supply. The blocks of ice were at first stored in a log building, but it was later replaced by one made of stone and located just south of the pond. The stone ice house was destined to become a historic link between the Ranch School era and the Manhattan

Project. During wartime construction, Ashley Pond was scheduled to be bulldozed to allow for the necessary technical buildings, but at the last minute the order was rescinded. The pond was deemed useful for fire protection, so the new buildings were constructed around it. The Ranch School's ice house was also preserved, and in 1945 the nuclear components for the first atomic bomb were checked and assembled in that small stone building beside the pond. (See Janie O'Rourke and Georgia Strickfaden, "Ashley Pond: The unlikely history of a small body of water," *Los Alamos Monitor*, July 25, 2003.) In 2000, the pond was a source of water for fighting the Cerro Grande forest fire, fulfilling its once-proposed use. Helicopters dipped their huge buckets into the pond many times in a valiant effort to check the flames which ultimately destroyed more than 400 homes.

13. Peggy Pond Church, "Early Days at Los Alamos," 1973, LAHMA. Peggy remembered the saddle with a certain sadness and lamented, "The saddle, which I doted on as though it were part of myself, is now in possession of my brother's family, but his children, like mine, turned out to be skiers, not horseback riders, and so are our grandchildren." In 2009, the saddle was donated by the family to the Los Alamos Historical Museum Archives.

14. Peggy Pond Church, "Yesterday" (1926), *Accidental Magic* (2004).

15. The Smithwicks left the plateau in 1937 and moved to Desert Hot Springs in southern California. Their three sons attended St. Michael's College in Santa Fe. When the property was condemned by the government in 1943, the family of Alex Ross bought another ranch for the young man near Silver City, where Alex lived out his life on a second Anchor Ranch.

16. The poet friend was Haniel Long, whose wife, Alice, was noted for establishing an environment in which Haniel could find the peace and quiet needed to write. One might wonder how Alice Long found the time to be creative in her own right, for she, too, was a poet and an artist.

17. Lawrence Hitchcock become headmaster at Los Alamos in 1926, following the death of the school's first headmaster, Fayette Curtis, who died of tuberculosis (see Aldrich and Wirth, *Los Alamos: The Ranch School Years*, 2003). Hitchcock began his tenure as headmaster in February of 1927 and held the position until he was called to active duty during World War II.

18. Ashley Pond Jr. was turned down for pilot training in World War I because of his age, but he never gave up the dream of flying. He finally earned a pilot's license in 1932 and bought his own plane, which he landed proudly in the outer fields at Los Alamos Ranch School. In his obituary in the *Santa Fe New Mexican* of June 22, 1933, he is credited with having "secured money for the improvement of the large local flying field beyond the Indian School and in every possible way helped to put New Mexico and Santa Fe on the air map."

CHAPTER 7

1. Shelley Armitage, "Introduction," *Wind's Trail: The Early Life of Mary Austin* (1990) by Peggy Pond Church, Santa Fe: Museum of New Mexico Press, p. xi.

2. John Gaw Meem also designed Fuller Lodge (1929) for the Los Alamos Ranch School.

3. Nancy Cook Steeper, *Gatekeeper to Los Alamos*, Los Alamos Historical Society, 2003.

4. Peggy Pond Church, "Invitation" (1932), unpublished poem, CFP.

5. Peggy Pond Church, "For D." (ca. 1932), unpublished poem, CFP.

6. Peggy Pond Church, "What Do I Know?" (1932), unpublished poem, CFP. In looking back at the idyllic two weeks that Dorothy and Peggy spent together in the summer of 1932, one cannot help but focus on the irony that history held for these two women, that both would be deeply affected by the Manhattan Project but in such different ways. For Peggy, the project's location on the Pajarito Plateau meant

the loss of the only place to which she had ever felt connected. For Dorothy, the project established her sense of belonging, identifying her as the "Gatekeeper to Los Alamos." Despite the opposite emotions of Dorothy's successful involvement with the Manhattan Project and Peggy's bitterness toward it, the two remained close friends throughout their lives.

7. Peggy Pond Church, "Portrait of My Father" (1956), *This Dancing Ground of Sky* (1993).

8. Haniel Long to Peggy Pond Church, Mss 231, CSWR.

9. Haniel Long to Peggy Pond Church, Autumn 1933, Haniel Long Papers (Collection 672), Department of Special Collections, Charles E. Young Research Library, University of California, Los Angeles. (Folder 3 in Box 33 of this collection contains photocopied material added to the Haniel Long Papers by Peggy Pond Church, with the stipulation that they not be open to researchers until after her death.)

10. Easson, Kay Parkhurst and Roger R. Easson, Commentary in *Milton: A Poem by William Blake*, Random House, 1978. Whether Peggy was already familiar with this work by Blake or read it because of Haniel's prompting is not known, but she was a lifelong admirer of Blake.

11. In the journals of Peggy Pond Church, this man remained a mystery, referred to only as "Bill" or simply "B," but in 1993 a biography titled *Jane Abbott Paul: An Unexpected Life* by Nancy Bondurant Jones (self-published), pp. 38, 136–137, gave further details of the affair, revealing the man to be Bill Barker, a faculty member at Belmont Hill School in Massachusetts. Jane Abbott Paul was the granddaughter of Ida and Judge A. J. Abbott of Ten Elders Ranch, Frijoles Canyon, and a childhood friend of young Peggy Pond in Santa Fe, ca. 1917.

12. Peggy Pond Church to Lawrence Clark Powell, ca. 1978, UCLA.

13. Florence Pond's cousin, Florence Converse, was an editor for *The Atlantic* in 1922 when Peggy was in her senior year of high school and considering which college to select. Pond took it upon herself to send three of Peggy's poems to Converse and tell her a bit about her niece. Converse was herself a respected poet and the author of several acclaimed novels. She wrote back with hopeful comments and advice for Peggy's college studies. Letter from Florence Converse to Florence Pond, 1922, CFP:

> 30 Leighton Road
> Wellesley, Mass.
> January 24, 1922

> Dear Florence: —
> I liked Peggy's verses so much that I tried "Desert Prayer," "The Piper," and the one about the mesa in the moonlight on Mr. Sedgwick, and I send you the memorandum which I found on my desk yesterday. I did not tell him how young Peggy was, or anything about her. You see he takes her seriously. And I, too, take her seriously. Her verse is youthful, of course . . . but it has imagination, and lyrical, musical quality, and simplicity . . . I may be heretical, but I think that the elaborate courses in *how* to write stories, dramas, etc., don't do very much for the people who really have it *in* them to write. But the study of English Literature, and European Literatures, and the Classics, helps immensely.

Converse thought that Peggy's choice of Smith College was a good one, despite her own well-recognized affiliation with Wellesley, and she continued to encourage Peggy's writing along the way, accepting occasional submissions to *Atlantic*.

14. Now a part of El Dorado business district at Wilmot and Speedway in Tucson, Stone Ashley has been used as a guest ranch, office space, restaurants, and a private club since it was sold by Florence Pond in 1948. Much of the surrounding property has been sold to developers, but outwardly the house looks as it did when it was finished in 1936 at a cost

of $67,000. It was designed by Grovenor Atterbury of New York and built by the Sundt Construction Company. Just more than a decade later, it sold for $200,000, including most of the furnishings. It was bought by a group of New York partners who turned it into a guest ranch called El Dorado Lodge in 1949. Several of Florence Pond's tapestries and furnishings still remained in Stone Ashley as late as 1999. In Florence Pond's day, a cypress-lined cobblestone drive led to a large circular fountain and the imposing front of the home with its façade of four stone arches and a second-floor balustrade. The ornate glass, wood, and iron door reportedly cost $1500 in 1934! Dark slate flagstones imported from Italy paved the entryway, and fountains accented the lawn and its sculpted shrubs that seemed strangely out of place in their desert setting.

15. Interview by the author with Julie Essroger, hostess for Charles Restaurant at Stone Ashley, Tucson, Arizona. Julie Essroger, long-time resident of Tucson, knew the history of Stone Ashley because she had visited the mansion when Florence Pond lived there. Ms. Essroger was eighty years old and still working as the hostess when the author visited Charles Restaurant for the interview in June 1998. She was a delight and a vast source of information.

16. *The Secret of the Golden Flower, A Chinese Book of Life* was first published in the United States by Harcourt, Brace & Company in 1932. The text was translated and interpreted by Richard Wilhelm. The book is still in print today.

17. Haniel Long, "The Rose Will Be Born Out of Roses," a poem written for Peggy Pond Church, ca. 1934, found in a folder of poems exchanged between the two, CFP.

18. Peggy Pond Church, "There Was Nothing" (1935), *Familiar Journey* (1936).

19. Comments from the book jacket of *The Burro of Angelitos* by Peggy Pond Church, Suttonhouse, Ltd., Los Angeles, 1936.

20. Lawrence Clark Powell, "Southwest Classics Reread: Haniel Long and *Interlinear to Cabeza de Vaca,*" *Westways*, April 1971.

21. Ibid. Lawrence Clark Powell, remembered as a writer and reviewer and as a noted librarian at UCLA, befriended Haniel Long in the last three years of Long's life, visiting often in Santa Fe. Powell was impressed by Long as a human being as well as an author. In his *Westways* article, Powell wrote, "My discovery of *Interlinear to Cabeza de Vaca* happened thirty years ago, on the shelf of a Los Angeles bookstore which had a goodly supply of unsold copies. I bought one at the published price of $1.50, more for its desert-colored format, I must admit, than for its contents. A reading of it, however, led me to go back and buy the rest of the copies—a dozen, I recall—to give to friends . . . " The friendship between the two men led to Long presenting his literary archives to the UCLA Library. In addition to Powell's writings on Haniel Long, a more in-depth commentary of Long's relationship with Witter Bynner can be found in *Who is Witter Bynner?* by James Kraft, University of New Mexico Press, 1995.

22. Ibid.

23. Marta Weigle and Kyle Fiore, *Santa Fe & Taos: The Writer's Era 1916–1941*, Santa Fe: Ancient City Press, 1982, p. 38–39.

24. Peggy Pond Church Collection, Mss 231, CSWR.

25. Ibid. Another particularly supportive note, and one that must have given Peggy a warm feeling when she read it, was sent from the New Mexico Normal University in Las Vegas in July 1934.

Mrs. Peggy Pond Church

Otowi, New Mexico

My dear Mrs. Church:

I want to tell you how much I enjoyed the reading of your two poems
at the Writers Round Table in Las Vegas Saturday. Believe me, I was

delighted with both of them. The poems were so full of feeling, sincerely and poetically expressed, and I particularly liked your presentation of detail. And you read them beautifully. I hope it is not asking too much to request that you drop me a card whenever you have something coming out which I might have the pleasure of reading.

With kindest regards and admiration, I remain,

Yours truly,

W. S. Campbell

"Stanley Vestal"

26. Peggy Pond Church Collection, Mss 231, CSWR.
27. Ibid.
28. A paper entitled "Who Was Haniel Long?" was presented by Dr. John R. Slater, professor emeritus of English at the University of Rochester, to the Fortnightly Club on January 12, 1965, in Rochester, NY. Dr. Slater gave his permission for a limited number of copies of the paper to be reproduced for family and friends of Haniel Long. A copy of the paper exists in MSC 513, Box 38, John Towner Frederick Collection, Special Collections, University Libraries, University of Iowa.
29. Haniel's thoughts on love and how he related those thoughts to his relationship with Peggy and her relationship with Bill Barker are stated in the pages of his journal that were shared with her in 1934, as well as in letters written to Peggy in that time frame. In 1983, Peggy donated Haniel's letters and the copies of his journal pages that were still in her possession to UCLA as an addition to Manuscript Collection 672, Haniel Long Papers. These materials are found in Folders 2 and 3, Box 33. Haniel's homosexual liaison with Witter Bynner occurred in his Harvard days after they met in 1908 (see James Kraft's *Who is Witter Bynner?*, UNM Press, 1995). Haniel's journal also refers to an affair in 1934, though the name of the man is not mentioned. (Haniel Long Papers, UCLA).
30. The thoughts expressed here are from Section X of *A Letter to St. Augustine after re-reading his confessions*, New York: Duell, Sloan and Pearce, 1950.
31. Peggy Pond Church, "Oh Night of Despair" (1934), *Accidental Magic* (2004), and Haniel Long, "The Rose Will Be Born Out of Roses" (1934), unpublished poem, CFP.
32. Journal, Haniel Long Papers, UCLA.
33. Peggy Pond Church, "More Than Mortal" (1934), unpublished poem, CFP. Haniel was moved by this tribute, writing Peggy to say, "I want to talk about this lovely thing." Also, "The Sister's Song" (1934), *Familiar Journey* (1936).
34. Promotional material for the release of *Familiar Journey* (1936), CFP.
35. Mary Austin, *Everyman's Genius*, Indianapolis: Bobbs Merrill, 1925.
36. Peggy Pond Church, "Here Is Ground Juniper" (1939), *Ulltimatum for Man* (1946) and *This Dancing Ground of Sky* (1993).
37. Connie Smithwick to Peggy Pond Church, January 1959, CSWR.
38. Peggy Pond Church, *The House at Otowi Bridge*, Albuquerque: University of New Mexico Press, 1960.
39. Email from Ted Church to the author, October 22, 2002. Ted never thought to question the stories about spiders and frogs when he was one of those little boys "helping" Tilano, but later he remembered that other adults getting water from the well would just let the bucket drop full speed with a splash! As for leaning over the wall and seeing the water down below, Ted remembered even decades later that "it was scary!"
40. Oscar Steege to Peggy Pond Church, January 4, 1961, CSWR.
41. Peggy Pond Church, "Some Lines Suggested for a Boarding-School Prospectus" (1939), *Accidental Magic* (2004).
42. Peggy Pond Church to Virginia Wirth, September 22, 1939, personal papers of John

Davis Wirth, used with permission.
43. Peggy Pond Church, "Letter to Virginia" (1944), *Ultimatum for Man* (1946) and *This Dancing Ground of Sky* (1993).
44. Peggy Pond Church, "Now You Are Dead" (1938), unpublished poem, CFP.
45. Peggy Pond Church, "For a Son in High School A.D. 1940," *Ultimatum for Man* (1946).
46. Peggy Pond Church to Hazel Pond, November 23, 1942, CSWR.

CHAPTER 8

1. Los Alamos Ranch School records that Fermor Church, A. J. Connell, and Fred Rousseau worked to organize in 1943 are kept in the New Mexico State Records Center and Archives in Santa Fe. Ferm sought employment at other private schools because he wasn't certified to teach in public schools.
2. Peggy Pond Church to Ted Church, February 15, 1943, CFP.
3 Peggy Pond Church to Ted Church, May 9, 1943, CFP.
4. Peggy Pond Church to Ted Church, ca. March 20, 1943, CFP. *How to Cook a Wolf* by MFK Fisher was published by North Point Press, Farrar, Straus and Giroux, New York, 1942.
5. Peggy Pond Church to Ted Church, June 21, 1943, CFP.
6. Peggy Pond Church to Ted Church, March 1943, CFP.
7. Email from Cate School archivist David Harbison to author, November 8, 2001. After the war, the Catalina school was never reestablished, and the name was simplified to Cate School, which still exists today.
8. At "almost forty miles an hour," Peggy and Ferm would have been speeding slightly! During World War II, a National War Time Speed Limit of 35 mph was mandated nationwide by Congress. The slower speed helped save gasoline and preserve tires, which was important in view of the fact that Japan had cut off access to Southeast Asia's natural rubber.
9. Thomas R. Waring Jr., LARS 1926–39, founded the Waring School in Santa Fe (1939–1941) and relocated to the Waring Ranch School in Pojoaque (1941–49). See Wirth and Aldrich p. 194.
10. Peggy Pond Church, "Of the Dust of the Ground" (1944), *Accidental Magic* (2004).
11. Email from Hugh Church to the author, August 5, 2005.
12. Beginning the late sixteenth century and spanning almost 300 years, El Camino Real de Tierra Adentro served as a route for settlers, livestock, the Spanish language, Christianity, agricultural methods, and cultural differences. Connecting Mexico City to Santa Fe and beyond as far as the San Luis Valley, El Camino Real (1598–1885) was the oldest of the long trails leading into North America.
13. John J. Cape was Fermor's half brother. He was eager to accept Ferm's offer to come to New Mexico because he needed time away from home in new surroundings. His son, navy pilot Lt. John J. Cape Jr. had been killed in action in the Aleutian Islands two years earlier.
14. Peggy Pond Church, "Enchanted" (1924), Southwest Review, April 1925. Also titled "Like the Pines" and "Perhaps I Will Take Root."
15. The phrase about a "power unleashed that men could not deal with" is quoted from Peggy's time line, where she kept notes about her activities and events. This dream is also discussed in the author's email files from February 27, 2007, in emails from Peggy's sons to the author.
16. Review of *Ultimatum for Man* by Florence Converse in *Survey Graphic*, November 1946.
17. "Peggy Church Makes First Return Hill Visit" by Hazel Hughes, *Los Alamos Times*, June 7, 1946. This article had some inaccuracies. The author mentioned that Peggy had

"tremendous pride" in the atomic laboratory, to which Peggy's son Hugh commented in 2004, "Good gracious, NO!" He added, "Especially as a devout Quaker and pacifist." Email exchange between Hugh Church and the author, January 24, 2004.

CHAPTER 9

1. Peggy Pond Church to William Carson, St. Louis, Missouri, 1946, CSWR. Carson's sons were not Los Alamos Ranch School students but attended the separate summer camp provided by the school.
2. Association of Los Alamos Scientists Records, 1945–1948, University of Chicago Library, 2009.
3. Robert R. Davis, Association of Los Alamos Scientists, to Peggy Pond Church, January 17, 1947, CSWR.
4. Peggy Pond Church, "Morning on Tseregé" (1945), *Ultimatum for Man* (1946;), *This Dancing Ground of Sky* (1993), and "Morning on Tshirege" in *Birds of Daybreak* (1985).
5. Though the title poem of the book, "Ultimatum for Man," describes well the world situation just after World War II, with the nuclear potential for destruction, the poem and its plea for unity was conceived in 1939.
6. Peggy Pond Church, "The Nuclear Physicists" (1945), *Ultimatum for Man* (1946), *New and Selected Poems* (1976), and *This Dancing Ground of Sky* (1993).
7. The stationery mentioned by Robert R. Davis was Los Alamos Ranch School letterhead.
8. Kit Carson Electric Cooperative was formed in 1944.
9. The Evenings hosted by Mabel Dodge in New York, prior to World War I were famous. Modeled after the salons of Europe, they attracted the intellectual elite. Writers, artists, poets, anarchists, socialists, suffragists, unionists, and more gathered in her large, old-fashioned apartment on lower Fifth Avenue for stimulating conversation, which was largely managed by their hostess, although she generally did not enter into the exchange of opinions and ideas. For more description of the Evenings, see by Van Deren Coke, *Andrew Dasburg*, University of New Mexico Press, 1979, p. 28, and Mabel Dodge: Biography at http://www.spartacus.schoolnet.co.uk/USAdodge.htm.
10. Dasburg first met John Reed at the McDowell Club in New York in 1913. Reed invited Dasburg to his first Evening at Mabel Dodge's home, setting in motion a friendship with Mabel that would be life changing. She introduced the "immensity and openness" of Taos to him in 1917 via a telegram from her that read, "Taos is a wonderful place. You've got to come. I am sending you tickets." After a few long-term yearly visits, Dasburg moved to Taos permanently. From *Oral history interview with Andrew Dasburg*, March 26, 1974, Archives of American Art, Smithsonian Institution, and Andrew Dasburg by Van Deren Coke, UNM Press, 1979, relationship with Mabel and Reed pp. 29–36, Addison's disease pp. 95–99.
11. Mabel Dodge became Mabel Dodge Luhan when she married Tony Luhan of Taos Pueblo, after moving to New Mexico in 1923.
12. Van Deren Coke, *Andrew Dasburg*, University of New Mexico Press, 1979, "judgment of the well-regarded critic and art historian Alfred Frankenstein," p. 1, originally quoted from *San Francisco Sunday Examiner and Chronicle*, April 17, 1966.
13. Peggy Pond Church, "Andrew's Tree in the Moonlight" (1951), published in the Taos newspaper *El Crepusculo*, October 14, 1954.
14. Ibid.
15. Originally called the New Mexico College of Agriculture and Mechanic Arts in Las Cruces, the school became New Mexico State University in 1960.
16. Life history of Corina Santistevan of Taos, New Mexico, established through personal interviews in 2008 by the author with Joan Pond (niece of Peggy Pond Church) and

Liz Cunningham (author of *Stones Into Bread: The Correspondence of Peggy Pond Church and Corina Aurora Santistevan*, publication pending). Recordings on compact discs in possession of the author.

17. Ibid.
18. Ibid.
19. Recollections of Joan Pond, Taos resident, 1937–1956.
20. Peggy Pond Church, "Peñas Negras" (1948), *New and Selected Poems* (1976) and *This Dancing Ground of Sky* (1993).
21. Ibid.
22. Corina Santistevan interviews, 2008.
23. Susan Sherman, Ed., *May Sarton: Selected Letters 1916–1954*, (New York: W.W. Norton and Company, Inc., , 1997), p. 320.
24. May Sarton, *After the Stroke: A Journal*, (New York: W.W. Norton & Company, 1988), pp. 193–195.
25. May Sarton, *A World of Light*, (New York: W.W. Norton & Company), 1976), pp. 123–143.
26. Shelley Armitage, "The Correspondence of May Sarton and Peggy Pond Church," in *Women's Work: Essays in Cultural Studies*, (West Cornwall: West Cornwall Press, 1995), p. 302.
27. Sherman, *May Sarton: Selected Letters 1916–1954*, 320.
28. Margot Peters, *May Sarton: a biography*, (New York: Ballantine, 1997); Lenora P. Blouin, "May Sarton: A Poet's Life," *A Celebration of Women Writers*, Digital Library, University of Pennsylvania, 1999, at http://digital.library.upenn.edu/women/sarton/blouin-biography.html#dedication.
29. Armitage, "The Correspondence of May Sarton and Peggy Pond Church," p. 306.
30. Sherman, *May Sarton: Selected Letters 1916–1954*, p. 304.
31. May Sarton, "*The Land of Silence*," *The Land of Silence and other poems*, Rinehart & Company, Inc., New York, 1953.
32. May Sarton, "Letter to an Indian Friend," *The Land of Silence and other poems*, Rinehart & Company, Inc., New York, 1953.
33. To date, there are two more Ashleys on the family tree, making a total of six. Ashley D. Pond had a son, Ashley Evan Pond, and in turn he had a son, Ashley Finn Pond.
34. The recollections of events surrounding Hugh Church's bout with polio and Peggy's reactions to it come from two, one-page remembrances that she wrote in early January 1950 (the first one titled "The Cold Room" and the second one simply "The Room") as well as from Hugh's memory of those weeks, shared in emails in 2010.
35. This opening is from "The Cold Room," a page-long story that Peggy wrote to vent her pain over Hugh's illness in the days she prepared for his return from the hospital.
36. Ibid.
37. This section of quotes is from the "The Room," the second page-long story that Peggy wrote in the days preceding Hugh's return from the hospital, a variation on "The Cold Room." The two versions were combined in this vignette.
38. Peggy Pond Church to Virginia Wirth, September 11, 1950, personal papers of John Davis Wirth, used with permission.
39. Peggy Pond Church to Ted and Liz Church, October 30, 1950, CFP.

CHAPTER 10

1. The people of San Ildefonso Pueblo call this place Po-sah-con-gay in their Tewa language, "the place where the river makes a noise."
2. Peggy Pond Church, *The House at Otowi Bridge*, Albuquerque: University of New Mexico Press, 1960, p. 18.
3. Peggy Pond Church Papers, CSWR

4. Edith Warner to Peggy Pond Church, December 1936, Peggy Pond Church Papers, CSWR.
5. Peggy Pond Church to Elizabeth Church, February 19, 1951, CSWR.
6. Ethel Froman to Peggy Pond Church, May 1, 1941, CSWR.
7. Peggy Pond Church to Virginia Wirth, April 2, 1951, personal papers of John Davis Wirth, used with permission.
8. Ibid. Rafael and Juanita Estevan of San Ildefonso cared for Tilano after Edith died. Rafael had been very close to Edith and Tilano since spending time with them during his coming-of-age years. He benefited greatly from their guidance. This information is from *In the Shadow of Los Alamos*, edited by Patrick Burns and email from Burns, 2011. Also, Henrietta Miller was known by everyone as "Peter," a childhood nickname.
9. Aileen O'Bryan was previously mentioned in Chapter 5 as Aileen Baehrens and as Aileen Nusbaum in Chapter 6. When she divorced Jesse Nusbaum, Aileen took back her maiden name of O'Bryan.
10. Peggy Pond Church to May Sarton, May 8, 1951, CFP.
11. Peggy Pond Church to Virginia Wirth, May 8, 1951, personal papers of John Davis Wirth, used with permission.
12. Dr. Philip Morrison to Peggy Pond Church, May 1959, CSWR.
13. Peggy Pond Church to Elizabeth Church, 1951, CFP.
14. Peggy Pond Church to May Sarton, October 4, 1951, CFP.
15. The England Journal, a separate journal from Church's daily entries, CFP.
16. Peggy Pond Church to May Sarton, December 15, 1952, CFP.
17. Ibid.
18. Kathleen Ferrier was a British contralto who rose to fame in 1937 as the result of winning a singing competition at the Carlisle Festival, which she had actually entered as a pianist! She became an immediate sensation, but her career was cut short in 1953 when she died of cancer. Ferrier is mentioned in an unfinished poem titled "An Elegy," dated April 2, 1978.
19. "Kew Gardens" remains unpublished, but "St. Paul's London" appeared in the Taos newspaper *El Crepusculo*, August 7, 1952.
20. The England Journal, CFP.
21. Peggy Pond Church to Virginia Wirth, September 11, 1950, personal papers of John Davis Wirth, used with permission.
22. Peggy Pond Church, "For Tilano of San Ildefonso" (1953), *The House at Otowi Bridge* (1960).
23. "On Building a Bridge," *New America*, University of New Mexico, Spring 1979, p. 45.
24. Peggy Pond Church to Peter Miller, February 12, 1954, and February 24, 1954; "On Building a Bridge," *New America*, University of New Mexico, Spring 1979, p. 45.
25. Speech presented at Los Alamos on the occasion of the Army-Navy E Award, October 16, 1945, in *The making of the atomic bomb* by Richard Rhodes, p 758.
26. Peggy Pond Church, "Ultimatum for Man" (1939), *Ultimatum for Man* (1946) and *New and Selected Poems* (1976).
27. Peggy Pond Church, "AEC Acted According to Standards But Men Not Made Loyal by Rules," *Santa Fe New Mexican*, published first week of July 1954.
28. Peggy Pond Church, "Sonnet I" of The Ripened Fields: Fifteen Sonnets of a Marriage, *Inward Light*, Autumn 1954. The spelling of the word "defences" is the poet's choice for this poem.
29. Fermor Church to Ted Church, October 11, 1946, CFP.
30. Haniel Long to Peggy Pond Church, October 5, 1954, CSWR.
31. Peggy Pond Church to Kathleen Decker, December 6, 1954, CFP.
32. Peggy Pond Church to Kathleen Decker, February 17, 1955, CFP.
33. Peggy Pond Church to Kathleen Decker, February 20, 1955, CFP.
34. "On Building a Bridge," *New America*, University of New Mexico, Spring 1979, p. 45.

35. Ibid.
36. Koshares are the clowns at Pueblo feast days and dances.
37. Peggy Pond Church to Kathleen Decker, October 18, 1955, CFP.

CHAPTER 11

1. Peggy Pond Church to Corina Santistevan, March 4, 1956, CAS.
2. Corina Santistevan to Peggy Pond Church, July 1956, CAS.
3. Corina Santistevan to Peggy Pond Church, October 31, 1956, CAS.
4. Peggy Pond Church to Corina Santistevan, October 2, 1956, CAS
5. "A Greeting" (1956), Christmas Poem, CFP.
6. Haniel Long to Peggy Pond Church, October 14, UCLA.
7. Peggy Pond Church Journal excerpt from November 22, 1956, placed in Haniel Long Papers, UCLA.
8. Borestone Mountain Poetry Awards were an annual series of poetry anthologies first published in 1949. The poems were selected from those published in a given year in English-language magazines and books. The awards continued until 1977. "Elegy in Three Movements" was published also in *New and Selected Poems*, Ahsahta Press, Boise State University, 1976, and *This Dancing Ground of Sky*, Red Crane Press, Santa Fe, 1993.
9. May Sarton to Peggy Pond Church, November 5, 1956, UCLA; and Ruth Swaine of Talpa, New Mexico, no date, UCLA.
10. Interpretation of "Song of the Unicorn" comes from *The Holy Grail: imagination and belief*, Richard W. Barber, Cambridge: Harvard University Press, 2004, p. 344.
11. Peggy Pond Church, "Elegy in Three Movements—Elegy II, The Unicorn" (1956), *New and Selected Poems* (1976) and *This Dancing Ground of Sky* (1993).
12. Dorothy McKibbin to Peggy Pond Church, November 2, 1956, UCLA.
13. Peggy Pond Church to May Sarton, April 14, 1985, CFP.
14. Peggy Pond Church, "Thirteen Year Old" (1925), published in *Children's* magazine, August 1927.
15. Email between Katherine Pond and the author, November 2010.
16. Ibid.
17. Peggy Pond Church, "Perhaps in Our Old Age" (1982), *Birds of Daybreak* (1985) and *This Dancing Ground of Sky* (1993).
18. Peggy Pond Church to Corina Santistevan, December 27, 1957, CAS.
19. The Nut Tree is a legendary road stop in Vacaville, California. It evolved from a family fruit stand in 1921 to a well-known northern California restaurant.

CHAPTER 12

1. Peggy Pond Church, "On Building a Bridge," *New America, The Southwest: A Regional View*, Vol. 3, Nov. 3, 1979, p. 46, CSWR.
2. Ibid., p. 44.
3. Ibid., p. 46.
4. Ibid., p. 46.
5. Ibid., p. 47
6. Ibid., p. 47
7. "Sylvia" to Peggy Pond Church, November 11, 1959, Haniel Long Papers, UCLA.
8. Spud Johnson, Erna Fergusson, Dorothy Pillsbury, and Dorothy McKibbin to Peggy Pond Church, 1959, CSWR.
9. Peggy Pond Church, "On Building a Bridge," *New America, The Southwest: A Regional*

View, Vol. 3, Nov. 3, 1979, p. 46, CSWR.
10. Ibid., p. 48.
11. Ibid., p. 48.
12. Ibid., p. 49.
13. Ibid., p. 50.
14. Witter Bynner, James M. Gilchrist Jr., May Sarton, and Ruth Laughlin to Peggy Pond Church, 1960–1967, CSWR.

CHAPTER 13

1. Peggy Pond Church to May Sarton, January 19, 1960, CFP. The comment that Arthur Ortiz made about the fire department was in reference to Ashley Pond Jr. organizing a group of volunteers in 1922 that eventually became the Santa Fe Fire Department. He was the fire chief for the volunteers for several years and even had a fire pole installed in his upstairs bedroom so that he could slide to the garage below to answer calls in the night!
2. Peggy Pond Church, "White Dog with Mushrooms" (1962), *Birds of Daybreak* (1985) and *This Dancing Ground of Sky* (1993), also published in *New and Selected Poems* (1976) as "December" and published in the *Los Alamos Monitor* under that name in an essay by John Bartlit, December 2001.
3. Peggy Pond Church to Corina Santistevan, July 8, 1961, CAS.
4. Peggy Pond Church to May Sarton, March, 25, 1968, CFP.
5. Peggy Pond Church to Harry James, November 3, 1967, Harry C. James Papers, Collection 111, used with permission of Special Collections, University Library, University of California, Riverside.
6. Ibid. Harry James was founder in 1926 of The Trailfinders School for Boys in Altadena, California, a private school that stressed an extensive outdoor program. James brought his boys for summer camping to New Mexico and, through camping in the Jemez region, became friends with Edith Warner. James was upset by the publication of *The Woman at Otowi Crossing* and wrote a critical book review the Pasadena newspaper ("Frank Waters Volume Leaves Reviewer Sad," *Pasadena Independent Star-News*, May 7, 1967).
7. Spud Johnson, "The Santa Fe GADFLY," *Santa Fe New Mexican*, October 23, 1966, p. 9.
8. Ferenc M. Szasz, *Larger Than Life: New Mexico in the Twentieth Century*, Albuquerque: University of New Mexico Press, 2006, p. 34.
9. John Bartlit, NMCCAW Columnist, "In memoriam: Remembering the Ranch School's last headmaster," *Los Alamos Monitor*, February 9, 1975. John Barlit and his wife, Nancy, were also founding members of this dedicated group. Through the years, several members have been from Los Alamos.
10. T. M. Pearce, Introduction, *The Land of Little Rain*, Albuquerque: University of New Mexico Press, Zia Edition, 1974. Dr. Pearce published *Mary Hunter Austin* (Twayne Publishers, NY, 1965), *The Beloved House* (Caston Printers, Ltd., ID, 1940), and edited *Literary America, 1903–1934: The Mary Austin Letters* (Greenwood Press, Westport, CT, 1979).
11. Peggy Pond Church to Elizabeth Riley, Crowell Publishing Company, July 14, 1967, CWSR.
12. Mary Austin, *The Land of Little Rain*, New York: Houghton Mifflin Company, 1903.
13. Peggy Pond Church to Elizabeth Riley, Crowell Publishing Company, July 14, 1967, CSWR.
14. Mary Austin, *The Land of Little Rain*, New York: Houghton Mifflin Company, 1903.
15. Peggy Pond Church, *Wind's Trail: The Early Life of Mary Austin*, Santa Fe: Museum of New Mexico Press, 1990; Augusta Fink, *I-Mary: A Biography of Mary Austin*, Tucson: University of Arizona Press, 1985.
16. T. M. Pearce, *Mary Hunter Austin*, New York: Twayne Publishers, Inc., 1965.

17. Ibid.
18. Peggy Pond Church to T. M. (Matt) Pearce, March 12, 1968, CSWR.
19. Richard Conner, *Jack London*, Little Brown & Co., 1964, CSWR.
20. Peggy Pond Church to Harriet Stoddard, June 17, 1972, CSWR.
21. Albert Genthe, *As I Remember*, John Day in association with Reynal and Hitchcock, 1936.
22. Ibid.
23. Peggy Pond Church to Virginia (Wirth) Wiebenson, February 19, 1973, personal papers of John Davis Wirth, used with permission. In 1953, Virginia Wirth remarried and became Mrs. John Wiebenson.
24. Peggy Pond Church to Elizabeth Riley, , Crowell Publishing Company, May 3, 1967, CSWR.
25. New Mexico Office of the State Historian, "1925—Spanish Colonial Arts Society Founded," http://www.newmexicohistory.org/filedetails.php?fileID=424.
26. Notes from Louis Adamic, *My America*, New York: Harper and Bros, 1938, CSWR.
27. Peggy Pond Church to Harriett Stoddard, June 17, 1972, CSWR.
28. Peggy Pond Church to Lawrence Clark Powell, February 17, 1973, CSWR.
29. Lawrence Clark Powell to Peggy Pond Church, August 22, 1973, CSWR.
30. Peggy Pond Church to May Sarton, December 17, 1978, CFP.
31. Frances Howard Shaw, "Who Loves the Rain," *Poetry, A Magazine of Verse*, Chicago, March 1914.
32. Margaret Craven, *I Heard the Owl Call My Name*, New York: Dell Publishing, 1980.
33. Peggy Pond Church, "Sonnet XV: For F.S.C. 1900–1975," *The Ripened Fields*, Santa Fe: Lightning Tree, 1978.
34. Robert R. White, "A Remembrance of Peggy Pond Church, *Book Talk* (Newsletter of the New Mexico Book League), September 1994, p, 4.
35. Peggy Pond Church to Virginia (Wirth) Wiebenson, April 27, 1978, personal papers of John Davis Wirth, used with permission.
36. Peggy Pond Church to Harriett Stoddard, June 17, 1972, CSWR.

CHAPTER 14

1. Peggy Pond Church, "The Rito: Frijoles Canyon" (1980), *Birds of Daybreak* (1985).
2. Ibid.
3. Peggy Pond Church, "Morning on Tsérege" (1945), *Ultimatum for Man* (1946) and *This Dancing Ground of Sky* (1993).
4. Peggy Pond Church and Jeannie Pear, *A Rustle of Angels*, Peartree Press, 1981.
5. Peggy Pond Church, "Sandhill Cranes in February" (1981), *Birds of Daybreak* (1985) and *This Dancing Ground of Sky* (1993).
6. Michael Mauldin, "Enchanted Land" (CD cover), 2000.
7. Peggy Pond Church to Dody Waring, November 16, 1971, personal papers of John Davis Wirth, used with permission.
8. Peggy Pond Church to Corina Santistevan, April 14, 1960, CAS.
9. Peggy Pond Church to Dody Waring, November 16, 1971, personal papers of John Davis Wirth, used with permission.
10. Peggy Pond Church, "For a Mountain Burial" (1984), *Birds of Daybreak* (1985) and *This Dancing Ground of Sky* (1993); "For Gus" (1971), *Accidental Magic* (2004).
11. Peggy Pond Church, "The Agéd Man" (1982), *This Dancing Ground of Sky* (1993).
12. Peggy Pond Church, "Old Man by the River," unpublished poem, CFP.
13. Peggy Pond Church to Virginia (Wirth) Weibenson, 1983, personal papers of John Davis Wirth, used with permission.
14. Peggy Pond Church to Ted Church, April 26, 1983, CFP.

15. Peggy Pond Church to May Sarton, November 7, 1983, CFP; "Silly Song for My Eightieth Birthday" (1983), *This Dancing Ground of Sky* (1993).
16. Peggy Pond Church, "On Putting to Death an Old Dog" (1983), *Birds of Daybreak* (1985) and *This Dancing Ground of Sky* (1993).
17. Peggy Pond Church, "Lines for a Granddaughter Age Twenty" (1984), *Birds of Daybreak* (1985).
18. Julia Church (Hoffman) to Peggy Pond Church, January 29, 1984, CFP.
19. Telephone interview of Shelley Armitage, September 2010; Shelley Armitage, *Bones Incandescent: The Pajarito Journals of Peggy Pond Church*, Lubbock, TX: Texas Tech University Press, 2001
20. Larry Hagman (telegram) to Peggy Pond Church, October 1984, CSWR.
21. Jill Gyngell to Peggy Pond Church, July 13, 1985, CSWR.
22. Peggy Pond Church to May Sarton, April 14, 1985, CFP.
23. Peggy Pond Church, *Birds of Daybreak*, Santa Fe: William Gannon, 1985.
24. Peggy Pond Church to Tony Long, February 12, 1986, UCLA.
25. Peggy Pond Church, "For D." (1932), unpublished poem, CFP.
26. Mary Bryan to Peggy Pond Church, March 21, 1978, CSWR.
27. Peggy Pond Church to May Sarton, October 12, 1986, CFP.
28. May Sarton to Peggy Pond Church, October 19, 1986, CFP.
29. Excerpts from suicide note left by Peggy Pond Church, October 23, 1982, CFP.
30. Peggy Pond Church, "I Have Looked at the Earth" (1930), *Foretaste* (1933), *New and Selected Poems* (1985), and *This Dancing Ground of Sky* (1993).
31. Peggy Pond Church, "Elegy for a Willow Tree" (1983), *Birds of Daybreak* (1985).

Published Works of Peggy Pond Church

Poetry
Foretaste (Rydal Press, Santa Fe Writers' Editions, 1933)
Familiar Journey (Rydal Press, Santa Fe Writers' Editions, 1936)
Ultimatum for Man (James Ladd Delkin, Stanford University, 1946)
New and Selected Poems (Ahsahta Press, Boise, 1976) *
The Ripened Fields: Fifteen Sonnets of a Marriage (Lightning Tree, Santa Fe, 1978)
The Lament at Tsankawi Mesa (Thistle Press, Santa Fe, 1980)
A Rustle of Angels (Peartree Press, Denver, 1981)
Birds of Daybreak (William Gannon, Santa Fe, 1985)
This Dancing Ground of Sky (Red Crane Books, Santa Fe, 1993) *
Accidental Magic (Wildflower Press, Albuquerque, 2004) *

Memoirs
The House at Otowi Bridge (University of New Mexico Press, 1960) *
"On Building a Bridge" in *New America* (University of New Mexico Press,
    Spring 1979)
When Los Alamos was a Ranch School (with Fermor S. Church, Los Alamos
    Historical Society Publications, 1998, Second Edition) *

Children's Books
Shoes for the Santo Nino (Rio Grande Books, 2010) *
The Burro of Angelitos (Suttonhouse, Ltd., London, 1936)

Biography
Wind's Trail: The Early Life of Mary Austin (Edited by Shelley Armitage,
    Museum of New Mexico Press, Santa Fe, 1990) *

* Still available

Selected Bibliography

Armitage, Shelley. *Bones Incandescent: The Pajarito Journals of Peggy Pond Church*. Lubbock: Texas Tech Press, 2001.

———. *Peggy Pond Church*. Western Writers' Series. Boise State University, 1993.

———. "The Correspondence of May Sarton and Peggy Pond Church," in *Women's Work: Essays in Cultural Studies*. West Cornwall: West Cornwall Press, 1995.

Baldinger, JoAnn. "Austin, Church: Spinners of legends." *Santa Fe New Mexican Pasatiempo*, August 31, 1990.

Bowman, Jon. "Peggy Pond Church: She draws inspiration from nature." *Santa Fe New Mexican Pasatiempo*, December 9, 1983.

Burns, Patrick, Ed. *In the Shadow of Los Alamos*. Albuquerque: University of New Mexico Press, 2001.

Elkins, Andrew. *Another Place: An Ecocritical Study of Selected Western American Poets*. Fort Worth: Texas Christian University Press, 2002.

———. "So Strangely Married: Peggy Pond Church's The Ripened Fields: Fifteen Sonnets of a Marriage." *Western American Literature* (1996).

Fink, Augusta. *I-Mary: A Biography of Mary Austin*. Tucson: University of Arizona Press, 1985.

Gumert, Shirley. "Dreaming of the Wind: Peggy Pond Church reflects on the world Los Alamos changed." *Santa Fe Reporter Voices*, 1985.

Henderson, Alice Corbin. *The Turquoise Trail*. New York: Houghton Mifflin Co., 1928.

Martin, Craig and Heather McClenahan. *Of Logs and Stone*. Los Alamos: All Seasons Publishing, 2008.

Mauldin, Michael. *Enchanted Land: Suite for Narrator and Orchestra* on Enchanted Land Compact Disc, performance by New Mexico Symphony Orchestra, words from *The House at Otowi Bridge* narrated by Kathleen Church, 2001.

Pearce, T. M. *Mary Hunter Austin*. New York: Twayne Publishers, Inc., 1965.

Sarton, May. *A World of Light*. New York: W.W. Norton & Company, 1976.

———. *After the Stroke: A Journal*. New York: W.W. Norton & Company, 1988.

———. *The Land of Silence and other poems*. New York: Rinehart & Company, Inc., 1953.

Shearer, Mike. "Death has rights, too." *Albuquerque Tribune*, August 7, 1987.

————. "Peggy Pond Church: An 'Octogeranium' Speaks." *New Mexico Magazine,* February 1985, 23, 58–59.

Sherman, Susan, Ed. *May Sarton: Selected Letters 1916–1954*, New York: W. W. Norton and Company, Inc., 1997.

Trusky, A. Thomas, Ed. *Women Poets of the West.* Boise: Ahsahta Press, 1981.

Weigle, Marta and Kyle Fiore. *Santa Fe & Taos: The Writer's Era 1916–1941.* Santa Fe: Ancient City Press, 1982.

Wirth, John D. and Linda Harvey Aldrich. *Los Alamos: The Ranch School Years 1917–1943.* Albuquerque: University of New Mexico Press, 2003.

Index

Index

Index